Rock Climbing
Tahquitz and Suicide Rocks

Help Us Keep This Guide Up to Date

Every effort has been made by the authors and editors to make this guide as accurate and useful as possible. However, many things can change after a guide is published—trails are rerouted, regulations change, techniques evolve, facilities come under new management, etc.

We would love to hear from you concerning your experiences with this guide and how you feel it could be improved and kept up to date. While we may not be able to respond to all commments and suggestions, we'll take them to heart. Please send your comments, suggestions, and new route information directly to the authors to the following address:

Randy Vogel
P.O. Box 4554
Laguna Beach, CA 92652

Thanks for your input, and happy travels!

Rock Climbing Tahquitz and Suicide Rocks

Third Edition

Randy Vogel and Bob Gaines

GUILFORD, CONNECTICUT
AN IMPRINT OF THE GLOBE PEQUOT PRESS

A FALCON GUIDE®

Previously published as *Guide to Tahquitz and Suicide Rocks* by Chockstone Press/Falcon Publishing

Library of Congress Cataloging-in-Publication Data
Vogel, Randy.
Rock climbing Tahquitz and Suicide Rocks/by Randy Vogel and Bob Gaines.—3rd ed.
p. cm.—(A Falcon guide)
Rev. ed of: Tahquitz & Suicide. 1993.
Includes index.
ISBN 1-58592-087-8
1.Rock climbing—California—San Jacinto Mountains—Guidebooks. 2. San Jacinto Mountains (Calif.)—Guidebooks. I. Gaines, Bob, 1959- II. Vogel, Randy. Tahquitz & Suicide. III. Title. IV. Series.

GV199.42.C22 S2886 2001
796.52'23'0979497—dc21

2001023720

Manufactured in the United States of America
Third Edition/First Printing

CONTENTS

Preface and Acknowledgments vi
Introduction 1
Topo and Map Legends 3
Los Angeles Climbing Areas Map 4
Idyllwild Area Map 6
Idyllwild Detail Map 7
Approach Information 16
Descent Routes 16
History 16

TAHQUITZ ROCK 37
Approach Information 37
Tahquitz Rock Overview Map 38
Northeast Buttress 40
Upper Northeast Buttress 43
North Face 45
North Buttress 52
Northwest Recess 55
Bulge 75
Royal's Arches 85
West Face 87
South Face 109
Tahquitz Summit Block 128

SUICIDE ROCK 132
Approach Information 132
Suicide Rock Overview Map 133
Winter Slab 132
Arpa Carpa Cliff 134
Le Dent Pinnacle Area 136
Deception Pillar 139
South Face 140
The Limp Dick 145
Smooth Sole Walls 146
My Obsession Boulder 152
Below Smooth Sole Wall (BSSW) Face 153
Sunshine Face 154
Buttress of Cracks 168
Paisano Pinnacle 176
The Weeping Wall 179
Rebolting Face 183
The Godzilla Face 186
Sunkist Face 188
Sideshow Slab 192
Tiny Pillars 194
Eagle Pinnacle 194
Upper East Face 198
North Side 199
Northeast Buttress 200
North Face 203

Index 209

PREFACE AND ACKNOWLEDGMENTS

This is the eleventh comprehensive guidebook published for the beautiful granite of the Idyllwild area. It has been sixty-five years since the first climb was established at Tahquitz (*The Trough*). Although much has changed about climbing since 1936, in its essence, climbing remains much the same as it has always been. More than just a sport, climbing is a passion. In this respect, the climbers of today share a bond with those of the past, and just as important, with each other.

And as with our predecessors, most climbers today have a strong commitment to the natural environment. In an age where climbing is seen by some as antithetical to conservation, each of us has a duty to share our commitment to the environment with our peers. Please keep these crags clean, dispose of human waste properly, and stay on all established trails to avoid soil erosion. Volunteer your time to upcoming trail projects, and make yourself aware of access issues. Always keep in mind that by our example we exert the most powerful influence.

Since the last edition of this guide, more than seventy-five new routes have been established. And though it appears that the potential for new lines is limited, perhaps it will always be premature to declare the area "climbed out."

It would be impossible to put together any guidebook without the help of other climbers. Darrell Hensel, Clark Jacobs, and Kelly Vaught should be particularly thanked for the detailed topos, rating charts, and other assistance provided. We'd also like to thank Kevin Powell, in particular, for his excellent photographs, and Leonard Gaines for piloting several aerial photography missions.

Other people who provided additional information include: Rick Accomazzo, Bob Austin, Terry Ayers, Alan Bartlett, Tom Beck, Christian Burrell, Charles Cole, Scott Erler, Dave Evans, Tom Gilge, Mark Hubbard, John Long, Troy Mayr, Mike Ousley, Kurt Stitz, Kelly and Kendell Vaught, and Jonny Woodward. We also owe a debt of gratitude to Chuck Wilts, who from 1956 to 1979 edited five editions of this guide and who established the Decimal Rating System.

The detailed history section was the result of many conversations with a number of people. In particular, special thanks go to the late Chuck Wilts, Ellen Wilts, Royal Robbins, Dick Jones, Ivan Couch, Pat Callis, Tom Higgins, Glen Dawson, Bob Kamps, Rick Accomazzo, Tony Yaniro, Darell Hensel, Larry Reynolds, Mike Dent, and Jim Smith.

The many fine photographs in this guide were graciously provided by Royal Robbins, Kevin Powell, Ellen Wilts, Rick Accomazzo, Larry Reynolds, John Harlin, Clark Jacobs, and Tom Frost.

Randy Vogel and Bob Gaines

May 2001

WARNING:
CLIMBING IS A SPORT WHERE YOU MAY BE SERIOUSLY INJURED OR DIE. READ THIS BEFORE YOU USE THIS BOOK.

This guidebook is a compilation of unverified information gathered from many different climbers. The author cannot assure the accuracy of any of the information in this book, including the topos and route descriptions, the difficulty ratings, and the protection ratings. These may be incorrect or misleading and it is impossible for any one author to climb all the routes to confirm the information about each route. Also, ratings of climbing difficulty and danger are always subjective and depend on the physical characteristics (for example, height), experience, technical ability, confidence, and physical fitness of the climber who supplied the rating. Additionally, climbers who achieve first ascents sometimes underrate the difficulty or danger of the climbing route out of fear of being ridiculed if a climb is later down-rated by subsequent ascents. Therefore, be warned that you must exercise your own judgment on where a climbing route goes, its difficulty, and your ability to safely protect yourself from the risks of rock climbing. Examples of some of these risks are: falling due to technical difficulty or due to natural hazards such as holds breaking, falling rock, climbing equipment dropped by other climbers, hazards of weather and lightning, your own equipment failure, and failure or absence of fixed protection.

You should not depend on any information gleaned from this book for your personal safety; your safety depends on your own good judgment, based on experience and a realistic assessment of your climbing ability. If you have any doubt as to your ability to safely climb a route described in this book, do not attempt it.

The following are some ways to make your use of this book safer:

1. Consultation: You should consult with other climbers about the difficulty and danger of a particular climb prior to attempting it. Most local climbers are glad to give advice on routes in their area and we suggest that you contact locals to confirm ratings and safety of particular routes and to obtain first-hand information about a route chosen from this book.

2. Instruction: Most climbing areas have local climbing instructors and guides available. We recommend that you engage an instructor or guide to learn safety techniques and to become familiar with the routes and hazards of the areas described in this book. Even after you are proficient in climbing safely, occasional use of a guide is a safe way to raise your climbing standard and learn advanced techniques.

3. Fixed Protection: Many of the routes in this book use bolts and pitons which are permanently placed in the rock. Because of variances in the manner of placement, weathering, metal fatigue, the quality of the metal used, and many other factors, these fixed protection pieces should always be considered suspect and should always be backed up by equipment that you place yourself. Never depend for your safety on a single piece of fixed protection because you never can tell whether it will hold weight. In some cases, fixed protection may have been removed.

Be aware of the following specific potential hazards which could arise in using this book:

1. Incorrect Descriptions of Routes: If you climb a route and you have a doubt as to where the route may go, you should not go on unless you are sure that you can go that way safely. Route descriptions and topos in this book may be inaccurate or misleading.

2. Incorrect Difficulty Rating: A route may, in fact, be more difficult than the rating indicates. Do not be lulled into a false sense of security by the difficulty rating.

3. Incorrect Protection Rating: If you climb a route and you are unable to arrange adequate protection from the risk of falling through the use of fixed pitons or bolts, by planning your own protection devices, do not assume that there is adequate protection available farther up the route just because the route protection rating indicates the route is not an X or an R rating. Every route is potentially an X (a fall may be deadly), due to the inherent hazards of climbing—including, for example, failure or absence of fixed protection, your own equipment failure, or improper use of climbing equipment.

THERE ARE NO WARRANTIES, WHETHER EXPRESS OR IMPLIED, THAT THIS GUIDEBOOK IS ACCURATE OR THAT THE INFORMATION CONTAINED IN IT IS RELIABLE. THERE ARE NO WARRANTIES OF FITNESS FOR A PARTICULAR PURPOSE OR THAT THIS GUIDE IS MERCHANTABLE. YOUR USE OF THIS BOOK INDICATES YOUR ASSUMPTION OF THE RISK THAT IT MAY CONTAIN ERRORS AND IS AN ACKNOWLEDGMENT OF YOUR OWN SOLE RESPONSIBILITY FOR YOUR CLIMBING SAFETY.

Mark Hoffman and Cheryl Basye on Bibliography *(5.10b), Tahquitz.* PHOTO BY BOB GAINES

INTRODUCTION

HOW TO GET TO THE ROCKS

Tahquitz and Suicide Rocks are located on the high western slope of the San Jacinto mountain range in Southern California, above the mountain town of Idyllwild. These mountains lie east of Los Angeles, just west of Palm Springs and southwest of Joshua Tree National Park. Joshua Tree is about one hour away from Idyllwild. The overview map of Southern California shows major road and freeway approaches to Idyllwild.

From the town of Hemet, take California Highway 74, 14 miles to the junction with California Highway 243 at Mountain Center. Head north for 5 miles on CA 243 to the town of Idyllwild. From the town of Banning along United States 10 take CA 243 south for 26 miles to Idyllwild.

From the town of Idyllwild, drive up North Circle Drive (the Fern Valley Road) through town to Humber Park, where the road ends (see map). Humber Park is a trailhead for the San Jacinto Wilderness, and consists of a small loop road and parking area. Toilets and trashcans are the only facilities at Humber Park.

Currently a Forest Adventure Pass is required for day-use parking at Humber Park. It is not required for parking for Suicide Rock. Annual and day-use Forest Adventure Passes are available at the Forest Service station in Idyllwild and at various retail establishments in town.

CAMPING

Camping is not permitted at **Humber Park,** although climbers often bivouac in their cars anyway. There are several campgrounds within a short driving distance of Humber Park and near the town of Idyllwild.

Idyllwild (County) Park is located 0.5 mile west of Idyllwild on Riverside County Playground Road, within walking distance of town. Camping fees are currently $15 per night. The campground also offers hot showers (extra) and excellent bouldering. Open year round. Telephone (909) 659–2656.

Mount San Jacinto State Park has two state park campground locations, both open year round:

1) The Idyllwild Campground is located just north of town along California Highway 243 (25905 Highway 243). Summer rates are $16 Friday and Saturday nights, and $15 the rest of the week. Off-season is $12 per night. Hot showers, flush toilets, tables, etc. In the summer reservations may be necessary. For reservations call 1 (800) 444–7275, the Key # for the campground is 6872. Telephone for the campground is (909) 659–2607.

2) **The Stone Creek Campground** is located about 6 miles north of Idyllwild on California Highway 243. Summer rates are $11 Friday and Saturday nights, and $10 the rest of the week. Winter rates are $7 per night. No showers. Pit toilets, tables, fire rings, etc.

Boulder Basin Campground (at Black Mountain) is operated by the Forest Service. Located along a dirt road (Black Mountain Road, 4601) off California Highway 243, approximately 14 miles north of Idyllwild. Excellent bouldering and a number of short sport climbs are found in the immediate area. Rates are $10 per night, no reservations taken. Open from May to October (approximately). Pit toilets, fire rings, tables, and no showers. One car and up to eight persons per site. Group camping at Black Mountain Campground is also available. Call (909) 659–2117 for prices and reservations.

HOW TO USE THIS BOOK

This guide is divided into two sections, one for Tahquitz Rock and one for Suicide Rock. To get to the base of each rock, see the **Approach Information** at the beginning of each section. As a general rule, informal trails exist along the bases of each rock. These trails provide access to the various routes. The text of the guide will provide approach information to a particular route(s) or section of the rock along these trails.

This guide uses a combination of written and topographic descriptions as well as photographs to describe the start and line of ascent of each route. Suggested equipment needed for each route is usually listed.

Most of the routes described in this guide are multipitch climbs. Because many of the climbers attracted to the long, moderately difficult routes at Tahquitz may not have good route-finding skills, the written descriptions accompanying these routes are more detailed than would ordinarily be provided.

Nevertheless, no combination of topos, photos, or written descriptions can relieve YOU of the responsibility of making good route-finding decisions. It is not uncommon for route descriptions to be in error or unclear. Also, the complex terrain at Tahquitz makes it very easy to make errors in following a particular route. For information on how to use the topos and maps, see the **Topo and Map Legends** on page 3.

Often, directions are given in the descriptions of routes. If "right" or "left" is used, this refers to the direction assuming you are facing the rock. Additionally, north, south, east, and west (and combinations thereof) are used. These may only be approximations. Likewise, distances between routes,

TOPO AND MAP LEGENDS

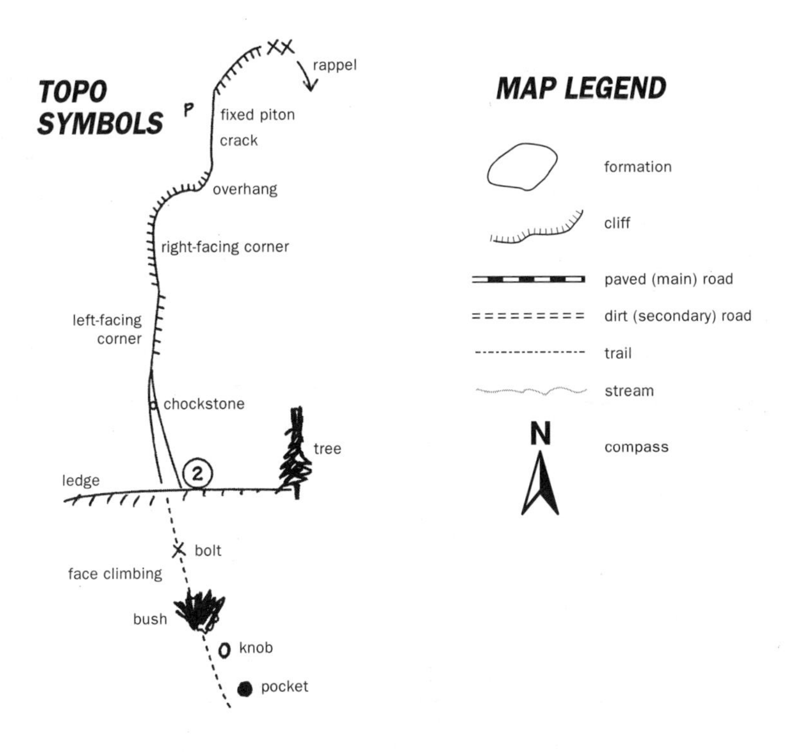

on the route, or along the base of the rock may only be approximate. Directions and distances should be used in conjunction with maps, photographs, topos, and other written descriptions to locate or follow routes.

Routes at Tahquitz and Suicide are described left to right along the respective rock. Therefore, at Tahquitz, this means that routes will be described starting at the North Face first, and finishing with routes on the South Face. At Suicide, this format dictates that routes are described starting at the South Face and ending at the North Face. Overview maps and drawings of Tahquitz and Suicide Rocks are provided to assist in route location. Additionally, written descriptions of the locations and particular approaches to various portions of each rock accompany the topos and maps.

LOS ANGELES CLIMBING AREAS MAP

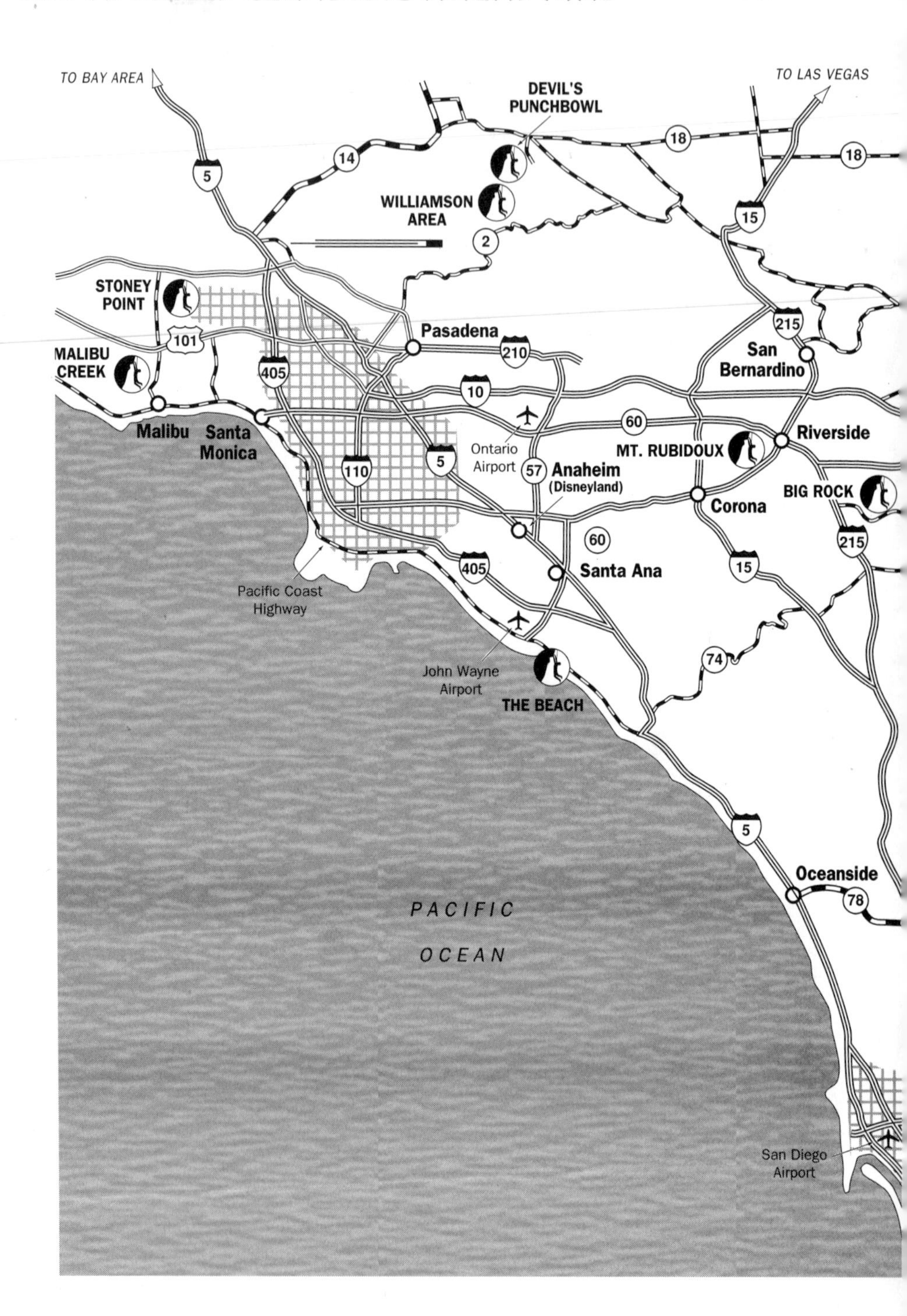

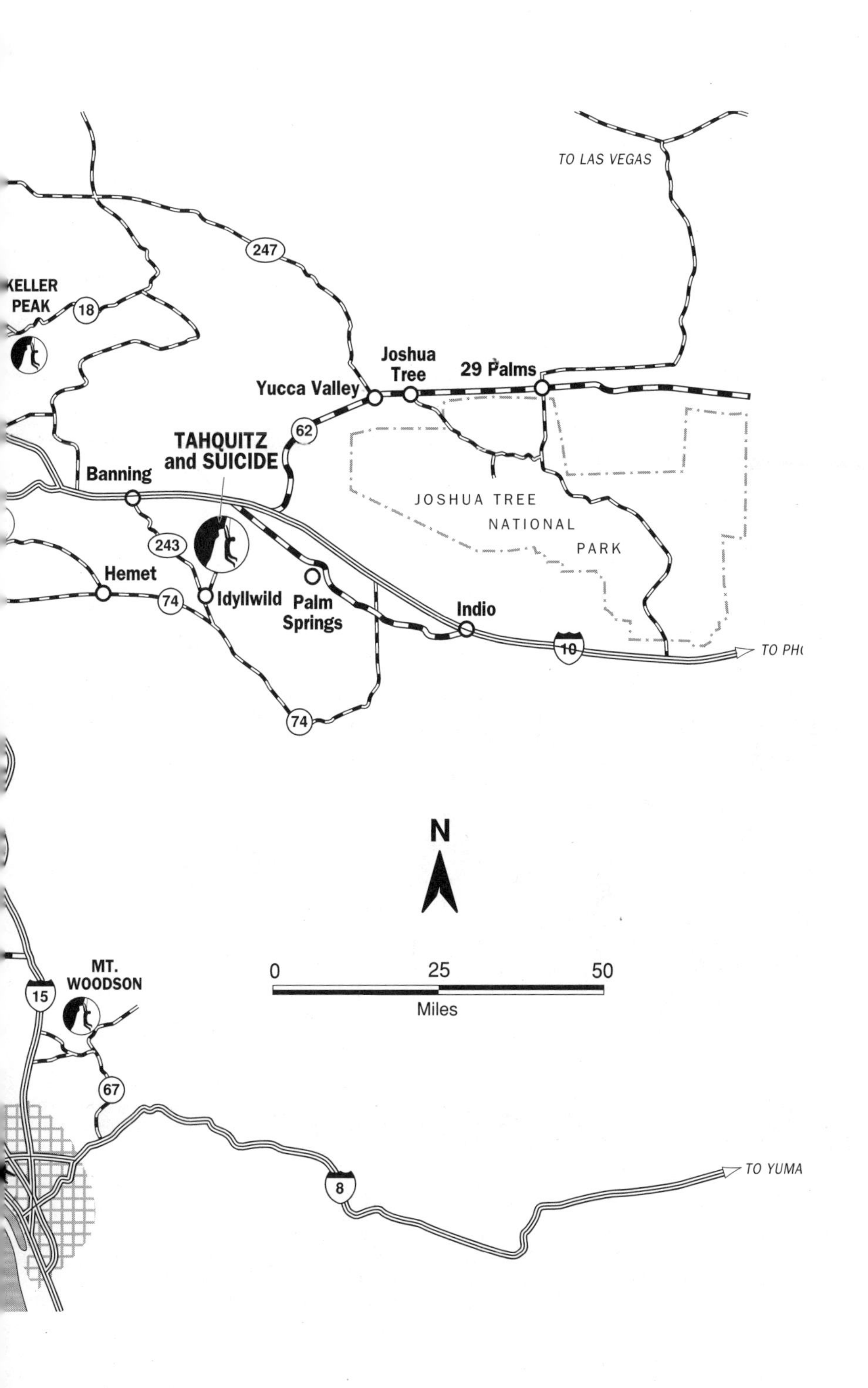
TO LAS VEGAS
247
KELLER PEAK
18
Joshua Tree
29 Palms
Yucca Valley
62
TAHQUITZ and SUICIDE
Banning
JOSHUA TREE NATIONAL PARK
243
Hemet
74
Idyllwild
Palm Springs
Indio
10
TO PH
74
N
0
25
50
Miles
MT. WOODSON
15
67
8
TO YUMA

IDYLLWILD AREA MAP

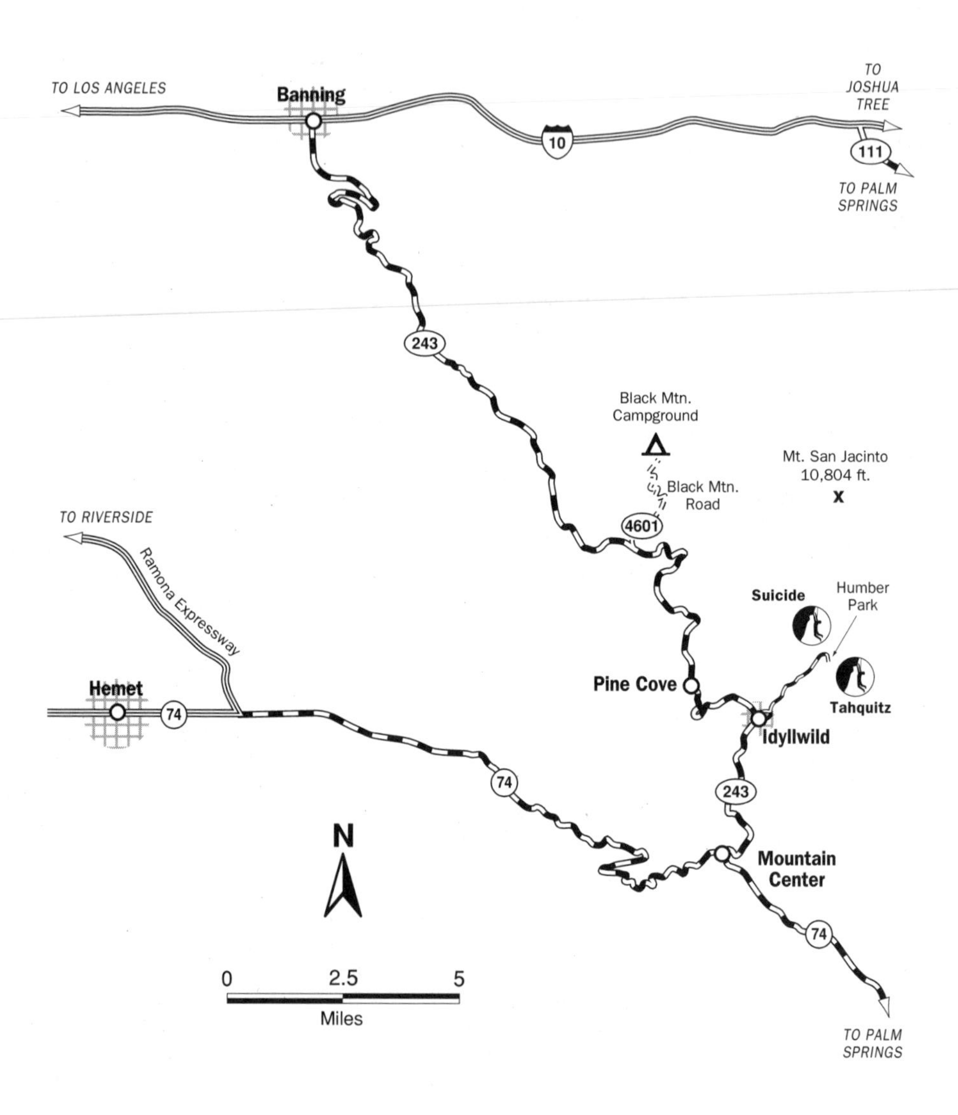

IDYLLWILD DETAIL MAP

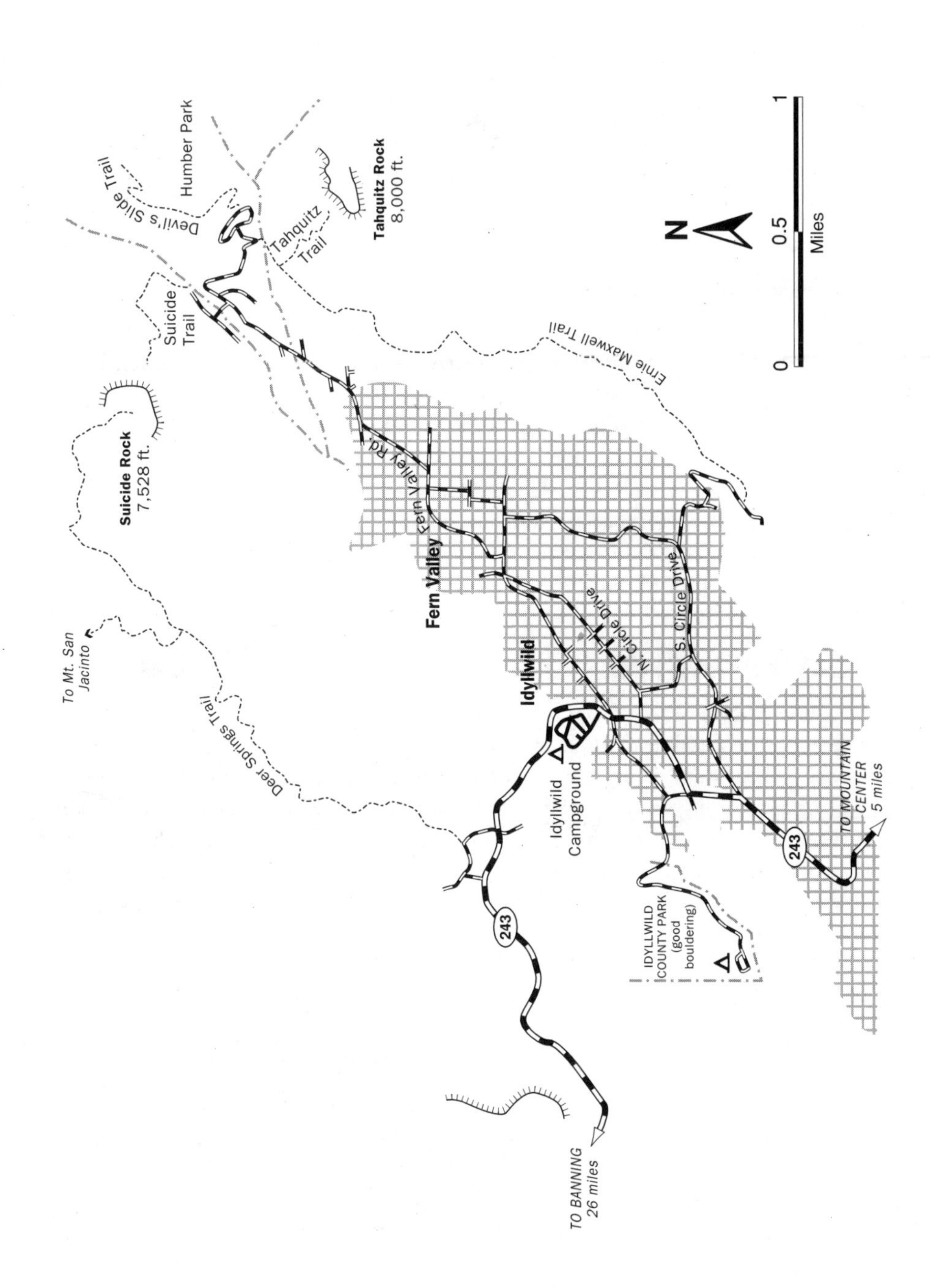

PERMITS

Although Tahquitz and Suicide Rocks are both located in wilderness areas, currently no permit is required for climbers. Trailhead registration may be implemented in the near future. For further information contact the Idyllwild office of the Forest Service at (909) 659–2117. A Forest Adventure Pass is currently required for day-use parking at Humber Park. It is not required for parking for Suicide Rock. Annual and day-use Forest Adventure Passes are available at the Forest Service station in Idyllwild (54270 Pine Crest) and at various retail establishments in town.

EMERGENCIES

In the event of a medical emergency (climbing accident), litters have been placed at both Tahquitz and Suicide. A litter will be found at Lunch Rock at Tahquitz, and near The Weeping Wall at Suicide Rock. Please make sure that these are returned to where they were found if used. For rescues or other more technical emergencies, climbers are fortunate to have the services of the Riverside Mountain Rescue Unit, which can be reached through the Riverside County Sheriff's Office Dispatch by dialing 911 or (800) 950–2444 (then #9 when prompted). Cell phones may have trouble getting through on the 800 number and should dial (909) 776–1099 (then #9 when prompted).

EQUIPMENT

Routes at both Tahquitz and Suicide can require a considerable amount of traditional protection. This is particularly true for routes at Tahquitz. A good selection of nuts, from tiny brass/steel nuts to large camming devices (3 inches or more) may be required. Obviously, the selection of gear and number of pieces will depend on the particular route as well as the individual climber's habits in protecting leads. Slings (that fit over your shoulder) are also useful in reducing rope drag. Equipment suggestions are made for many of the routes. Sizes are given for the particular width of a crack (i.e. "Pro to 3 inches" signifies a crack 3 inches wide).

Climbing and camping equipment can be purchased at Nomad Ventures in Idyllwild. It is located at 54415 North Circle Drive. Telephone (909) 659–4853.

RATINGS

All the climbs listed in this guide are given a difficulty rating, and, where applicable, a quality and/or protection rating.

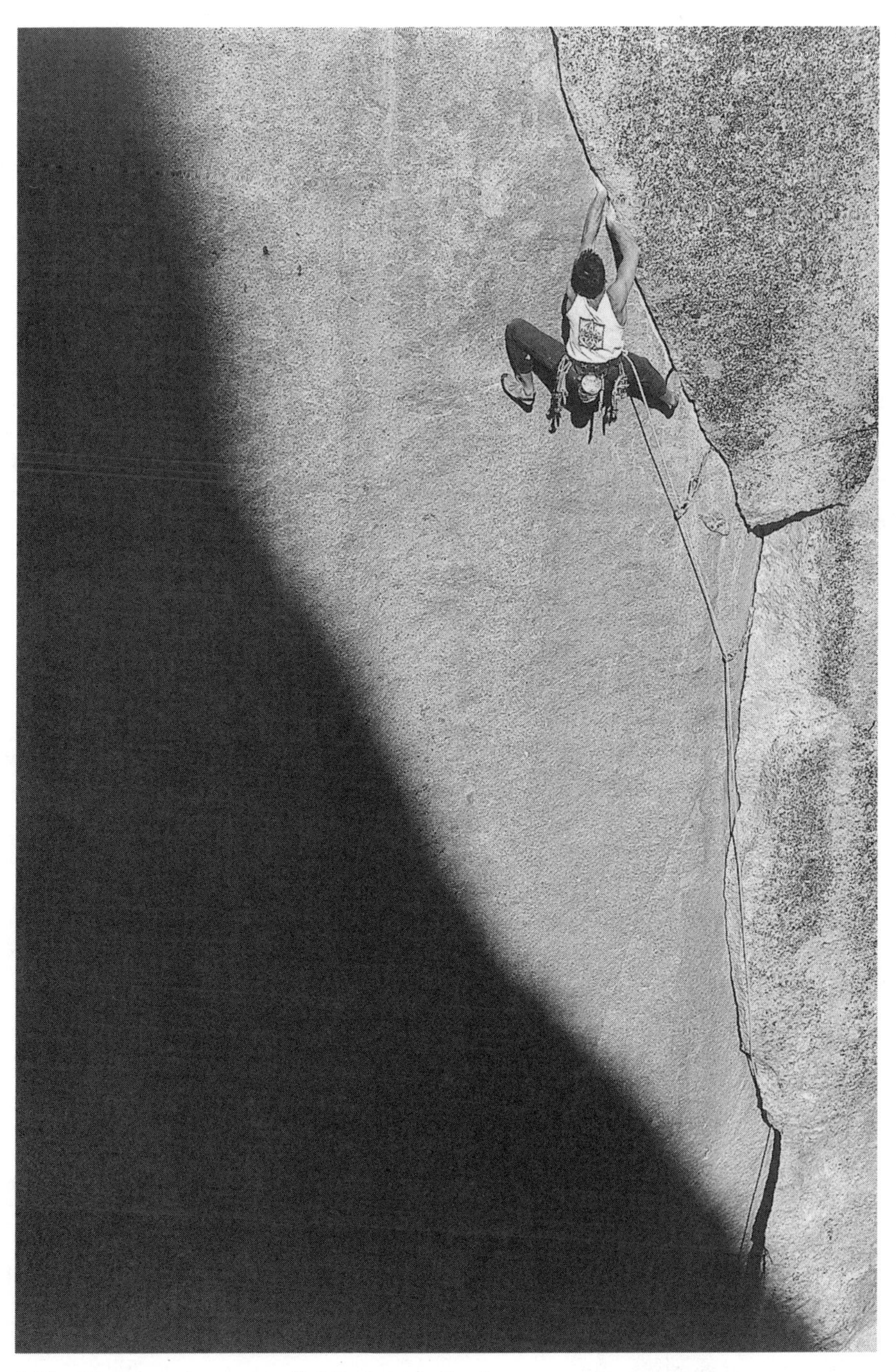

Mike Waugh on Insomnia *(5.11), Suicide Rock.* PHOTO BY KEVIN POWELL

Difficulty

Climbs at Tahquitz and Suicide Rocks use the Tahquitz Decimal System (erroneously referred to as the Yosemite Decimal System) to rate the difficulty of a particular climb. The decimal system was devised at Tahquitz in the early 1950s. In general, the rating given to each climb rates the most difficult move or series of moves on that climb. Sometimes a route with sustained climbing at a particular grade will be given a higher overall rating.

Although ratings at Tahquitz were the "standards" to which other routes were compared, in practice, climbers may find the ratings at Tahquitz and Suicide harder or easier than those to which they are accustomed. Although the ratings given to routes are generally consistent, THE RATINGS GIVEN TO SOME ROUTES MAY JUST BE WRONG. Inconsistent ratings have many causes. Some first ascensionists chronically overrate or underrate difficulty. Just as often, climbers have different opinions based upon their own strengths and weaknesses. Keep this in mind—take the ratings as a guideline only and use your own judgment.

A Rating Comparison Chart is included to assist foreign climbers in determining the relative difficulty of the climbs listed.

Quality Ratings

As with the last several editions of the guide to Tahquitz and Suicide Rocks, climbs that are thought to be of above-average quality are assigned anywhere from 1 to 3 stars. A one-star route is above average in quality; a two-star route is a very good, well-above-average climb; and a three-star route is a classic.

Of course, this is a highly subjective rating system. Few people will completely agree as to what appeals to them in a climb. Nevertheless, the purpose of the use of a quality rating is to direct climbers to routes generally acknowledged to be better in quality.

Please note: Many of the routes at both rocks are quite good. The quality ratings are assigned only in comparison to other climbs at Tahquitz or Suicide. Many unstarred routes may in fact be quite good compared to climbs at other climbing areas.

Protection Ratings

Most climbs at Tahquitz and Suicide tend to be reasonably well protected. However, this is not a sport-climbing area and many climbers may find even the bolt-protected routes to be "run-out." Other climbs in this guide that are poorly protected may have protection ratings. These ratings are tentative and should be used in conjunction with sound judgment. In reality, any climb is potentially dangerous, and the absence of a protection rating does not necessarily mean a climb is safe.

INTERNATIONAL RATING SYSTEMS COMPARED

West German	YDS	British	British	Australian	East German	French
	5.0					
	5.1					
	5.2					
	5.3					
	5.4					
	5.5					
	5.6					
5+	5.7	4b	VS		VIIa	5a
6-	5.8	4c		16	VIIb	5b
6	5.9		HVS	17		5c
6+	5.10a	5a		18	VIIc	6a
7-	5.10b	5b	E1	19	VIIIa	6a+
7	5.10c			20	VIIIb	6b
	5.10d		E2	21	VIIIc	6b+
7+	5.11a	5c		22	IXa	6c
8-	5.11b		E3	23		
8	5.11c			24	IXb	6c+
8+	5.11d	6a		25	IXc	7a
9-	5.12a		E4	26	Xa	7a+
9	5.12b	6b		27	Xb	7b
	5.12c			28		7b+
9+	5.12d		E5	29	Xc	7c
10-	5.13a	6c		30		7c+
10	5.13b		E6	31		8a
	5.13c	7a		32		8a+
10+	5.13d		E7	33		8b
11-	5.14a			34		8b+

The bottom line is that what constitutes good protection for one climber may be poor protection to another. This is especially true for climbers trained on well-bolted sport climbs. If your protection skills are rusty or undeveloped, you may find some routes very difficult to protect adequately. Also, little consensus exists for protection ratings. As stated above, never rely on the absence of a protection rating to indicate good protection. Use your own judgment.

In this guidebook, R and X ratings are given. The definitions for R and X ratings for this guidebook may be slightly different from those used by other guidebook authors. To understand the use of these protection ratings please read this section carefully.

Note: This guide does not use either the G or PG protection ratings. Once again, the protection ratings in this guide are NOT intended to tell you that a climb is well protected. You should NEVER presume that a route is well protected just because it is not given an R or X rating.

R ratings: If a route is poorly protected (AT THE DIFFICULT SECTIONS), but not without some protection, it will be given a R rating. Falling at the wrong place on an R-rated route could result in a very long or serious fall that may result in injury or worse. (Remember, a long or even deadly fall *could* occur on almost any route.)

X ratings: If a climb is so poorly protected (AT THE DIFFICULT SECTIONS) that a severe fall makes hitting the deck possible, it will be given an X rating. A fall from the wrong place on a route with an X rating could result in severe injury or death.

The R and X ratings in this is guide are intended to be used as guidelines only. Only *you* can be the judge of whether a route is adequately protected for you. Please note, many easier routes that deserve a protection rating may not have them. NEVER ASSUME A ROUTE WITHOUT A PROTECTION RATING IS SAFE. You alone are responsible for your own safe climbing. Comments that may improve this tentative rating system are welcome.

Climbing Safely

A guidebook is not an instruction manual, nor is it any protection against having a climbing accident. Experience and careful thinking (sound judgment) are probably the best form of protection for any climber.

Climbing at Tahquitz and Suicide Rocks is largely "traditional" climbing. This means that not all protection is fixed, nor are all routes extremely well protected. Even on the bolted face climbs at Suicide Rock, run-outs of 15 to 20 feet are not uncommon. Few of the bolted routes at either crag could be legitimately termed a "sport" climb. For these reasons, leading confidence and well-developed protection skills will help you avoid a climbing accident.

Remember that these crags involve approaches, descents, and complex rope management. If your climbing experience is limited to a local climbing gym or even a sport-climbing crag, you may lack the skills required to climb safely on a multipitch route at these crags. Professional instruction or climbing routes that are several grades below your normal leading level may be necessary to safely gain experience.

Loose Rock

Loose rock, although not common, has been a major cause of accidents (and fatalities) at Tahquitz. Loose rocks on a ledge can be accidentally knocked off, or larger blocks may dislodge when weighted. This is particularly true on the easier routes at Tahquitz. Even a small falling rock will quickly gain velocity, and if it strikes a climber below, it could be fatal.

When climbing, ALWAYS be careful not to dislodge rocks, even small ones. This also means that you should take care that your rope does not run over loose rocks. Avoid holds or blocks that appear or sound loose. Make sure your belayer is aware of any loose rock you find. If you accidentally dislodge a rock, ALWAYS yell **"ROCK!!"** to warn those below.

Unplanned Bivouacs

It is increasingly uncommon for climbers to get benighted on route. Yet at Tahquitz, every year climbers have unplanned bivouacs. Remember that some of the routes at Tahquitz are relatively long (up to 1,000 feet). If your party is slow and/or inexperienced, start up a climb early. If it is clear that you are moving too slowly to reach the top, an early retreat may be prudent. Seek a rescue if weather or other conditions would not permit you to continue the next day on your own.

Guide Services

There are several climbing schools that operate in the Idyllwild area. Vertical Adventures (800–514–8785) offers classes, guided climbs, and private instruction.

ABOUT BOLTS AND CHIPPING

Bolts

Many of the routes at both rocks were established 10 or more years ago. As a result, most bolted climbs had ¼-inch bolts. In recent years, several local climbers (Clark Jacobs, Bob Gaines, John Barbee, Kevin Powell, Dave Mayville, Mike Ousley, and others) have replaced many of the old bolts (and hangers) on the most popular routes with new ⅜-inch-diameter bolts. In most cases this was done at considerable expense in hardware and time.

However, there are still some original (old) ¼-inch bolts to be found on climbs at both rocks. These should be treated as suspect and replaced (in their original locations) whenever possible. When replacing an old bolt, it should be pulled directly out, not "chopped." The old hole can either be drilled out to a larger size, or if this is not possible, it can be filled with epoxy and the mouth covered with granite dust. (See *Climbing* magazine, Nov./Dec. 1992 for more information about bolts and bolt replacement.)

If establishing a new route (there aren't many good lines left, so use a little common sense), install (and buy) ONLY camouflaged hangers, and use only ⅜- or ½-inch-diameter bolts. Do not use homemade bolts or hangers.

Adding bolts to an established route (as opposed to replacing old bolts) is so seldom justified that it should rarely be considered. Additional protection bolts should generally not be placed on existing routes. Routes are now being given protection ratings to warn of some of the more run-out climbs. Because different people establish routes in different styles, some routes will be perceived to be "underprotected" by some people, and other routes will be considered to be "overprotected" by others. The boldness, or lack of boldness, used by the first ascent party when establishing a particular route should be respected.

Chipping

The chipping or "improving" of holds should never be acceptable. It robs future climbers of the ability to establish more and more difficult routes. Chipping or adding holds to a route or potential route presumes that no one will ever be able to climb at a higher standard, therefore it is okay to alter the rock. History has proven the falsity of such thinking. *The Man Who Fell to Earth* has chiseled holds, despite the fact it is possible to do the route without them.

If the above reasoning is not in any way compelling to you, also consider that the Forest Service, National Park Service, and other public land managers have placed climbing activities under microscopic scrutiny. Even the use of bolts for protection is under review. There is no defense for resource impacts caused by chipping holds. Chipping of holds will inevitably lead to overly restrictive regulation or banning of climbing. Your actions affect every other climber throughout the United States.

New Route Information

New route activity has waned considerably in the last few years, but it will probably always be premature to consider the area climbed out. This guide will be updated in the future. To ensure that new route information is received, all new route information should be mailed directly to: Randy Vogel, P. O. Box 4554, Laguna Beach, CA 92652.

When submitting new route information:

1. Provide the NAME of the route, the RATING (try to use a, b, c, or d rather than plus or minus), the approximate DATE of the first ascent, and the FULL NAMES of the first ascent party.

Clark Jacobs on Flower of High Rank (5.9), Suicide Rock. PHOTO: JACOBS COLLECTION

2. If the route lies adjacent to an existing route, give directions or reference in relation to an existing route. You should also give approximate distances (right or left) in feet or yards.

3. A topo of the route is vital. You may wish to photocopy the topo in this guide that covers the appropriate section of rock and draw the topo on the photocopy. A marked photocopy of a photograph in this guide is also helpful.

APPROACH INFORMATION

For approach information to the bases of Tahquitz and Suicide Rocks, see the overview maps and **Approach Information** at the beginning of each section.

DESCENT ROUTES

Since the routes at both Tahquitz and Suicide are generally multipitch, and the topography often complex, descents from some routes (most routes at Tahquitz) can be complicated. Climbers have devised many descent routes, ranging from walk-offs to technical downclimbs to rappels. The most frequently used descents are described in the text or on the topos. Some of the shown descents may be quite technical and may not be suitable for novice or inexperienced climbers. You may want to familiarize yourself with the descent you plan on using before starting to climb.

HISTORY

The history of Tahquitz Rock as a climbing area dates back to the earliest beginnings of technical rock climbing in the United States. The development of climbing at both Tahquitz and Suicide is intertwined with the history of rock climbing in the United States, with often profound influences on the sport as we now know it. Many of the first 5.8, 5.9, 5.10, 5.11, and 5.12 climbs in the country were established at these rocks by many of the sport's great innovators.

In the early 1930s, Robert Underhill introduced modern rope technique to Sierra Club members in California. Soon after, the Southern California Chapter of the club formed its own technical climbing branch, the Rock Climbing Section (RCS). By the mid-1930s, the RCS conducted an intensive search to ferret out every bit of climbable rock in Southern California.

The RCS had official "scouter report" forms which could be filled out by members to document potential climbing areas. The intent was for club members to further investigate the more promising sites, based upon these reports. As a direct result of this effort, Tahquitz Rock was "discovered" in June 1935 by Jim Smith, a member of the RCS. While on a trip in the San Jacinto Mountains east of Los Angeles, Jim immediately recognized the vast potential offered by Tahquitz.

In Jim's official scouter report he noted, "This rock offers by far the best in advanced rock climbing to be found in So. Calif." In fact, Jim was so excited by the climbing prospects that he made an on-the-spot attempt of the west face with his companion, Mary Jane Edwards. This attempt was ill fated from the beginning as Mary Jane had no climbing experience, Jim had no pitons and only carried a very short piece of rope. After a "rope-length" the difficulties increased, and it became apparent, "much to Mary's relief," that they were ill equipped to continue.

The same route saw another attempt later that year, but this time the climbers were stopped by ice and poor weather. The attempted climb was the most obvious line at Tahquitz and would eventually become the easiest route on the rock. But **The Trough** (5.4) would have to wait until the summer of 1936 before its first ascent. Later in the summer of 1936, Jim Smith, together with Bill Rice, climbed the classic corner system above Lunch Rock, **Angels Fright** (5.6), and with Bob Brinton and Art Johnson, discovered the exhilarating **Fingertip Traverse** (5.3). The climbers were ecstatic with their successes of that summer, and with the quality—but surprising ease—of their new climbs.

By 1937, there was a grand total of six routes, and the climbers were justifiably quite proud of their new crag. That same year, Jim reported in the Sierra Club Bulletin that "A complete Climber's Guide for Tahquitz Rock has been written, with the hope that climbers visiting the South will wish to test their ability on our pride and joy."

Although several reliable references confirm the existence of this first guidebook to Tahquitz, no known copies have survived. It is imagined that the guide would be no more than one sheet of paper (perhaps two sides) reproduced by mimeograph (as was common at that time). Discovery of the 1937 guide is consistent with publication of other small guidebooks by local RCSs during the late 1930s.

Without a doubt, the most impressive climb of this era was **The Mechanic's Route,** one of the country's first 5.8s. Climbed on October 3, 1937, it involved technically difficult climbing on an exposed and steep face. Dick Jones led both pitches and was followed by Glen Dawson, another prolific climber of the 1930s.

Dick demonstrated amazing control leading the second pitch. No piton cracks were available for protection. (Though a bolt was added on the fourth ascent, it has been removed.) Even a modern-day climber would find the runout 5.8 face climbing, in light tennis shoes and tied into a manila rope, more than a bit unnerving.

Glen Dawson recalls, "The climb was right at the limit of what I wanted to do, difficulty-wise. I think we may not have done it free if we had a good spot to put in a piton—the free climbing was really partly a result of necessity."

The late 1930s were exciting times for the infant sport of climbing in Southern California. The possibilities seemed endless and a very noncompetitive camaraderie pervaded the RCS. During this time, climbing at Tahquitz was featured in a film entitled *Three on a Rope.* The movie featured several local climbers, including Bill Rice. Most of the climbers worked on the

From left: Dave Sherrick, Harry Daley, Yvon Chouinard, Dick Erb, Dolt, and Tom Frost, 1959. PHOTO BY CHUCK WILTS

movie for free, but a few, including Rice, were promised nominal wages. In what were still the lean years in the aftermath of the Great Depression, the thought of climbers receiving money for doing what they liked to do was a fairly attractive proposition. When the film was completed, the film makers refused to pay. The climbers were forced to sue to collect what was really just a modest sum.

Development continued, and by 1940 approximately a dozen routes had been established. But activity soon slowed as World War II saw most climbers joining the armed forces. Nevertheless, a few people continued to climb. The best known and perhaps the most influential of these was Chuck Wilts.

Wilts recalled climbing in the 1940s: "I got started climbing in 1941 with the RCS. A friend of mine, Lester Grossman, persuaded me and a girl, who ended up being my wife, to go rock climbing. All three of us took to it immediately, but then the war came along and put a stop to it, just as we got started."

Since graduate work at Cal Tech had potential military applications, Wilts and a few of his climbing friends stayed in California for the duration. Four or five active RCS members kept the section alive, as those with nontechnical jobs went off to war.

Jim Gorin was one of those RCS members active during the war. Jim did not have a technical job, but was excused from military service—he had lost one leg. This did not seem to prevent Jim from climbing all the hardest routes of the time. His greatest difficulty climbing, apparently, was dragging his crutch to the top of the rock so that he could make the descent.

In 1941, local climber William Shand produced a guidebook for climbing at Tahquitz. Original mimeograph copies of this guidebook, listing approximately 15 routes, were distributed to RCS members. Unlike the first guidebook produced in 1937, several copies of this guide have survived. In 1945, Shand produced a two-page supplement to the guidebook listing new routes. Routes listed in this guide were rated either easy, moderate, or hard fifth class. This division of class five climbing into finer grades of difficulty was one of the first documented attempts to quantify the difficulty of technical rock climbs.

During the war years, gas rationing made the trip to Tahquitz a major undertaking, and restricted such ventures to once- or twice-a-year affairs. After the war, climbing returned to prewar levels, but motivation for new routes was absent. Most climbers were content to repeat established climbs, time after time.

"It wasn't until some of the young kids started pushing us that we got excited about new routes," recollected Wilts. These young "kids" who broke the complacent atmosphere were the likes of Royal Robbins, Jerry Gallwas, Don Wilson, and Frank Hoover. "They took to it and started trying new things. The older people just had to compete to survive. As a matter of fact, that is what really got me interested in new routes."

Improved equipment also played a significant role. The postwar years brought a large amount of surplus rope, pitons, and carabiners onto the domestic market. Prior to the war, these items had to be ordered from Europe and were often expensive. The ring-angle piton, developed during the war, was a great improvement. Leading was now safer, encouraging yet harder leads.

Wilts's accomplishments form quite a respectable list. **The Swallow** (5.10a) and **The Consolation** (5.9, later freed) are only two of his seventeen first ascents at Tahquitz. Perhaps the most classic of these routes was **The Ski Tracks** (5.6). This excellent, amazingly steep route was one of Wilts's personal favorites.

About this time, the leading climbers at Tahquitz began to place greater emphasis on free climbing. Wilts was quite conscious of pushing free climbing, feeling it was very important to do a route without aid if at all possible. His attitude was quite influential, beginning a tradition of high-standard free climbing which was soon exported to other areas. This emphasis on free climbing helped shape Tahquitz into a major spawning ground for successive generations of influential climbers.

While Wilts championed a new free climbing ethic, many members of the RCS were much slower to do so. Older members felt that young climbers like

Ellen Wilts on The Steparound (crux) of Left Ski Track, *Tahquitz.* PHOTO BY CHUCK WILTS

Royal Robbins on the second ascent of Jonah. PHOTO COURTESY OF ROYAL ROBBINS COLLECTION

Robbins had started out at too high a standard. Motivated by jealousy, the old guard labeled hard climbing "unsafe." This attitude was by no means uncommon in other climbing organizations at this time. Similar to the disenchantment felt in the Shawangunks due to the Appalachian Mountain Club's repressive attitudes, the RCS started to lose credibility.

Tahquitz during the 1950s was clearly the domain of one of the young upstarts: Royal Robbins. Royal recalls receiving positive feedback from the more progressive RCS members: "Chuck Wilts and John Mendenhall were good examples for me to follow. They were very positive—they just loved climbing."

Royal Robbins on Unchaste, *1964.* PHOTO BY TOM FROST

Robbins started climbing in 1950 with the RCS. By 1952, he had established one of the hardest free climbs in the United States, **The Open Book** (5.9). This aptly (though unimaginatively) named route climbs an elegant dihedral for three-and-a-half pitches, and is still regarded as one of Tahquitz's classic lines. Wilts quickly made the second ascent. "Our policy," states Royal, "was to try to free climb as much as possible. We really pushed climbing beyond what previous generations had tried. Doing new things was just natural for us, because we were young."

During the early 1950s, new climbs were constantly being added. The high concentration of difficult climbs led to the need for a better rating system. Up to this time, technical climbs were described as being either easy, moderate, or hard fifth class. So many routes of varying difficulty were being lumped together that the existing rating system was not very useful.

As a result, Robbins and Don Wilson had been devising a new rating system. When Wilts began work on his new guide, Wilts, Robbins, and Wilson put their heads together and the modern "Decimal System" was born. When a comprehensive new guidebook appeared in 1956, free climbs were rated the now familiar 5.0, 5.1, 5.2, etc. The top rating, 5.9, was assigned to the hardest routes, and 5.0 was assigned to the easiest fifth-class route. Climbs of certain difficulties at Tahquitz become the "standards" by which to rate new routes.

Some informally referred to the new rating system as the "Southern California" or "Wilts-Sierra" System. The unassuming Wilts refused to attach his name to the system. About this time, Tahquitz local Mark Powell became one of the early Yosemite climbing bums and is credited by some with introducing the decimal system to the Valley. In any event, Yosemite got credit for this innovation, and by the early 1960s, the Decimal System, devised at Tahquitz, became commonly known as the Yosemite Decimal System (YDS).

Robbins's reign at Tahquitz was to end by 1960, as he moved on to bigger climbs. But before he left, he established an imposing and serious aid route (5.9 A4) up to central bulge of Tahquitz's west face. Now regarded as one of the finest free climbs in California, **The Vampire** was a high point for Robbins. "We were so far out there, on those thin flakes. It was a new step for us, just like when we did Half Dome."

The Tahquitz scene of the 1960s witnessed a new group of climbers even less loyal to the increasingly restrictive environment of the RCS. Nevertheless, the values of their predecessors deeply influenced this new generation. Again, free climbing standards took a large leap forward, and Tahquitz continued to lead the country in pushing the free climbing scale. Bob Kamps, Mark Powell, TM Herbert, Tom Higgins, and Tom Frost were some of the individuals instrumental in continuing the free climbing legacy.

Style and free climbing were very important at the time. "There was no question about what was right," recalls Tom Higgins. Just as Wilts and

Chuck Wilts on Whodunit, *1962.* PHOTO BY TOM FROST

Mendenhall had influenced Robbins, Robbins influenced the next generation. As Higgins observes, the influence of Robbins and others "was so strong we wouldn't ever think about doing otherwise." But again, Higgins adds, there was "no rationale for considering other ethics, as plenty of challenges were left without violating the existing ethical standards."

Aid routes of earlier generations began to be freed and new, more difficult climbs established. Frost and Kamps's 1960 free ascent of **The Blank** (5.10a) was one of the first climbs in the country to be rated 5.10. By 1963, **Blanketty Blank** (5.10c), freed by Kamps and Higgins, firmly established Tahquitz as the center of hard face climbing in the country. "**Blanketty Blank** opened our eyes; you could get away from the cracks, out on the faces. When we later freed the **Powell-Reed** (5.10c) and **The Punch Bowl** (5.10a), both in Yosemite, we used the confidence from our experience at Tahquitz," says Higgins.

Shoe design also began to evolve about this time, which enabled climbers at Tahquitz to climb steeper, thinner, and more sustained pitches. The Zillerthal shoe was one of the first shoes specifically designed for climbing and was first used in the early 1960s by climbers at Tahquitz. Another very popular shoe during the 1960s was the Kronhoffer, and during the early and mid-1960s was the shoe of choice by most climbers.

However, Bob Kamps recalls that the "fit" of the Kronhoffer was not right for him, and he climbed most of his difficult routes in Pivetta Cortinas, a very stiff hiking shoe with a vibram sole.

In 1967, **Chingadera** (5.11a) was freed by Kamps and Powell. Kamps originally rated this route either hard 5.9 or 5.10. "I was reluctant to call it 5.10. In 1967 everyone was reluctant to call anything 5.10, although I felt it was harder than **Blanketty Blank,** which I did in 1963," states Kamps today.

In the mid-1960s climbers were extremely reluctant to rate any climb harder than 5.9, the upper limit of the Tahquitz Decimal System. However, it was very clear that climbs being established during this period were significantly more difficult than routes such as **The Open Book,** the standard 5.9 (established in 1952).

In fact, **Chingadera** was rated 5.10 until 1980. **Chingadera** was the next logical step in face climbing after the freeing of **Blanketty Blank.** But where **Blanketty Blank** had only one bolt placed on it, **Chingadera** had 8, away from any crack systems. This marked the line as the first in a genre of pure face routes. **Chingadera** was a significant advance in free climbing standards at Tahquitz, with Kamps leading the entire route (including placing of 3 new bolts above the end of the aid section) in one push.

"I remember being really frightened, especially placing the last bolt. I was forced to sit in a crouched position to place that bolt. My feet were so sore that I couldn't even feel them when going out on the traverse (one of the cruxes)."

Chuck Wilts on an early ascent of Traitor Horn *(5.8), Tahquitz.*

As impressive as the unprotected tennis-shoe lead of **Mechanic's Route** in 1938, few modern climbers would be able to climb **Chingadera** in the inflexible Pivetta hiking boots used by Kamps on his first free ascent.

Unlike Tahquitz, which is rife with crack systems, Suicide Rock's steep, flawless faces presented a rather formidable obstacle. Despite the advances made at Tahquitz in face climbing, other than an impressive 1955 ascent of **Paisano Jam Crack** (5.10a; Powell, Wilson, and Hoover), Suicide Rock was all but ignored. But in 1965, a climber from the Northwest began his post-doctoral work at Cal-Tech, and things were due to change. That climber, Pat Callis, remembers those next few years well. After climbing at Tahquitz for awhile, he began to ask about that big rock across the valley. "The common lore was that the faces at Suicide were too steep and blank to climb. This was an amazing mental barrier; we were held back from climbing there by this." Bob Kamps recalls that the reason he did not climb there was that he did not know anybody else who had ever been there and from across the valley "it didn't look that worthwhile."

But Callis wasn't put off for long. Used to establishing new routes, he hiked up to Suicide one day with Larry Reynolds to have a look for himself. "I wandered up this face a ways just for fun, and realized that it was climbable. It was tremendously exciting." The route they climbed that day was aptly named **Surprise** (5.8), the first face climb on the rock.

"We began putting routes up at will. Although large numbers of bolts were required, this wasn't a barrier, as Kamps and Powell were doing bolted routes at Tahquitz. When you are young and don't have a reputation, you are open to creating new stuff; your imagination isn't limited." Over the next three years, Callis, usually climbing with Charlie Raymond and Lee Harrell, put up over thirty new routes at Suicide.

The Iron Cross (later freed at 5.11a), **Sundance** (5.10b), **Hesitation** (5.10a) and **Serpentine** (5.9) were only a few of the classics established by Callis, Raymond, and Harrell. **Sundance** remains one of Pat's "special" routes. Established in the winter months, it was an extremely bold line for the time, ascending the center of the Sunshine Face, Suicide's largest expanse of unbroken rock, well away from any other routes. **Hesitation,** also on the Sunshine Face, was a product of perhaps Callis's boldest moment. "I soloed the first ascent—by accident, really. I was supposed to climb with Lee Harrell, who didn't show up. I just couldn't deal without climbing that day so I did it solo. It was a real adventure; I used a 5⁄16 prussik from my swami, and actually took a couple of short falls, maybe 5 or 6 feet, at the crux."

By the late 1960s and early 1970s, most new route attention had shifted to Suicide. In addition to Callis, Raymond, and Harrell, Ivan Couch—usually partnered with Mike Dent and Larry Reynolds—began to spearhead further development. In all, Couch was involved in 14 first ascents at Suicide, including the intimidating **Hair Lip** (5.10a), **Miscalculation** (5.10c), and in November 1970, his last route and *piece de resistance,* **Valhalla** (5.11a).

Valhalla took a line up the center of the Sunshine Face, to the right of **Sundance.** The route avoids any weakness exploited by previous routes on the face. Sustained, difficult, and extraordinary climbing immediately marked **Valhalla** as the classic of the area. Although Couch continued to climb after his ascent of **Valhalla,** he never again pushed himself as before.

Most of Ivan's climbing was done in brown leather RD rock shoes—excellent for edging, but poor for smearing. The late 1960s saw the common use and development of other specialized rock shoes. The red PA was a popular and early "smooth-soled" shoe. Perhaps the most popular shoe of the late 1960s was the blue suede RR (Royal Robbins). These specialized rock shoes clearly had a big effect on the advancement of face (and crack) climbing standards.

With the rapid establishment of bolted face routes, bolting technology began to advance. Bolts were hand drilled from stances on the rock. Many bolt hangers were homemade models, cut from "L" stock aluminum. ¼-inch by 1-inch Rawl compression bolts were almost universally used; few people questioned the security of these bolts and hangers. Until the 1960s, most bolts were used for direct aid, and the existing technology was adapted for protecting face climbs without much consideration of how bolts would hold up to repeated falls.

Ivan Couch on the first ascent of Valhalla. PHOTO BY LARRY REYNOLDS

Bolts were not accepted by climbers without some controversy. Some climbers felt that bolts destroyed the element of the unknown in climbing and were concerned about the excessive use of bolts, especially for aid. For many years climbers even felt that replacing even poor bolts was questionable.

A short period of quiescence settled on the crags after **Valhalla.** Little new-route activity was occurring, and most climbers knew each other—it was a friendly fraternity. Some observers even declared the area "climbed out." The most noteworthy route established during this lull was the elegantly thin **Rebolting Development** (5.11a), done in 1971 by D. Wert, Mike Kaiser, and Greg Bender. The run-out first pitch and sustained climbing on the thinnest of edges produced an instant test piece. Until it was replaced, a spinner (poorly placed bolt) protecting the crux of the second pitch long demanded competent climbing.

About this time, the seeds of a new climbing revolution were being planted in the vast urban sprawl of greater Los Angeles, and the beginning of the modern free climbing movement was just around the corner. With its long history of pushing free climbing standards, Tahquitz and Suicide provided the perfect breeding ground for this free climbing metamorphosis.

In 1971, a young Eric (Rick) Accomazzo enrolled in a high school climbing course, taught by fellow student John Long. What Rick didn't know was that John had started the course to find a partner. When Rick inquired of John's experience, Long—true to form—professed to "years." Only later did he confess that a month had been closer to the truth!

Accomazzo was suspicious: "John was interested in climbing with me because I had a car." A short time later, the two young climbers met Richard Harrison, who was also psyched to climb as much as possible, and the three began to climb together regularly. This new generation of climbers was irreverent, talented, and willing to try anything.

In 1972, the first specialized technical rock boot became available. The "E.B." had a profound impact on climbing—not unlike what happened in 1983 when the super-sticky Fire shoes hit the scene. A large number of younger climbers found that they could climb even the hardest routes. For the most part, there was little socializing with the older climbers. A group of these young hotshots improved rapidly, and by 1972 a few had climbed **Valhalla,** the undisputed hardest climb in the area.

Long, Accomazzo, Harrison, Gib Lewis, John Bachar, Tobin Sorenson, Mike Graham, Rob Muir, and Jim Wilson were the core of this counter-culture new generation. Climbing **Valhalla** was the unofficial rite of passage into this unofficial conglomeration of friends known as The Stonemasters. In 1972, Jim Erickson's first free ascent of **Insomnia** (5.11b), an overhanging and beautiful thin-hands crack on Suicide, had a big effect. A Colorado climber had snatched a prize route, shocking the locals who, frankly, were not good enough at cracks to have climbed it free. A summer in Yosemite was to change that, and once again Tahquitz and Suicide came into national prominence.

A banner year was 1973. At Tahquitz, free ascents were made of the strenuous **Le Toit** (5.12a), by Long and Accomazzo; **Lower Royal's Arch** (5.10d), by Sorenson and Accomazzo; **The Flakes** (5.11c), by Long, Sorenson, Harrison, and Bill Antel; and the formidable and imposing **The Vampire** (5.11a), by Accomazzo, Long, Graham, and Antel.

This last route was a mental breakthrough as well. Clearly, **The Vampire** was the hardest of Robbins's legacy; its first free ascent was clear evidence that free climbing could know no bounds. Accomazzo comments: "John was really the driving force behind all these free ascents. We were really happy to do a Royal Robbins route free; it made us think we were hot stuff. It had a great reputation as an aid climb. In fact, we didn't know anyone who had aided it."

At Suicide, Long and Harrison freed **The Drain Pipe** (5.11a), and Graham and Sorenson made the first ascent of a new climb on the Sunshine Face, **New Generation** (5.11c). This latter route, to the right of **Valhalla,** combined bold climbing with what was then the highest standards of difficulty. Like **Valhalla** before it, **"New Gen"** established the new mark for others to meet.

In 1974, in a Herculean effort and braving poor protection, John Long led the first free ascent of **Paisano Overhang** (5.12c). Even though Long has since disdained the climb as "a miserable climbing problem—an utterly insignificant route," it ushered in the 5.12 rating, and remained unrepeated for many years. Long led the offwidth splitting the 220-degree roof wearing leather gloves wrapped with electrical tape. The shear audacity of such a project so many years ago compels one to believe his comment, "The jams were hardly any better."

By 1975, most of the action had begun to subside. Accomazzo succeeded in free climbing the steep dihedral of **The Green Arch** (5.11c) at Tahquitz. The crack in the corner starts as thin fingers, then becomes thinner, as does the dihedral, which arches to the right, eventually forming a tiny roof.

But that year Tobin Sorenson led what is arguably the most outstanding first ascent ever made in the Idyllwild area, **The Edge.** Although technically "only" 5.11a, this climbs remains one of the most psychologically demanding routes in Southern California.

The Edge ascends a beautiful arete left of **The Open Book,** and sports two 40-foot run-outs on continuous 5.10 while palming the edge. As the story is recounted, Sorenson was so scared upon reaching the only bolt stance—a marginal sloping area on the arete—that he broke into tears. After nearly an hour of desperate drilling, the drill bit broke, and only after considerable coaching from his belayer was the bolt finally placed.

Sorenson's enthusiasm knew few bounds, and he lived his life on and off the crags at the limit. Whether doing the flying leap of **Super Fly,** unroped and with a full body twist, or leading with a noose around his neck, Tobin always upped the ante. Sorenson took his tremendous talent and go-for-it attitude to the Alps, where he scored a list of impressive solo and important alpine climbs. Tobin died in 1980 while attempting the first solo ascent (and second overall) of the north face of Mt. Alberta in the Canadian Rockies.

Harder climbs followed harder climbs throughout the 1970s. Most of the climbers pushing standards were about the same age, and were in great competition with each other. But even the brilliant Rick Accomazzo admits there was one that eventually stood out: "Then [John] Bachar came along and drove the competition even more—until he passed all of us, of course."

Although Bachar directed most of his energies into projects in Yosemite, he left an indelible mark on the Idyllwild scene. He joined with Sorenson to do the coveted first free ascent of **Black Harlot's Layaway** (5.11d) in 1974. But certainly his most impressive lead was the 1978 first ascent of the demanding **Caliente** (5.12b), perhaps the most difficult pure face route in California at the time.

In 1976, a 15-year-old boy started climbing at Suicide. Not part of The Stonemasters, or one of the resident hard men, Tony Yaniro would go on to change the face of climbing by establishing the world's hardest route in 1979 (**Grand Illusion** on Sugarloaf, near Lake Tahoe) and promoting the pursuit of pure difficulty. In his first year of climbing, he and Dick Leversee made the first ascent of **Gates of Delirium** (5.11c) on the left side of the Sunshine Face. Tony had never climbed a 5.11 before. "I cranked so hard on that route that at the belay I noticed blood coming out from underneath my fingernails," says Tony.

"After we completed the route we told Kevin Powell and Darrell Hensel about it; we told them it was 5.10d. We just didn't know any better." The same year, Matt Cox and Hensel freed **Magical Mystery Tour** at Tahquitz (5.11c) and Lewis, Accomazzo, and Wilson established **Quiet Desperation** (5.11c), which links **Iron Cross** and **Ishi** on Suicide's Sunshine Face. Hensel and Kevin Powell (no relation to Mark) began their reign over the hard face climbs of Suicide about this time as well.

In 1978 Yaniro added another route to the top standard at Suicide with his first free ascent of **The Pirate** (5.12c). Many locals had doubted that this thin, 100-foot stopper crack up a flawless, 85-degree face would go free, and there were rumors that Tony climbed outside of Idyllwild's well-established traditions. Consequently, some doubted the truth of the ascent. In reality, Tony did the climbing in good style. "I wasn't into hang-dogging at the time, and actually took some hard long falls, slamming down on the face, trying to lead it," Tony remembers, adding, "After the first ascent, I did it three or four times more." But he started visiting the area less frequently and stopped altogether within a few years.

Darrell Hensel, regarded by many as the ultimate master of thin face, recalls looking up to The Stonemasters in his early years: "Accomazzo, Long, and Sorenson were the biggest influences on my climbing, but mostly Accomazzo—his technical ability, and the fact that long falls never seemed to bother him. He had really clean style."

In 1979, Hensel and Powell continued The Stonemasters' tradition by pushing free climbing, and perhaps even more than The Stonemasters, they eschewed poor style. Powell could be brought to near fits of rage when he fell on a route or in some other manner "tainted" an ascent.

John Long on Hades, *1984.* PHOTO BY DWIGHT BROOKS

Darrell Hensel on the first free ascent of Ishi, *Sunshine Face.* PHOTO BY KEVIN POWELL

Their first free ascents of **Knocking on Heaven's Door** (5.11d) in 1979 and the first pitch of the **Direct South Face** (subsequently renamed **Hades,** 5.12b) in 1980 are particularly significant. Hensel recounts that on **Knocking,** "I tried face climbing under the arch then finally got the idea of underclinging it. So I started underclinging out, but there was no way I could stop, I got myself committed, and couldn't let go to place pro. I fell off before reaching the end of the arch, took a pretty good sized swing and got bruised ribs from the rack."

We finally got a fixed pin in halfway across the arch. Five days later we came back, and the pin was gone. We thought someone had taken it, then we found it in the dirt at the base; it had fallen out on its own, the flake was so expanding." Similarly, on the **Direct South Face (Hades)** entire days were spent just placing fixed pins on the lead, only to have them removed by aid climbers. In 1985 Hensel scored a major *coup de grace* by freeing **Ishi** (5.12d). **Ishi** remains one of the ultimates in thin face climbing at Suicide and has seen few repeat ascents.

In the 1980s Tahquitz and Suicide both saw renewed new route activity, despite having been declared "climbed out." These include the 1981 ascent of **Fred** (5.11a), a superb two-pitch climb established by Charles Cole and Randy Vogel.

In 1984 John Long and Bob Gaines freed the **Stairway to Heaven** (5.12a) on Tahquitz and the second pitch of **Hades** (5.12+) on Suicide Rock. Long also led the direct start to **The Edge,** titled **Turbo Flange** (5.11c R).

In 1985, Charles Cole and Bob Gaines found **Scarface** (5.11d) on Tahquitz, and in 1986 Dave Evans (with Craig Fry and Darrell Hensel) added two classic routes to Suicide's Sunshine Face: **Moondance** (5.11c) and **Red Rain** (5.11b).

In the summer of 1986, Darrell Hensel and Jonny Woodward teamed up to establish several excellent Suicide Rock routes: **The Great Pretender** (5.12b) on Deception Pillar Buttress, **Archangel** (5.11d) on the South Face, and **The Untickable** (5.12a) on Eagle Pinnacle.

In 1987 Tom Gilge added **Pinhead** (5.12b), an overhanging test piece on Suicide's Limp Dick formation, and Bob Gaines added a beautiful slab pitch to Suicide's South Face with **Hell's Angel** (5.12a).

In 1988, Gilge led the spectacular **South Arete** (5.11d) on Suicide's Le Dent Pinnacle. While a teenager from Hemet, Gilge and the late Dan Osman could often be seen free-soloing **Insomnia** (5.11c) in tandem. Over on Tahquitz, Charles Cole and Troy Mayr discovered a great two-pitch route on the West Face: **Fright Night** (5.12a).

On Suicide Rock, perhaps the most significant first ascent of the 1990s was Hensel's completion of his long-standing project **Someone You're Not** (5.13a) in November 1991. **Someone You're Not** ascends an audacious line on superb rock to the right of **Caliente.** Considered by many to be one of

John Long on the first free ascent of Stairway to Heaven. BOB GAINES PHOTO

Suicide's last great projects, the second pitch has one of the area's most baffling cruxes, with no repeat ascents as of this writing.

In the 1990s, new route development continued, albeit at a slower pace, mainly on Tahquitz. In 1990 Bob Gaines and Charlie Peterson completed **Constellation** (5.12a), a five-pitch slab between **The Swallow** and **Consolation.** Several test piece aretes were done, including Dave Mayville's **Slapstick** (5.12b) and Gaines's **Point Blank** (5.12b). Gaines added several classic face routes, including the four-pitch **Heathen** (5.11b) on the South Face, **Crucifix** (5.11b) and **Field of Dreams** (5.11b) on the West Face Bulge, and the demanding **Bookworm** (5.12c) on the wall left of **The Open Book.**

It is also meaningful to note that many of the aging ¼-inch bolts at Tahquitz and Suicide have been systematically replaced with solid ⅜-inch bolts, thanks to the work of local climbers. This effort has been undertaken with great care to minimize damage to the rock and to preserve the original placements. In the future, some bolts should be upgraded to 1/2-inch diameter, especially where they see repeated falls.

In Chuck Wilts's sixth edition of the *Tahquitz and Suicide Guide* (published in 1979) Chuck wrote, "This may be the last edition of the *Tahquitz and Suicide Guide.* Even climbers of the present generation seem to agree that the basic purpose of the guide has been fulfilled, and that there is no real need to record more and more variations of existing routes." Since 1979 however, more than 300 new routes have been climbed, more than doubling the number of routes existing at the time.

Once again one is tempted to declare these crags "climbed out." The number of new routes has declined precipitously, particularly at Suicide Rock. However, there remains potential for short routes at both crags, some of these climbable at a very high standard of difficulty, and numerous smaller crags exist on the mountainside left of Tahquitz, making any such pronouncements always premature. No doubt the crags of Idyllwild will produce fine routes in the future, but more important, they contain one of the country's most superb collection of easy-to-difficult granite routes.

TAHQUITZ ROCK

The starts of the routes are described in the description of each climb. Tahquitz Rock is divided into several sections, corresponding to the rock's various aspects. These include The North Face, The Northwest Recess, The West Face Bulge Area, The West Face, and The South Face. The boundaries are described in greater detail in each section.

APPROACH INFORMATION

The following are the most commonly used approaches to the base of Tahquitz Rock. For approaches to particular routes or sections of the rocks, see the text.

The approaches to Tahquitz Rock are steep and at altitudes over 7,000 feet. If you are in poor physical condition, plan on taking extra time on the approach and descent. The "trails" have formed as a result of years of use, and are not maintained. It is hoped that a more formal trail system will be constructed in the future to reduce erosion. Use care to hike along only the established trail, and don't forge new paths. This will help avoid unnecessary soil erosion.

Lunch Rock Trail: The normal approach to Tahquitz Rock starts on the Ernie Maxwell Trail. The trailhead is located just before the first sharp bend at Humber Park, 0.25 mile up the road from the Suicide Rock parking area. Follow the Ernie Maxwell Trail across Strawberry Creek, then proceed about 200 yards (around a bend) along this well graded trail to a point where a very crude trail will be seen heading straight up the hillside on your left. This steep and rough trail heads about 0.4 mile up the hillside (staying right of a talus field). It eventually leads you to the base of Lunch Rock, where most climbers leave their packs, etc. Plan on about 30 minutes or more for the approach from the car. See Tahquitz Rock Overview Map.

North Face Trail: Climbers approaching directly to the North Face of Tahquitz may wish to avoid the Lunch Rock Trail. Instead, start at the Devil's Slide Hiking Trail. This is well marked and located at the top of the Humber Park Loop. After about 20 yards head right (southeast) to Strawberry Creek. A rough trail borders the creek, eventually fading out below talus fields which are taken directly uphill to the North Face. Plan on about 30 minutes for the approach from the car. See the Tahquitz Rock Overview Map.

TAHQUITZ ROCK OVERVIEW MAP

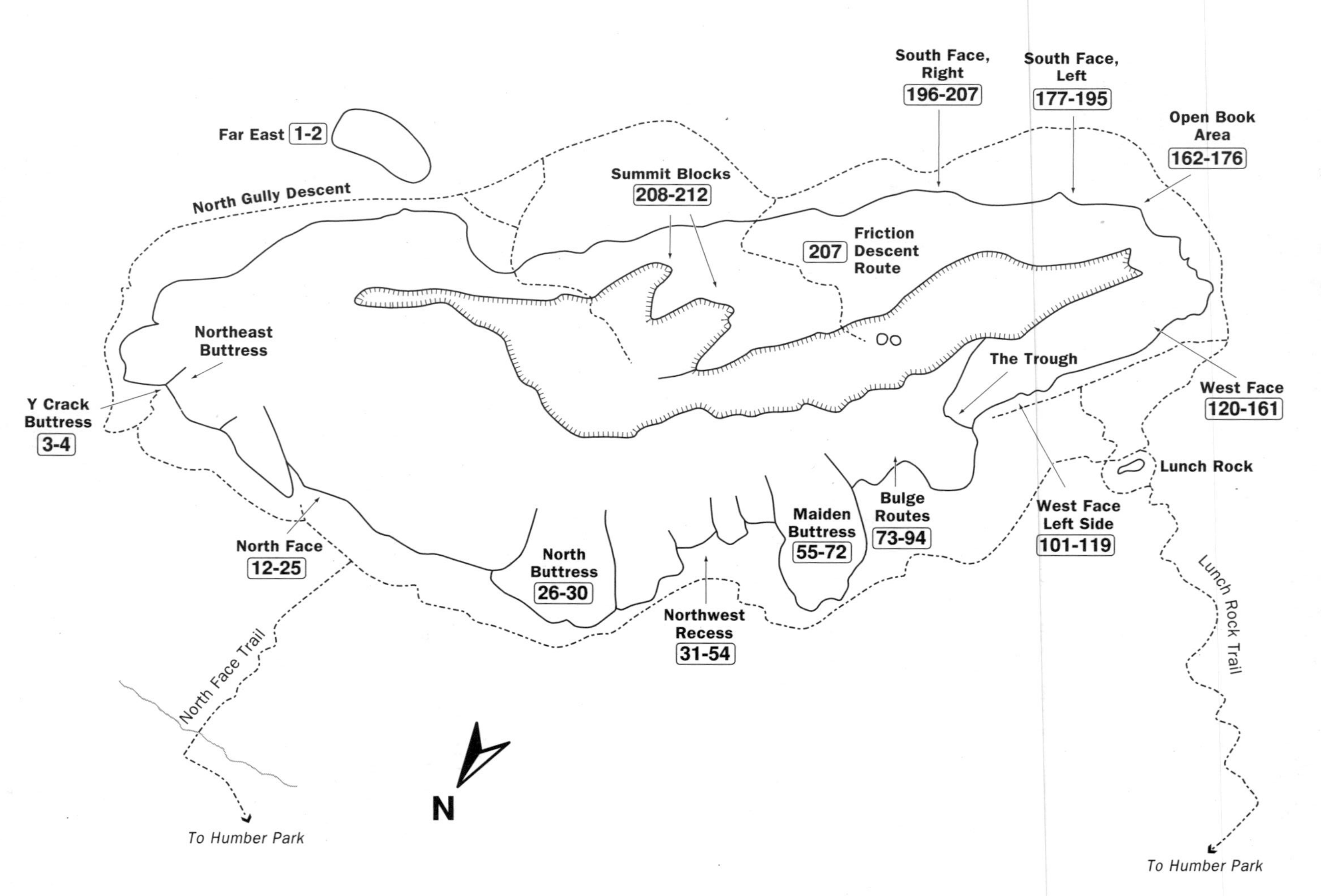

TAHQUITZ DESCENT ROUTES

The following are the most commonly used descent routes for Tahquitz Rock. Descents used for specific routes are listed in each section heading or route description. In addition to the written descriptions below, consult the photo on page 54 and topos for additional information.

The North Gully Descent (also referred to as The Notches Descent) from the North Face routes is generally down a steep gully to the left and behind the Northeast Buttress. This gully runs down from the summit area of the rock. The gully is probably class 3 in places.

The Friction Route Descent is a class-4 downclimb on the southern side of Tahquitz Rock. It is the most commonly used means of descent off Tahquitz Rock. More than a few climbers have inadvertently strayed while descending, sometimes with catastrophic results. Please descend carefully, or, if possible, follow other climbers familiar with the descent your first time down it.

From the summit area of Tahquitz Rock, head down and west (right) to where a large boulder on the brink of the South Face cliff will be seen. From the top of the West Face and South Face climbs, head up low-angle slabs (east) along the ridgetop of the rock, near the edge of the South Face. A very large boulder will be seen ahead. If you get near the larger summit blocks of Tahquitz, you have gone too far.

Shimmy down the far (northeast) side of this large boulder for about 30 feet to a ledge/ramp. Move right for about 50 feet down the ledge/ramp, then work diagonally left across ledges, then slabs that lead to the base of the cliff. Hike down along the South Face.

THE FAR EAST

This is the 200-foot-high face located immediately to the east (left) of the North Gully.

1. **Mercy of the Sisters** 5.8 Begin by traversing left along the base of the wall on class 3 slabs to a ledge in a corner just shy of a large tree. 1. Up a corner, over a bulge to small right-facing corner, then a seam, up to a wider crack. Work right and belay at the base of an arch/corner. 2. Up the ramp/arch (5.5) moving right at the top. Pro: to 4-inch. FA: Christian Burrell and Brian "Gonzo" Gonzales, June 1999.
2. **East Crack** 5.10a ★ This climb is located a short distance down from the notch of the North Gully, on the east side of the gully. Step left and climb a long, discontinuous finger crack to the top. FA: Unknown.

NORTHEAST BUTTRESS ROUTES

On the far left side of the somewhat slabby North Face of Tahquitz is an indistinct and large buttress of rock (The Northeast Buttress). Several routes have been established on various sections of the buttress. These routes lie a short distance left of the North Face. Most climbers will approach from Humber Park via the North Face Trail.

THE Y CRACK BUTTRESS

The very lowest and left-most part of the Northeast Buttress presents a small, steep, green-colored face with two cracks on its western aspect: this is the Y Crack Buttress. It is so named for the left-hand crack, which resembles an upsidedown Y. A short, moderate 5th-class scramble is required to reach the base of the routes. From the top, a 100-foot (30-meter) rappel from bolts leads to the base of the climbs; another short rappel from a tree leads to easy ground (a 160-foot rappel from the top would take you to the base of the 5th-class approach). Alternatively, 4th class climbing down the back of the buttress leads to the ground.

3. **The Y Crack** 5.10b ★ This is left-hand crack mentioned above. Either start is 5.9. Pro: medium to 3-inch. FA: Jim Wilson, et al., 1975.
4. **The Green Rosetta** 5.11c ★ This is the very thin crack on the right, that turns into a chimney near the top. Pro: many thin to 2-inch. FA: Mike Lechlinski and others, 1982.

NORTH FACE OVERVIEW
North Gully descent
12
13
Y Crack Buttress routes 3-4
18
14
17
21
22
20
The Larks Routes 23-25
Approach to routes 7-11

Y CRACK BUTTRESS

ROUTES

3. The Y Crack 5.10b★
4. The Green Rosetta 5.11c★

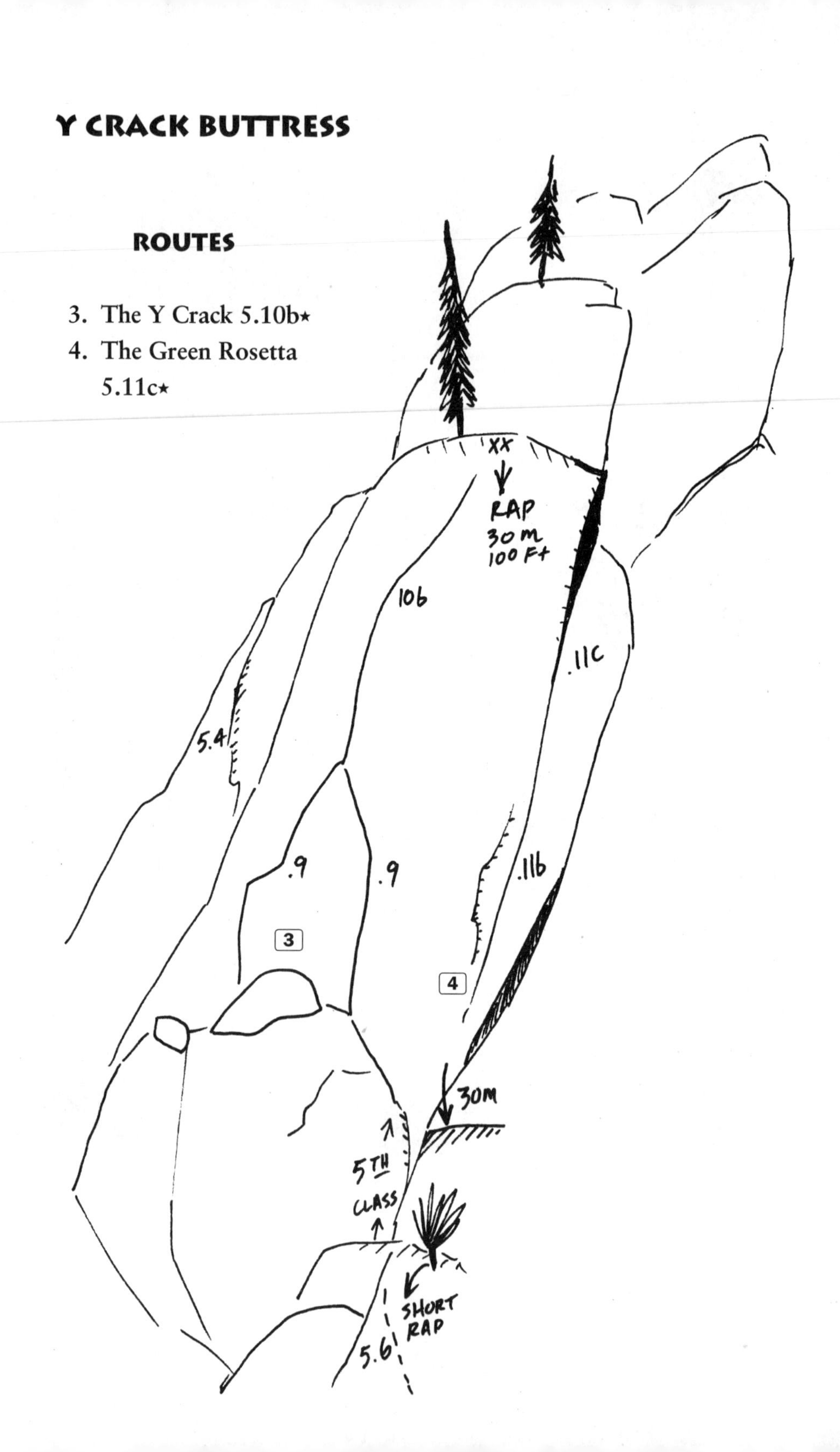

UPPER NORTHEAST BUTTRESS ROUTES

The following routes are located on the upper section of the Northeast Buttress. Near the left side of the North Face, near the base of the prominent line of *Northeast Face-East Variation* (Route 17), a very large sugar pine will be found. From this point proceed up and left up a Class 3 ramp/gully. After 200 feet, you pass beneath a very large right-facing dihedral/corner system (*The Northeast Farce,* Route 12). Fourth class climbing up and left from here leads to "Large Ledge." Most climbers will approach from Humber Park via the North Face Trail (See page 38). Descent is down the North Gully.

5. **Northeast Rib** 5.0 From Large Ledge continue up and left (Class 3-4) a short distance. At this point head up a broken series of corner systems to reach the crest of the Northeast Buttress. Above are several pitches of easy Class 5; many variations are possible. Descend the North Gully. Pro: to 2 inch. FA: John and Ruth Mendenhall, October 1940.
6. **Birdman Direct** 5.9 This is a two-pitch climb on the broken face a short distance to the right of the Y Crack Buttress leading to Large Ledge at the base of *Birdman.* Begin a few feet right of a vegetated, right-facing corner that leads to the Northeast Rib. Various routes on the broken face lead to a 3-bolt slab section (5.9) up to Large Ledge. FA: Unknown.
7. **Birdman** 5.11b ★ Climb the arete and face to the left of *Last Grapes,* past 5 bolts. Rappel 80 feet from 2 bolts. FA: Rick Linski, Dave Evans, and Bob Sachs, June 1989.
8. **Last Grapes** 5.9 ★ Starting directly from the middle of Large Ledge, climb the thin crack system to the *Birdman* anchor. 80 foot rappel. Pro: mostly thin to 2-inch. FA: Dave Evans and Tom Beck, 1980.
9. **My Pink Half of the Drainpipe** 5.10b ★ Start at the right end of Large Ledge, face climbing up to the large roof. 80 foot rappel. Pro: several thin to 2-inch, long runners (beware of rope drag). FA: Spencer Lennard and Randy Vogel, 1977.
10. **Lik'en to Lichen** 5.10b This route starts as *Northeast Farce,* but immediately climbs cracks on the left side of the huge dihedral. Pro: several thin to 2-inch. FA: Charles Cole, Dave Evans, and Randy Vogel, 1981.
11. **Bitchin Lichen** 5.10c This is a second pitch to *Lik'en to Lichen.* Traverse right to a thin crack with a pin, then up a corner past a bolt. Rappel 50 feet to the *Birdman* anchor. FA: Charles Cole and Gib Lewis, July 1987.

UPPER NE BUTTRESS

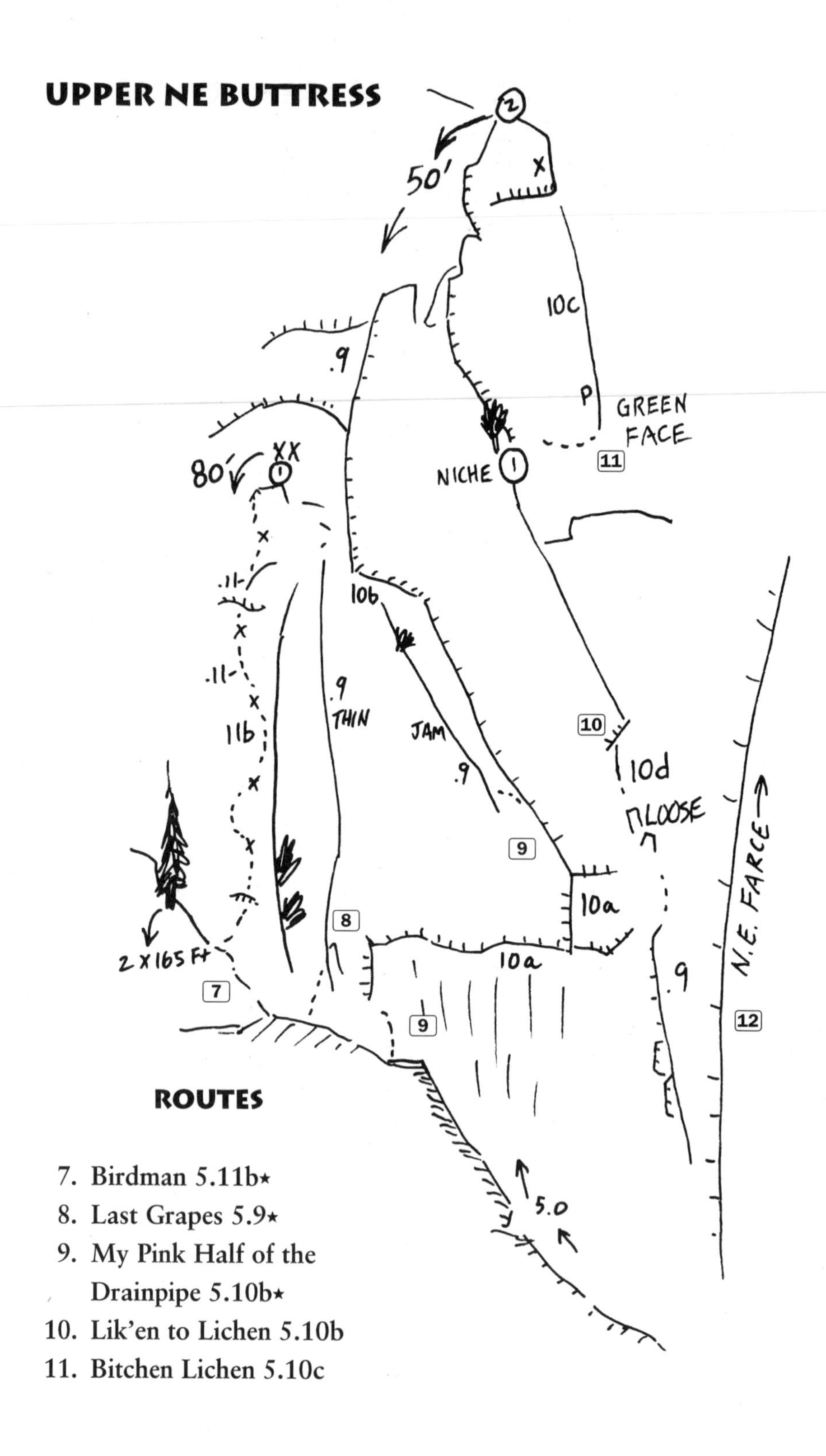

ROUTES

7. Birdman 5.11b★
8. Last Grapes 5.9★
9. My Pink Half of the Drainpipe 5.10b★
10. Lik'en to Lichen 5.10b
11. Bitchen Lichen 5.10c

NORTH FACE ROUTES

The North Face of Tahquitz is characterized as a large expanse of exfoliated slabs. It contains a myriad small corner systems and roofs, with small sections of blank slab. The *Northeast Face* routes (*East* and *West*) follow very obvious and continuous right-facing corner systems, which join, located near the center of the North Face. These routes are often used as reference points for the starts of other climbs. Most climbers will approach the North Face from Humber Park via the North Face Trail. Descent for most of these routes is down the North Gully.

12. **Northeast Farce** 5.3 Start up the huge dihedral (see Upper Northeast Buttress description for details). After one pitch, traverse right, across *El Whampo* to a huge crack. Pro: to 4-inch. FA: Don Wilson and Jerry Gallwas, September 1954.

13. **El Whampo** 5.7 ★ Start down and right of the huge dihedral of *Northeast Farce,* up shallow cracks; head left and over some small overlaps, belaying on *Northeast Farce.* Traverse right to the classic, straight-in 2-inch crack, which thins. Pro: thin to 3 inches. FA: Roy Coats, Larry Reynolds, Russ McLean, and D. Ross, 1964.

14. **El Grandote** 5.9 ★ Partway up the gully leading up to the upper Northeast Buttress is a right-facing corner leading to a prominent roof. Pitch 1: The trick is to climb up and left out of the corner before you reach the roof. Pitch 2: Up and right on discontinuous flake systems with

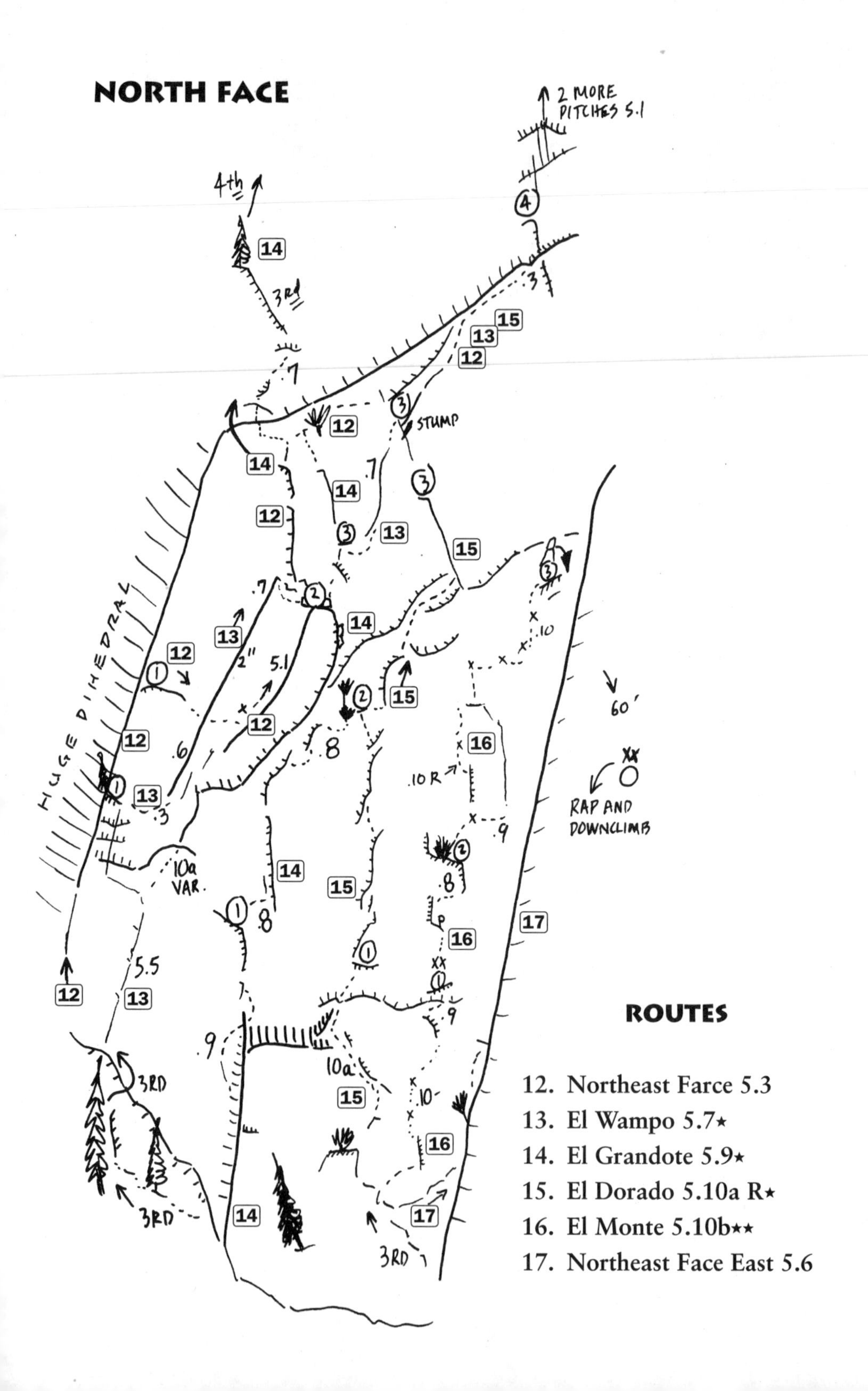
NORTH FACE
2 MORE PITCHES 5.1
4th
3rd
HUGE DIHEDRAL
STUMP
2"
5.1
10a VAR.
5.5
3RD
10R
60'
RAP AND DOWNCLIMB
ROUTES
12. Northeast Farce 5.3
13. El Wampo 5.7★
14. El Grandote 5.9★
15. El Dorado 5.10a R★
16. El Monte 5.10b★★
17. Northeast Face East 5.6

tricky route finding beneath a right-leaning arch system. Pitch 3: Undercling over the arch; above, go between *El Whampo* and *Northeast Farce,* then head left over the dihedral/roof. Pro: thin to 2.5-inch. FA: Yvon Chouinard and Harry Daley, May 1961. FFA: Bob Kamps and TM Herbert, 1963.

15. **El Dorado** 5.10a R ★ At the start of *Northeast Face East* (Route 17) Class 3 up and left leads to the start of the route on a broken ledge, below and right of a thin left-arching roof and crack. Pro: several thin to 2 inches. FA: Tom Higgins and R. Coats, 1963.
16. **El Monte** 5.10b ★★ Start as for *El Dorado,* but move right up to a crack, then left and up past 2 bolts (5.10) to an easy lieback, then a 5.9 move up to two-bolt belay (100-foot rap from here). 2. 5.8 face up to a ledge with a stout bush. 3. Up and right to a bolt, then traverse right, up a crack, then up past 3 bolts to a block with slings. Pitch 3 Direct variation: at the first bolt climb straight up a small left-facing corner (no pro) then traverse up and left (5.10b/c R) to a bolt. Continue up and right past 5 more bolts to the anchor. Rappel 60 feet to *Grace Slick*'s rappel anchors (165 feet to ground from here) or rappel 80 feet to and downclimb *Northeast Farce East.* Pro: quickdraws, several thin to 3-inch. FA: Fred Zeil, et al.,1979. FA: Direct Variation Pitch 3: Dave Evans and Rob Raker, 1987.
17. **Northeast Face East** 5.6 This route climbs the left of the two obvious and continuous right-facing dihedrals on the North Face. The beginning of the route is found near the bottom of the class 3 gully leading up and left to the upper Northeast Buttress. Climb up and right to the dihedral. Pro: to 2 inches. Note: the lower two pitches of this route are sometimes used as a downclimb for *El Monte* and *Grace Slick*. FA: Don Wilson and Royal Robbins, September 1954.
18. **Grace Slick** 5.10b ★★ Begin from a series of ledges above and to the right of a large dead pine tree. Climb a crack to a mountain mahogany beneath a slanting overhang. Once over the roof, follow a series of bolts. Many people do only the first two pitches, then rappel the route with two ropes (or downclimb the *Northeast Face* route to the left). Pro: bolts, thin to medium nuts. FA: Jim Wilson, Peter Wilkening, and Chris Wegener, 1975.
19. **Science Friction** 5.10a Little is known about this route except that it ascends the face for two pitches starting about 20 feet left of the *Northeast Face West* variation. The first pitch has several bolts for protection. FA: Clark Jacobs, Troy Martin, and John Edgar, 1977.
20. **Northeast Face West** 5.6 Climb the obvious right-facing corner near the center of the North Face, just left on an obvious large pine tree (the start

NORTH FACE

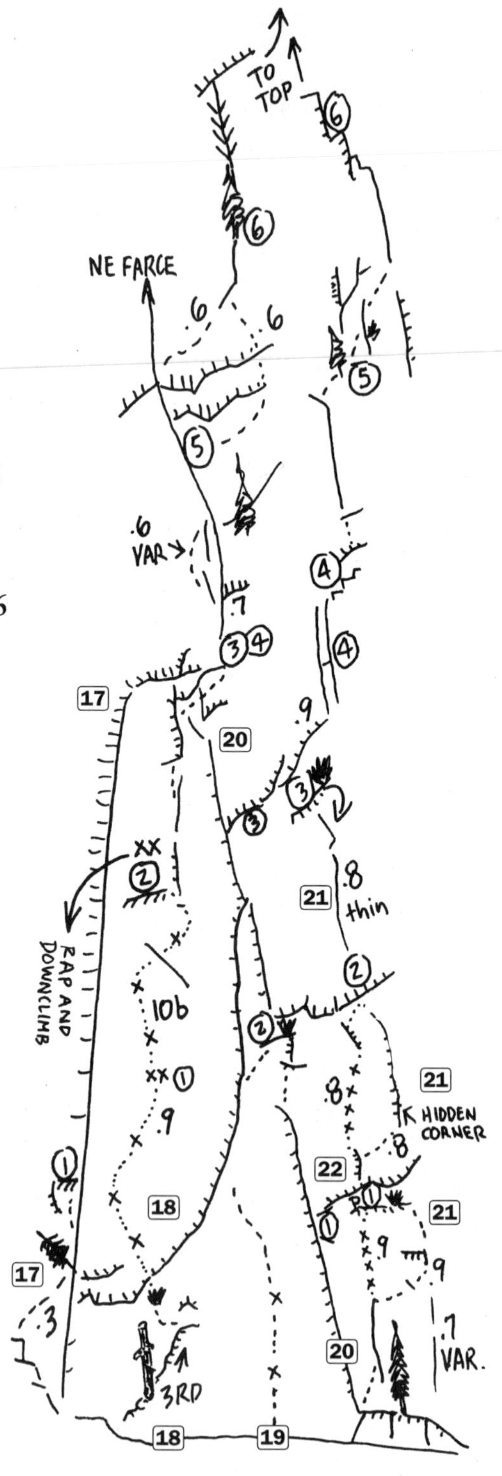

ROUTES

17. Northeast Face East 5.6
18. Grace Slick 5.10b★★
19. Science Friction 5.10a
20. Northeast Face West 5.6
21. Toe Bias 5.9 R
22. Too Biased 5.9

TOE BIAS AND TOO BIASED

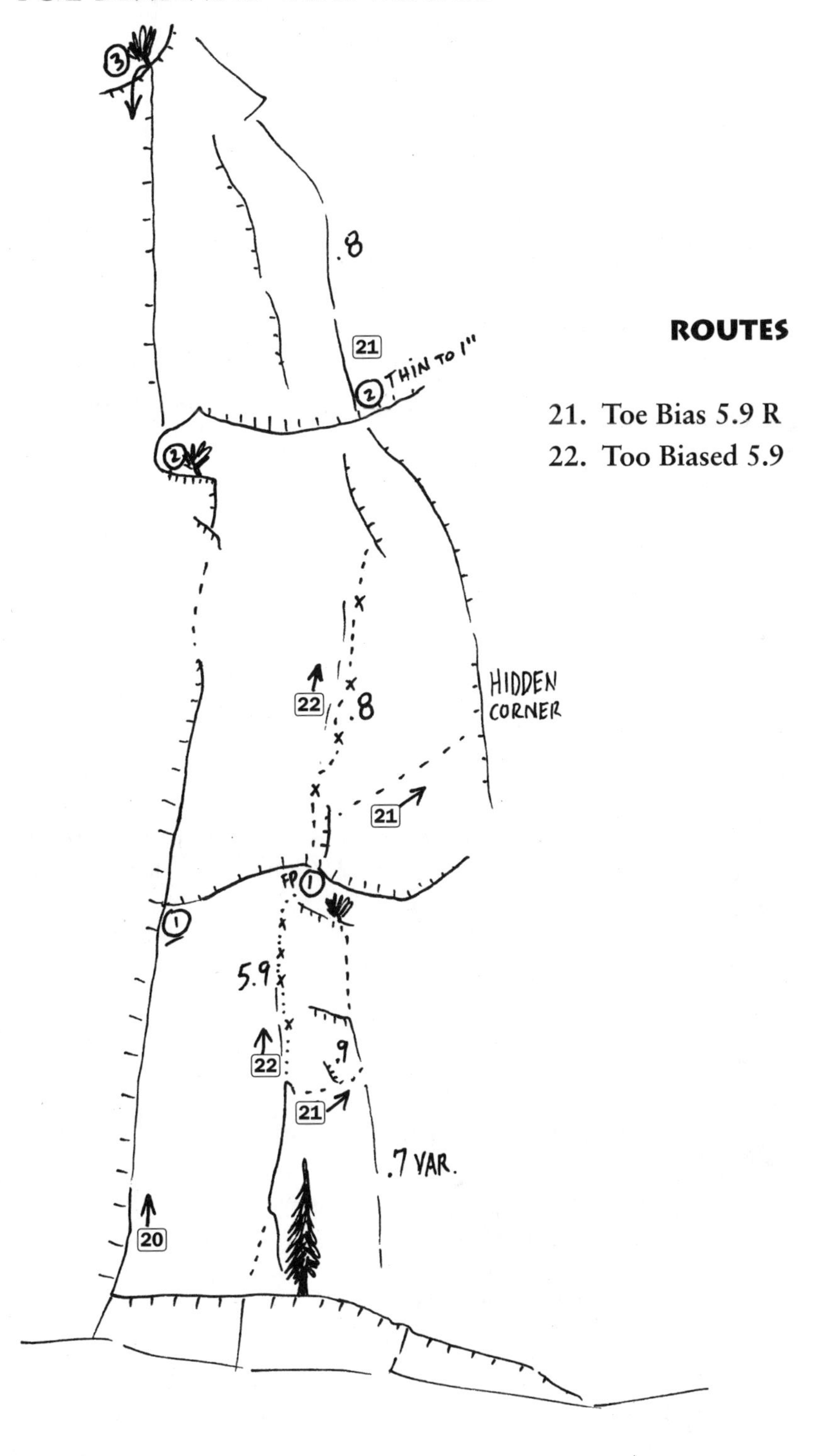

ROUTES

21. Toe Bias 5.9 R
22. Too Biased 5.9

of the corner actually faces left). Join with *Northeast Face East* after 3 pitches. Pro: thin to 2-inch. FA: Chuck and Ellen Wilts.

21. **Toe Bias** 5.9 R Begin 20 feet right of *Northeast Face West.* Climb a thin crack, then traverse right and up to a belay at a bush. 2. Over a roof, then traverse right to a lieback flake and belay at a small ledge. 3. 5.8 thin crack to belay bush. Rappel 85 feet or 165 feet plus some easy downclimbing. Pro: many thin to 2 inches. FA: Bob Kamps, Ivan Couch, and Tom Higgins, June 1966.

22. **Too Biased** 5.9 A two-pitch variation that straightens out the line of *Toe Bias.* 1. Where the normal route traverses right to a corner, continue straight up the face past 4 bolts up to the belay. 2. Where the original route moves right, continue up and right past 4 bolts. 3. Follow the 5.8 thin crack on *Toe Bias.* Descend by rapelling (85 feet or 165 feet) and some easy downclimbing. Pro: a #2 Loweball is reportedly useful on the first pitch below the first bolt. FA: Tom Beck and Mike McCoy, August 1993.

23. **Hard Lark** 5.7 ★ Probably the best of the *Lark* climbs. Climb the broken face left of the beginning of *East Lark,* crossing it where it traverses left on its first pitch, and belay a bit higher (bolt). Several moderate pitches lead up to a belay at a small tree (point where *East Lark* goes through the arch). Undercling right along the arch, past a bush to a delicate traverse to a right-facing corner, joining *West Lark.* Pro: to 2.5-inch. FA: B. Berry and J. Williams, 1966.

24. **East Lark** 5.5 Route finding is difficult, as the face is not marked by obvious features. Begin just left of the recess on the left side of the North Buttress. 1. Ascend a short crack to a bush, traverse left to another crack to a series of ledges leading up and left. 2. Climb a right-facing corner, then step left to a belay above bushes. 3. Proceed up a flake, but when the climbing appears more difficult, make a traverse slightly down and left to a belay stance. 4. Climb up a right-facing corner, over several overlaps. Belay below the arch system. 5. Traverse right under the arch, then directly up through the arch at an obvious break (at a small tree/bush). Several easier pitches lead to a deep chute, where a final 5.5 section is encountered. Pro: to 2.5 inches. FA: Chuck and Ellen Wilts, G. Harr, and B. Tory, November 1950.

25. **West Lark** 5.5 Start in the recess just left of the North Buttress. After two pitches, traverse right to a crack, which is followed for three more pitches (*Hard Lark* joins here). Near the top, finish up the chute. Mostly class 4, with a few easy class 5 sections. Pro: to 2.5 inches. FA: Roy Gorin, J. Hudson, William Dixon, and Ellen Wilts, 1954.

NORTH FACE

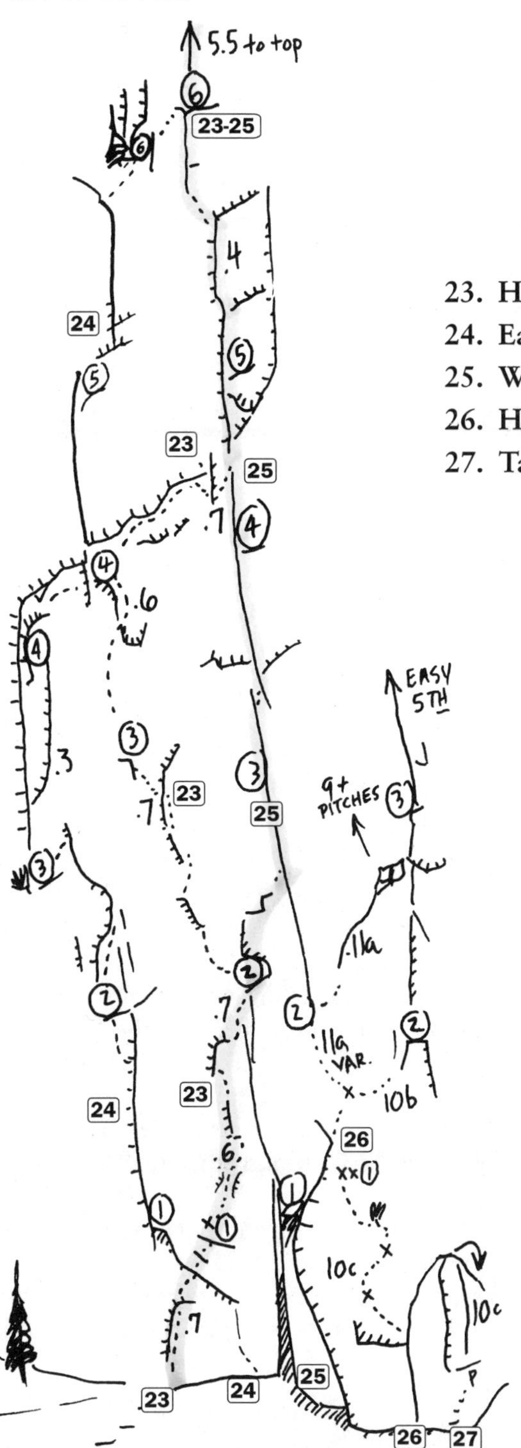

ROUTES

23. Hard Lark 5.7★
24. East Lark 5.5
25. West Lark 5.5
26. Hubris 5.10c (or 5.11a)★
27. Tank Mechanic 5.10c

THE NORTH BUTTRESS

The North Buttress of Tahquitz is the indistinct projection of rock that separates the lower-angled North Face and the steeper Northwest Recess. However, the base of the rock does extend down somewhat at the toe of the buttress, making finding it along the base relatively easy. Although one can approach from Lunch Rock, most climbers will approach directly from Humber Park via the North Face Trail. Descent is down either the *North Gully*, or a bit longer down the *Friction Route.*

26. **Hubris** 5.10c (or 5.11a) ⋆ On the left side of the lower North Buttress. Begin 35 feet right of *West Lark* and lieback a 4-inch left-leaning flake for about 40 feet, passing a small roof, then up past 2 bolts and a small bush to a 2-bolt belay. Above, a difficult lieback leads to a bolt; either traverse right (5.10b) to a belay on *Uneventful,* or head up and left (5.11a) to a belay. Other pitches and variations exist. Pro: thin to 4-inch. FA: Manuel Gonzales and Mike Heath, 1974.
27. **Tank Mechanic** 5.10c This one-pitch route face-climbs up to, then jams the straight-in thin crack just right of *Hubris.* There should be a fixed pin. Pro: small to 2-inch. FA: Dave Evans and John Casper, September 1984.
28. **The Uneventful** 5.5 The North Buttress is split into two ridges at the bottom, separated by a shallow gully. *The Uneventful* begins left of the gully and follows the left ridge for about 5 moderate pitches to a ledge system with two huge pine trees, the upper tree having a distinctive, twisted shape. At this point the *North Buttress* route is intersected (it proceeds up and left from here). *The Uneventful* ascends a 5.5 chimney directly above the upper tree, with several easier pitches leading to the top. FA: Harry Daley, Yvon Chouinard, C. Butler, and Dan Doody, October 1959.
29. **Lip Up Fatty** 5.8 Begin just left of stacked blocks at the "toe" of the North Buttress. 1. Start with (a) lieback on left, or (b) straight up an offwidth. Continue up a corner, past a bush, then pass the "angel wings" flake. Belay at highest ledge with bushes. 2. Follow crack system, stay left in crack to lieback over small roof. 3. Climb cracks left of the main corner to belay ledge with fixed pin and large dead tree (*The Uneventful* shares next pitch). 4. Wide crack to roof with pin (*The Uneventful* moves right from here) then over 2 more roofs, past a bush to a small ledge in mini cul-de-sac. 5. Follow seam up and right to the right of two similar crack systems, beware of the loose "kidney stone" flake, belay under small roof. 6. Over the roof, then class 4 to the top. A 60-meter rope was used on the FA. Pro: to 3.5 inches. FA: Christian Burrell and Brian "Gonzo" Gonzales, May 1999.

NORTH BUTTRESS

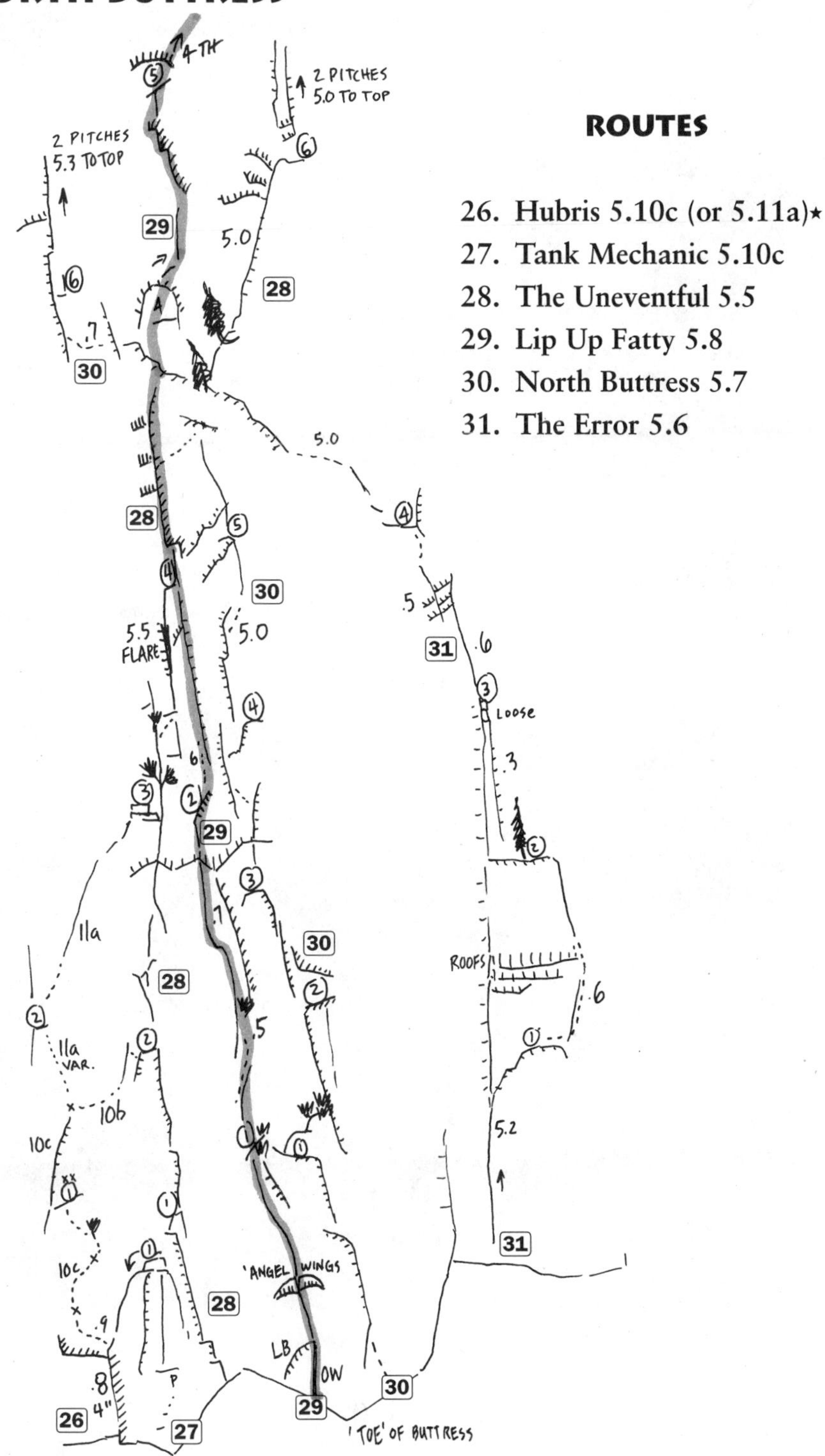

ROUTES

26. Hubris 5.10c (or 5.11a)★
27. Tank Mechanic 5.10c
28. The Uneventful 5.5
29. Lip Up Fatty 5.8
30. North Buttress 5.7
31. The Error 5.6

NORTH/NORTHWEST FACE OVERVIEW

30. **North Buttress** 5.7 The base of the North Buttress is split into two distinct ridges separated by a shallow gully. Climb the right ridge to a ledge system with two trees (See *The Uneventful* description). From the lower of the two trees, climb up and left about 40 feet on a discontinuous ledge system, then make an inobvious traverse 30 feet left across a smooth face to a gully/corner that is followed to the top. FA: R. Smith and Don Wilson, August 1952.

NORTHWEST RECESS

The Northwest Recess is located between the Maiden Buttress on the right and the North Buttress on the left. The rock is noticably steeper, especially near the right-hand section. The right-facing dihedral extending nearly all the way up the Northwest Recess is *Whodunit*. Approach is made either from Lunch Rock (Lunch Rock Trail) or the North Face Trail. From Lunch Rock, head straight left (and slightly down), then along the "toe" of the Maiden Buttress, then angle up and left. From the North Face Trail, head right along the base of the North Face, then around the base of the North Buttress. Descent is usually down the *Friction Route;* however, it takes roughly the same amount of time to descend the *North Gully*.

31. **The Error** 5.6 To the right of the North Buttress is a recess where a major crack system/corner shoots upward, intersecting the North Buttress at two large pine trees. Climb easy ground up the left side of the corner, then right to a belay ledge about 40 feet below large overhangs. Traverse right to a crack which heads around the right side of the roofs and leads to a ledge. Climb 2 pitches up a gully/crack system, then traverse left to ledges with 2 prominent pine trees. Join *North Buttress* or *The Uneventful* to the top. FA: Jerry Gallwas, Barbara Lilley, and G. Schlief, September 1952.
32. **The Souvenir** 5.10d ★★ A long route with great variety. 1. Up *The Error* (5.2) to a good ledge 40 feet below roofs. 2. Over the roofs on the left (5.8, fixed pins), or weave through the center (5.10c, fixed pins). Belay 40 feet higher at a large pine. Shift the belay to the far right of the ledge. 3. Fingertip traverse leads up and right to *Sahara Terror*'s dogleg crack, up a thin crack to a fixed pin (5.9 R), then slab (interspersed with thin crack) past 6 bolts to a tiny stance beneath a small overhang with a mountain mohogany (165 feet). 4. 60 feet up the obvious crack (5.8), taking care passing a loose chockstone at the second overhang. Belay at small ledge on the left. 5. Traverse right, up steep corner (5.9), over small roof, then up to a belay shared with *Sahara Terror.* 6, 7. Two 5.0 pitches up *Sahara Terror* to the top. Pro: medium nuts, 2 each CDs to 3.5 inches. FA: Bob Gaines and Charlie Peterson, August 1995.

SOUVENIR AND SAHARA TERROR

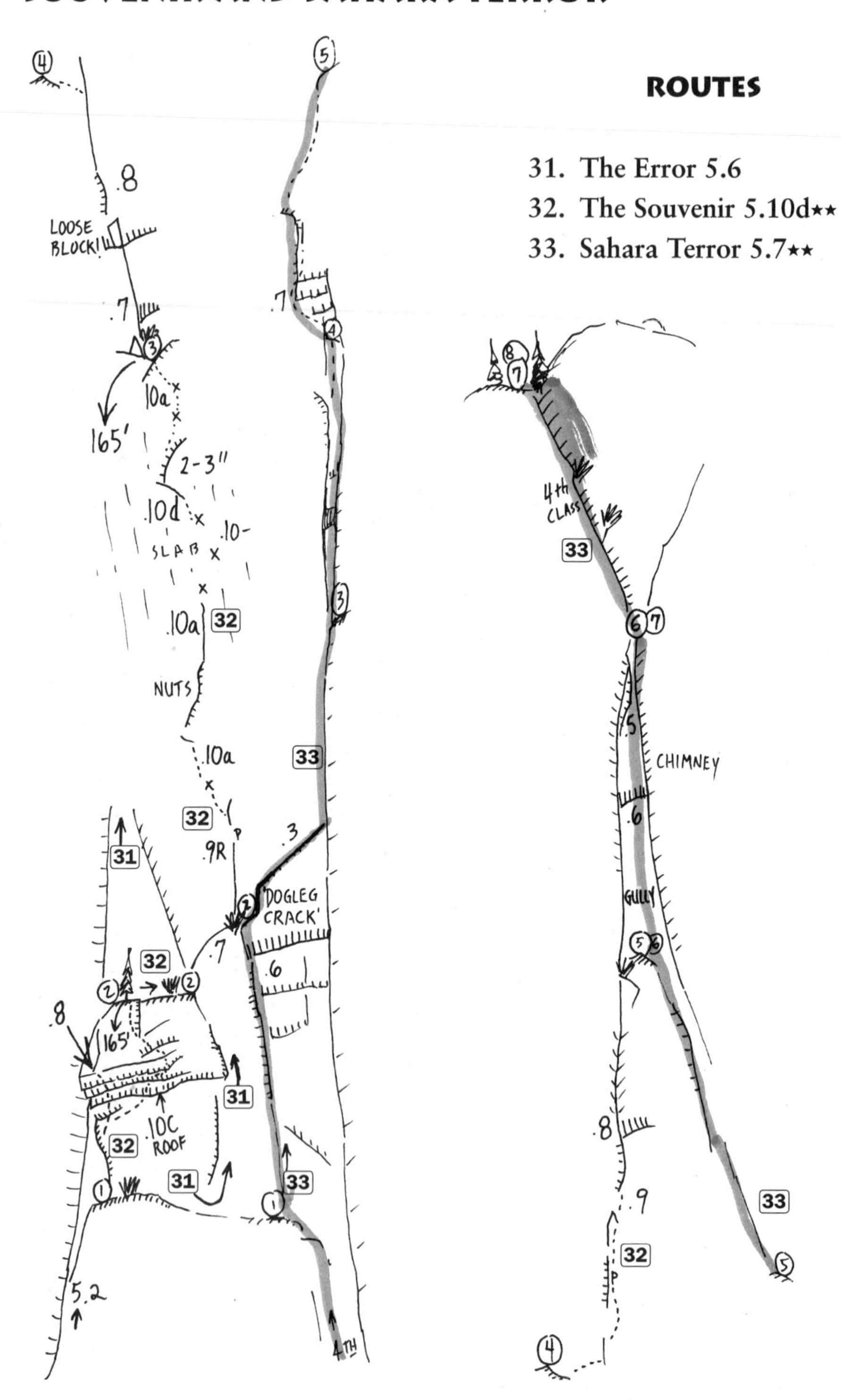

ROUTES

31. The Error 5.6
32. The Souvenir 5.10d★★
33. Sahara Terror 5.7★★

NORTHWEST RECESS
32
33
31
32
34-36
38
31
32
33
40
41
43

33. **Sahara Terror** 5.7 ★★ Begin about 45 feet right of *The Error* and 15 feet left of an obvious crack/corner system. An easy pitch leads to a belay beneath a series of overlaps. Follow a crack through the overhangs and belay at the base of a deep crack that doglegs sharply to the right. Take the dogleg crack to the left-facing corner and follow this crack system until progress is blocked by overhangs. Traverse 10 feet left, then up through the overhang; continue diagonally up and left for about 50 feet in a crack system, then up and right across a face to the base of an obvious chute, then up a deep chimney. A 4th-class crack diagonals up and left to the top. Pro: to 3 inches. FA: William Shand, Roy Gorin, and Paul Flinchbaugh, July 1942. FFA: Bill Pabst and Spencer Austin.
34. **Magical Mystery Tour** 5.11c R ★★ A long and serious route on the expansive slab between *Sahara Terror* and *Whodunit.* 1. Climb the nebulous face (5.9 R) left of the *Edgehogs*'s start to a two-bolt belay. 2. A thin crack with fixed pins (very thin nuts useful) protects crux face moves (11c) to a choice of routes. The original route moves far left to a crack, then traverses back right above an overlap to a bolt, then up to a two-bolt sling belay. A more direct variation surmounts the overlap directly above a bolt (11-). 3. Up a crack (fixed pins) to a bolt, move right to a bolt shared with *Edgehogs,* then up to a tiny belay ledge with 2 bolts. Two 165-foot rappels from here reach the ground. 4. Up a right-facing dihedral (5.7) with an unavoidable, dangerously loose block to another two-bolt anchor (or climb *Edgehogs's* third pitch). 5. A run-out 5.10 pitch with thin cracks and several small roofs leads to two easier pitches. Pro: many thin to 2-inch. FA: (5.10, A3) Matt Cox, Tobin Sorenson, Dave Evans, Mike Graham, and Jim Wilson, 1973. FFA: Matt Cox and Darrell Hensel, 1976. FA: Direct Variation Pitch 2: Bob Gaines and Charlie Peterson, August 1994.
35. **Three-Hour Tour** 5.10d ★ A two-pitch divergence beginning from *Magical Mystery Tour*'s third pitch. Climb past the fixed pins, then traverse left across an improbable, smooth face (10d) then up cracks to a bushy belay ledge. Jam a dogleg crack to a face/arete with 2 bolts (10-) to a two-bolt, semihanging stance at a mountain mahogany on the right. Two 165-foot rappels to the ground. Pro: thin to 2 inches. FA: Bob Gaines and Charlie Peterson, August 1994.
36. **Edgehogs** 5.10d ★★ This route climbs the striking arete on the left side of the *Whodunit* dihedral. 1. The first pitch lies just left of *Whodunit* and climbs easy flakes to a blank section with one bolt (5.10a) up to the two-bolt belay shared with *Whodunit.* 2. Climb the awesome arete and face past 10 bolts to a tiny two-bolt belay stance. 3. Slap up the rounded arete past 3 bolts (10c) to another two-bolt stance at a bush (a 1-inch CD for pro above the 3rd bolt). 4. Up to a fixed pin and bolt; move right

NORTHWEST RECESS

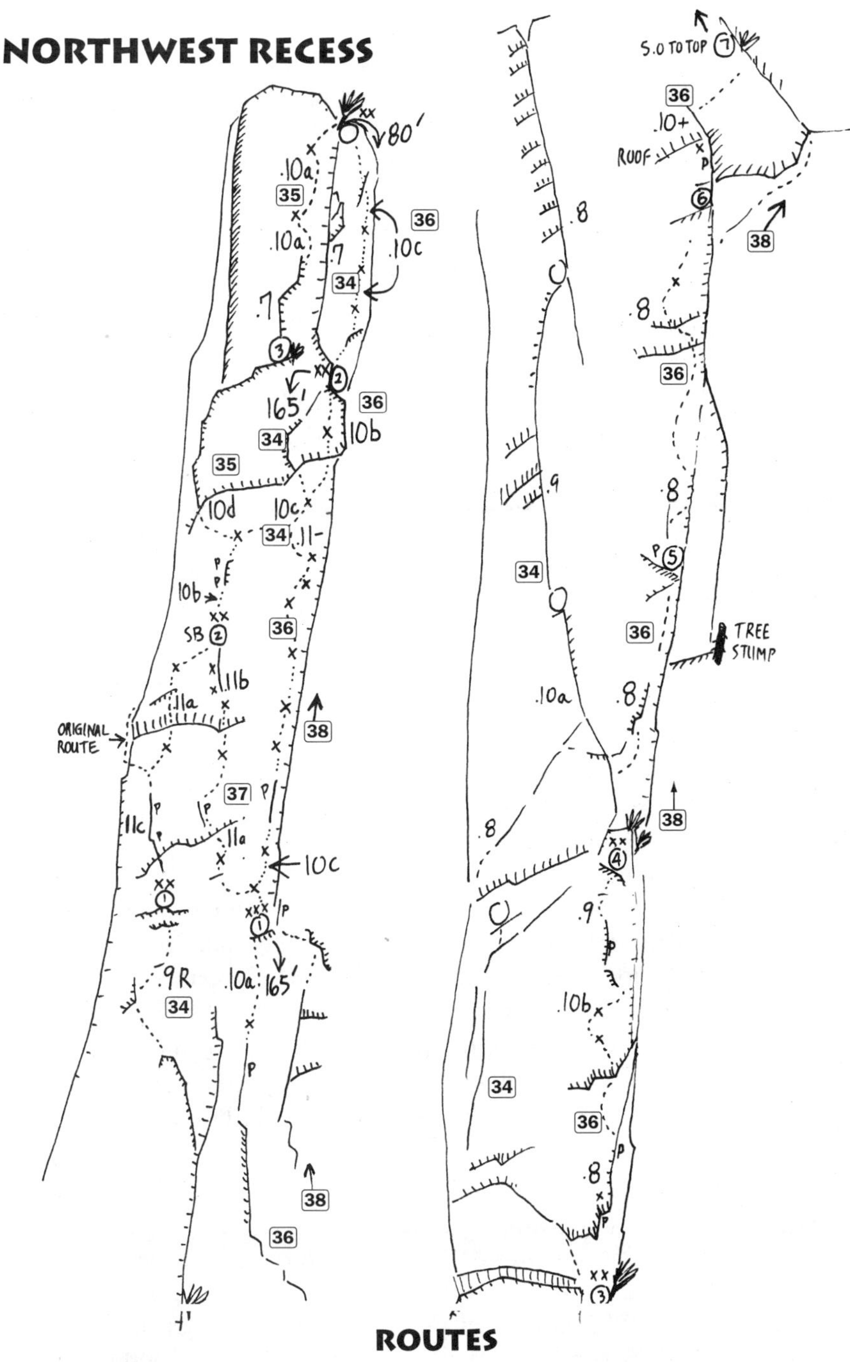

ROUTES

34. Magical Mystery Tour 5.11c R★★
35. Three-Hour Tour 5.10d★
36. Edgehogs 5.10d★★
37. The Incision 5.11c★
38. Whodunit 5.9★★★

(5.8) up to a roof, then step left over the lip (10-) to a bolt. Move right past another bolt to the arete (10b), then up a flake system (med. nuts, TCUs .4 to 1.5 inches) to the bolted belay. You can rap the route from here with two ropes. 5. Up 40 feet of easy ground, then move right and climb flakes on the arete (very close to *Whodunit* at this point) to a tiny belay stance at a fixed pin. 6. Step right and up (5.8) to a crack that fades into runout slab (5.4 R), then a 5.8 bulge to a slab with a bolt. Belay beneath the big overhang. 7. Over the roof (10+) to a belay on *Whodunit*. 8. Join *Whodunit* for its last pitch (5.0) Pro: thin to 3 inches. FA: Pitches 1 and 2: Bob Gaines and Clark Jacobs, August, 1992. FA pitches 3 and 4: Bob Gaines,Todd Gordon, and Bob Austin, July 1997. FA pitches 5, 6, 7: Bob Gaines and Charlie Peterson, August 1998.

37. **The Incision** 5.11c ★ From the first belay on *Edgehogs* climb up to *Edgehogs*'s first bolt, then move up and left over several overlaps to a hairline crack leading to the bolt belay on the second pitch of *Magical Mystery Tour.* Pro: 6 bolts, 1 fixed pin. FA: Bob Gaines and Clark Jacobs, 1992.
38. **Whodunit** 5.9 ★★★ Seen from Humber Park in afternoon light, this route is easily discerned as a right-facing, sunlit dihedral extending nearly all the way up the North Face. Begin by scrambling up and left on ledges from the Northwest Recess. The first pitch climbs easy flakes for about 100 feet until a difficult section is encountered: Follow a thin crack straight up over a small overlap (5.9), then traverse up and left to a two-bolt belay. 2. Up the right-facing dihedral to a series of ledges. 3. Up to a chimney that narrows, then awkward jamming (5.9) to exit. Continue up the crack system until reaching overhangs, then move about 15 feet right and climb through a weakness to easier terrain. Pro: to 3 inches. FA: (5.8, A1) Joe Fitschen and Royal Robbins, September 1957. FFA: Tom Higgins and Bob Kamps, 1966.
39. **Hog variation** 5.10b From a bushy ledge 2 pitches up *Whodunit,* climb a series of awkward cracks on the left wall of the dihedral to join *Edgehogs* at its second pitch belay. Pro: to 3.5 inches. FA: Bob Gaines and Todd Gordon, July 1997.
40. **The Swallow** 5.10a Begin about 40 feet right of *Whodunit* in a broken, left-facing corner system on the right side of a rock apron that leads upward to a steeper headwall. *The Gulp* continues up the corner and jamcrack above, while *The Swallow* makes a diagonal traverse up and left (touching *Whodunit*) then moves back up and right to rejoin the original crack system at a belay shared with *The Gulp*. Continue directly up 2 pitches up a deep crack and short overhang to a sloping belay ledge with a scrubby tree. Climb the right side of a triangular-shaped block, then jam a short, strenuous crack (10-) to a broad ledge system

WHODUNIT

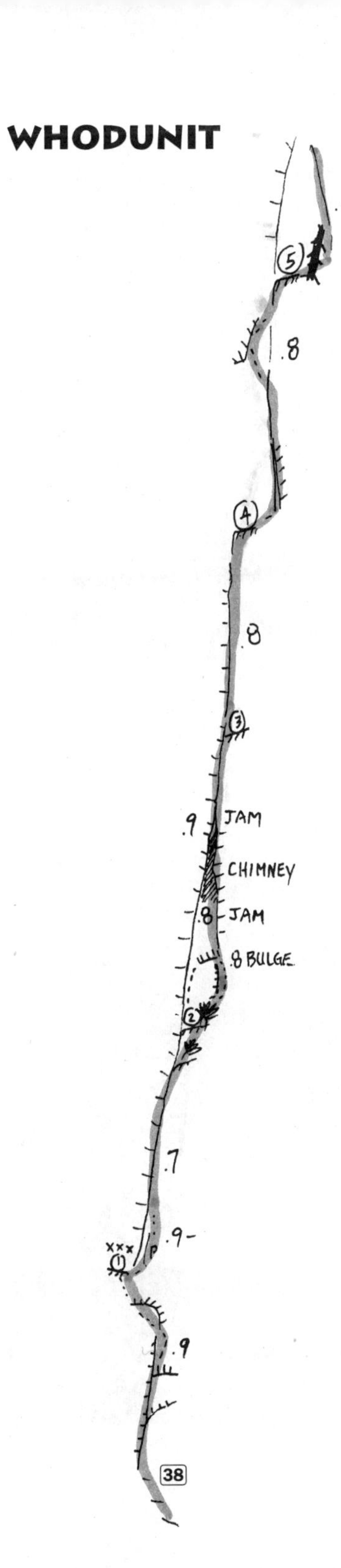

ROUTES

38. Whodunit 5.9★★★

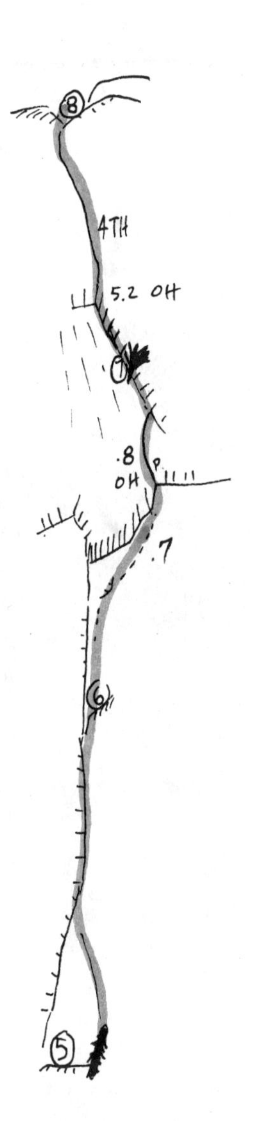

NORTHWEST RECESS
50
50
51
55
38
43
51
50
33

NORTHWEST RECESS

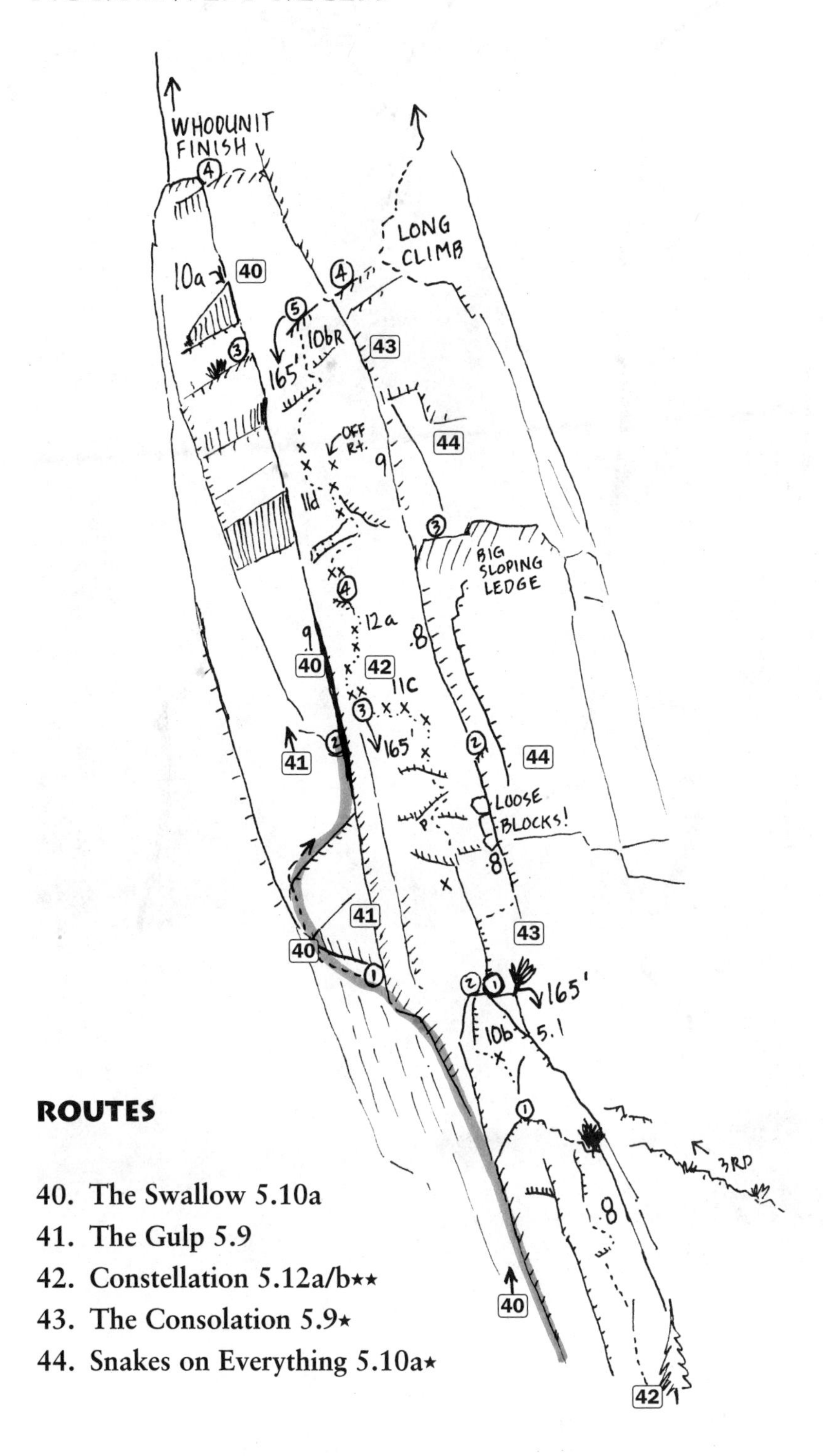

ROUTES

40. The Swallow 5.10a
41. The Gulp 5.9
42. Constellation 5.12a/b★★
43. The Consolation 5.9★
44. Snakes on Everything 5.10a★

NORTHWEST
RECESS
50
50
51
33
38
43

that extends across the Northwest Recess. Continue up the *Whodunit.* Pro: to 4 inches. FA: Chuck Wilts and Royal Robbins, June 1952.

41. **The Gulp** 5.9 This line is somewhat contrived, and the third pitch can actually be combined with *The Swallow* for a more direct and logical line. At the point where *The Swallow* loops back in from the left, *The Gulp* traverses down and left a few feet then ascends the crack system between *The Swallow* and *Whodunit* for about 70 feet until an undercling traverse right intersects *The Swallow,* which is followed to the sloping ledge with a bush. From here the route avoids the triangular-shaped block by traversing up and right on easier face climbing, then up to the broad ledge system extending across the Northwest Recess. Pro: to 4 inches. FA: P. Gerhard and D. Ross, 1965.
42. **Constellation** 5.12a/b ★★ One of Tahquitz Rock's most sustained face climbs, up the high-angle slab between *The Swallow* and *Consolation.* Begin at the lowest point of the narrow "slab" and climb a 165-foot 5.8 pitch up the center, belaying at a block on the highest ledge. Above are four difficult pitches protected with both bolts and natural pro. From the end of the fifth pitch, either rappel (three 165-foot rappels reach the deck) or continue to the top via *Consolation* or *The Gulp.* Pro: to 2 inches, including TCUs. FA: Bob Gaines and Charlie Peterson, 1990.
43. **The Consolation** 5.9 ★ This route essentially follows the long crack system bordering the right side of the *Constellation* slab. Begin with a 4th class pitch up a bushy corner system, set up a belay at a ledge on the left. Climb up, then right to reach the obvious 100-foot, left-facing dihedral, which ends on a wide, sloping ledge that extends to the *Long Climb* on the right. Continue up the crack system with a 5.9 pitch. Pro: to 3 inches. FA: (5.8, A1) John Mendenhall and Chuck Wilts, May 1953. FFA: Royal Robbins and TM Herbert, 1959.
44. **Snakes on Everything** 5.10a ★ From the belay halfway up the *Consolation* dihedral, climb a steep, left-facing dihedral that shoots upward just a few feet right of the main corner, exiting up and right to the big, sloping belay ledge. The next pitch jams the straight-in crack (10a) that angles up and left to intersect the *Consolation* after about 40 feet. Pro: to 3 inches. FA: Craig Fry, Dave Evans, and Jim Angione, 1979.
45. **The Sham** (Original Route) 5.10d R, A2 Ascend the initial section of the *Consolation* to a belay spot beneath the first level of overhangs. Lieback a flake up and right over the bulge onto a spectacular slab, traverse right to a flake system to run-out 5.8 face leading to a bolt. Traverse left (10+) to a thin crack leading up to a belay ledge (or finish up the last bolts of *Farewell Horizontal*). Protection on this pitch may be difficult without

NORTHWEST RECESS DETAIL

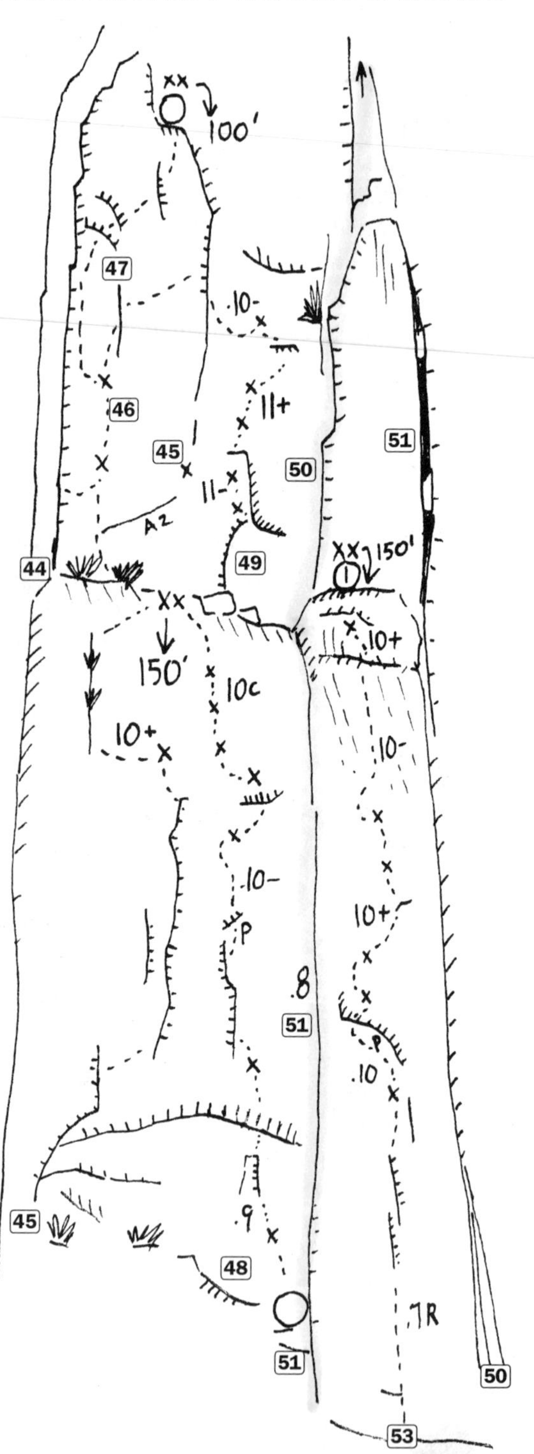

ROUTES

45. The Sham (original route) 5.10d R, A2
46. The Sham (free variation, pitch 2) 5.11c/d R★
47. The Scam 5.11d★ (TR)
48. Farewell Horizontal 5.10b★★
49. The Sting 5.11b/c★
50. The Long Climb 5.8★★
51. The Wong Climb 5.8 (★★for the first pitch)
53. Special K 5.10d R★★

pitons. The next pitch begins just left of *The Sting*. Aid a thin horizontal crack out right (A2) to a bolt (pins may be required), then up a vertical crack system to a big, sloping ledge. Jam a vertical crack that turns into a left-facing dihedral system up to the ledge system extending across the Northwest Recess. Finish up *Consolation* or *Long Climb*. Pro: to 3 inches. FA: Tom Higgins and Roy Coats, May 1964.

46. **The Sham (Free variation, pitch 2)** 5.11c/d R ★ Begin left of the *Original Route* and climb the face past 2 bolts to a thin crack (thin piton needed here for pro), traversing right to the vertical crack on *The Sham*. 2-bolt rap anchor, 90 feet. FA: Kevin Powell and Dan Leichtfus, 1983.
47. **The Scam** 5.11d ★ (TR) Climb past the first 2 bolts on *The Sham,* then move left to the arete, moving right at the top to the 2-bolt anchor (90 feet) FA: Bob Gaines, October 1999.
48. **Farewell Horizontal** 5.10b ★★ Fun face climbing on featured granite. Begin at the base of the *Wong Climb,* moving left past a bolt to a flake system. 2-bolt rap anchor (140 feet). Pro: 7 bolts, 1 fixed pin, thin nuts to 2-inch CDs. FA: Tom Beck and Scott Escher, July 1998.
49. **The Sting** 5.11b/c ★ The steep flake system and face between *The Sham* and The Mummy Crack. 5 bolts, medium nuts and CDs. 2-bolt rap anchor (90 feet) FA: Bob Gaines and Frank Bentwood, October 1999.
50. **The Long Climb** 5.8 ★★ At the far right side of the Northwest Recess are two parallel cracks that merge about two hundred feet up. 1. Take the wider right crack to a nice ledge with a two-bolt anchor. 2. Take the left crack system, the infamous Mummy Crack, to a wide, sloping ledge. 3. Up and right over a small roof to a mountain mahogany. 4. Friction up and left across a slab, then back right over a flake to a fir tree. 5. Above, a downpointing flake (with a fixed pin) is passed on the left, then up a thin corner (5.8), traverse right to an easy crack, belay above a notch. 6. Up and right (easy 5th) to the top. More difficult (5.9/.10) pitches can be done up and left to finish. Pro: to 3.5 inches. FA: Royal Robbins and Don Wilson, May 1952.
51. **Wong Climb** 5.8 (★★ for first pitch) Jam the classic, straight-in, hand-and-finger crack 30 feet left of the *Long Climb* (a great direct start for the Long Climb). 2-bolt rap anchor (150 feet). The second pitch (the right crack) is not popular, involving a strenuous squeeze chimney with several loose chockstones. Join the *Long Climb*. Pro: to 4 inches. FA: Tom Higgins, D. Molner, and R. Coats, 1963.
52. **Yellowjacket** 5.11a (TR) From the start of the 2nd pitch of the *Wong Climb* face climb diagonally up and left across the face of the slab to join the upper section of the Mummy Crack. FA: Bob Gaines, October 1999.

NORTHWEST RECESS

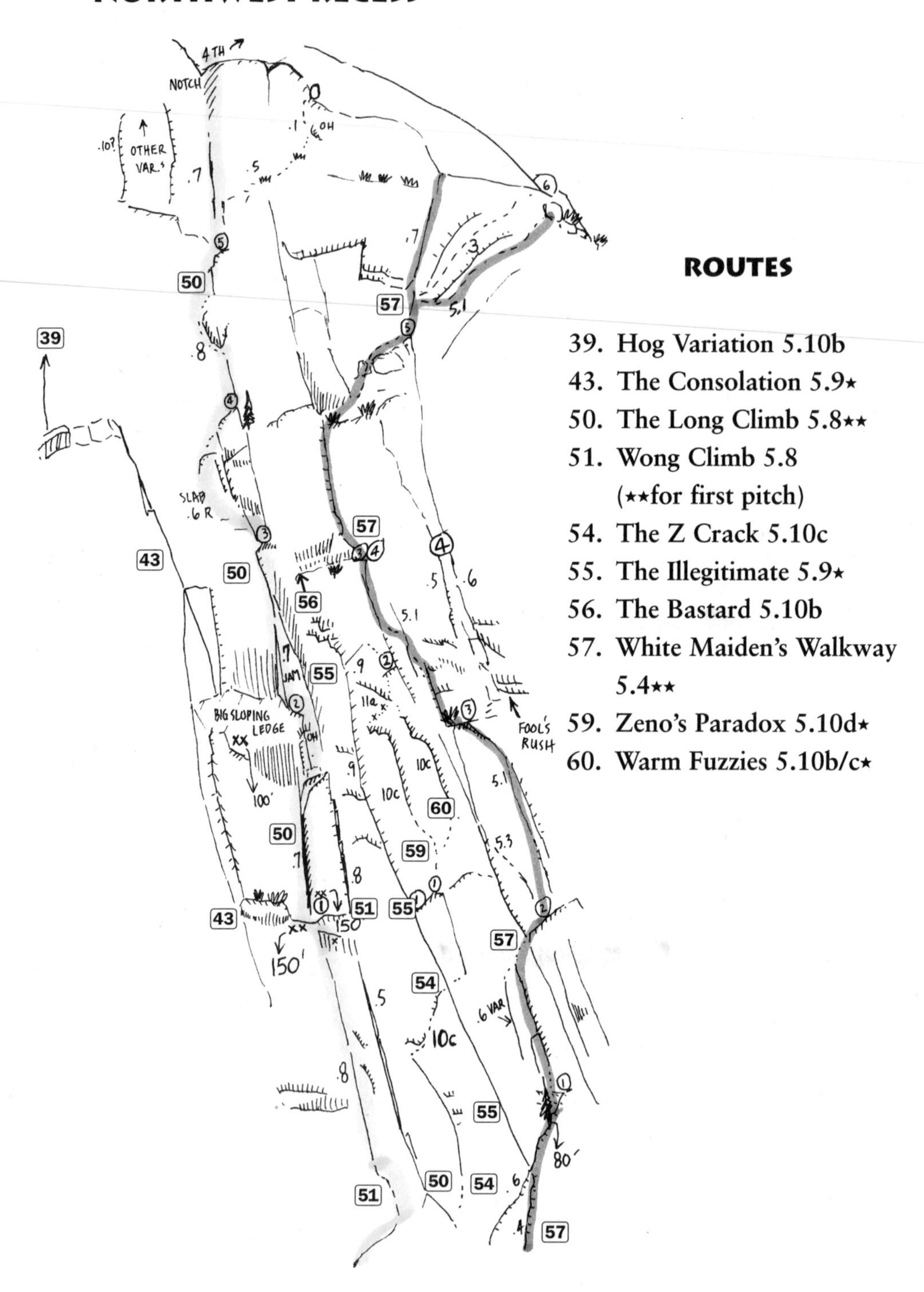

ROUTES

39. Hog Variation 5.10b
43. The Consolation 5.9★
50. The Long Climb 5.8★★
51. Wong Climb 5.8
    (★★for first pitch)
54. The Z Crack 5.10c
55. The Illegitimate 5.9★
56. The Bastard 5.10b
57. White Maiden's Walkway 5.4★★
59. Zeno's Paradox 5.10d★
60. Warm Fuzzies 5.10b/c★

53. **Special K** 5.10d R ★★ The narrow slab between the *Wong Climb* and the *Long Climb's* first pitches. Unprotected face (5.7) leads to a flake system (5.9), friction slab (10+), and short headwall (10+) finish. Beware rope drag. 2-bolt rap (150 feet). Pro: thin to 2 inches, 6 bolts, 1 fixed pin. FA: Bob Gaines and Frank Bentwood, October 1999.

54. **The Z Crack** 5.10c A good direct start to *Zeno's Paradox*. 1. Climb the dogleg crack system on the wall just right of the first pitch of the *Long Climb,* crossing *Illegitimate* up to a belay. Pitch 2 continues up an easier crack to intersect *Zeno's* at its crux pitch. Pro: thin to 2 inches. FA: Dave Evans, Craig Fry, Margy Floyd, Todd Battey, and Charles Cole, August 1985.

MAIDEN BUTTRESS

This long and very prominent buttress of rock separates the Northwest Recess and the West Face/West Bulge. A seven-pitch, easy, and classic route (*White Maiden's Walkaway*) starts on the left side of the Maiden Buttress. Several shorter routes start along the base or from several pitches up the Maiden Buttress. The Maiden Buttress forms the left skyline of the rock as seen from Lunch Rock. From Lunch Rock, head straight left; to reach the left side of the buttress, go along the toe of the Maiden Buttress, then angle uphill along the base. Descent is usually down the *Friction Route.*

55. **The Illegitimate** 5.9 ★ An intimidating route up the left side of the Maiden Buttress. Climb the first section of *White Maiden* (5.4) to a large tree. 1. Jam up the long diagonal crack to a semi-hanging belay up and right with less-than-perfect anchors. 2. Continue up the crack to steep face climbing over blocks, then up the corner to an improbable move right over the dihedral, traverse right, then down to a belay (so-so anchors) at the base of a corner. Follow the corner to easier pitches up and right that lead to the *White Maiden* finish. Pro: plenty of thin to 2 inches. FA: Royal Robbins and TM Herbert, May 1959.

56. **The Bastard** 5.10b On the second pitch of *Illegitimate,* instead of traversing right, continue straight up through the roof system to a belay ledge about 40 feet higher. Another moderate pitch wanders up to join the *Long Climb*. FA: Jay Smith and Terry Abahai, June 1987.

57. **White Maiden's Walkaway** 5.4 ★★ A popular introduction for novices to long, multipitch climbing, this route ascends the buttress that forms the left skyline when viewed from Lunch Rock. The normal line begins on the left side of the Maiden Buttress in the right corner of the Northwest Recess. 1. Climb up and right, past a tree, and up to a bushy ledge, above which is a large flake resting beside a dihedral. 2. Climb the deep crack on the right side of the flake, up the corner, then up and right on broken rock to a large belay ledge on top of a truncated rock tooth or

MAIDEN BUTTRESS

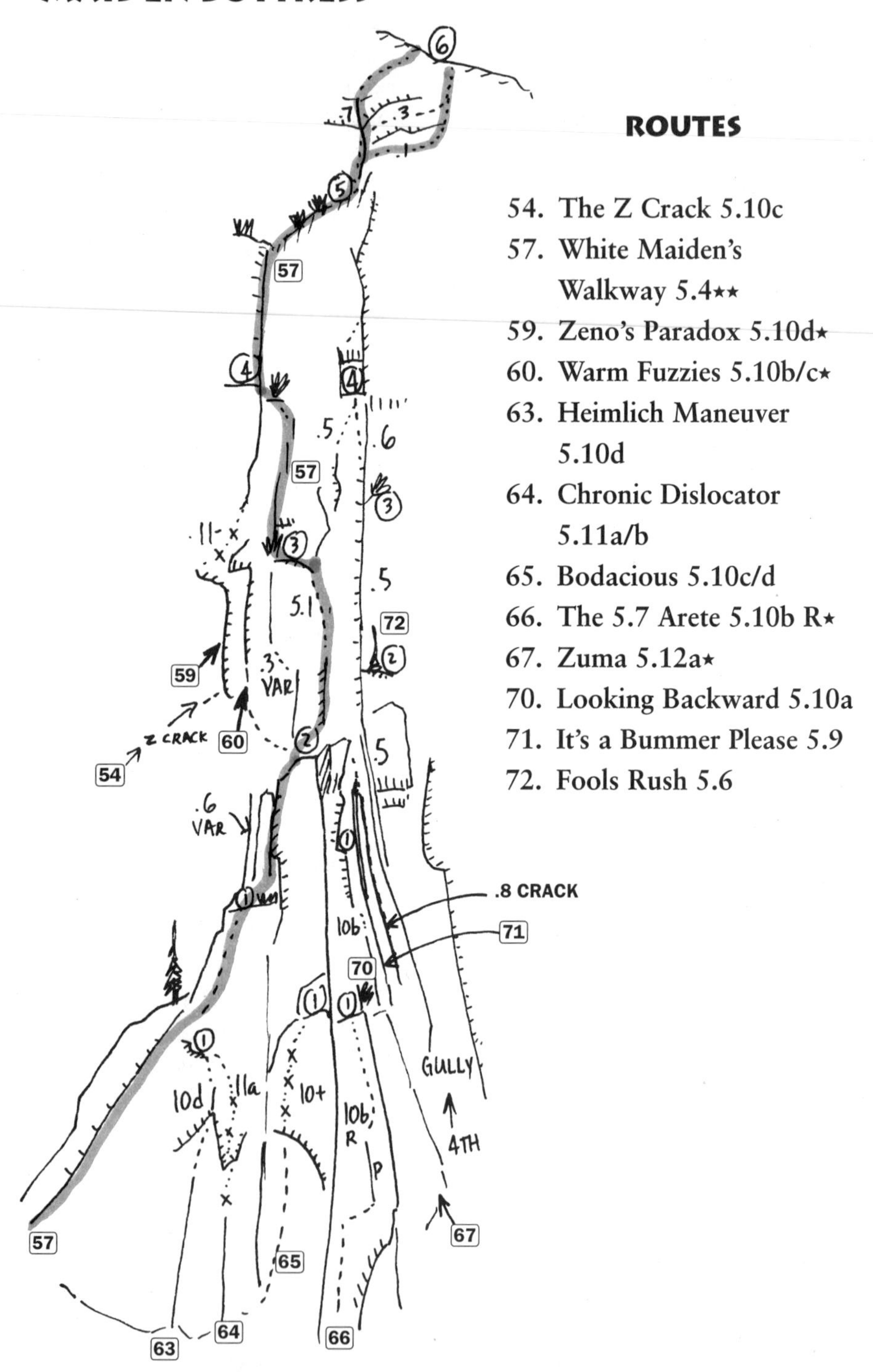

ROUTES

54. The Z Crack 5.10c
57. White Maiden's Walkway 5.4★★
59. Zeno's Paradox 5.10d★
60. Warm Fuzzies 5.10b/c★
63. Heimlich Maneuver 5.10d
64. Chronic Dislocator 5.11a/b
65. Bodacious 5.10c/d
66. The 5.7 Arete 5.10b R★
67. Zuma 5.12a★
70. Looking Backward 5.10a
71. It's a Bummer Please 5.9
72. Fools Rush 5.6

gendarme on the crest of the buttress. 3. Go directly up the broken corner system to a small tree and traverse left to a bushy belay ledge. 4. Up the corner until climbing becomes more difficult, then traverse left around a corner and up a crack to a belay at a tree. 5. (class 4) Continue up the crack system about 80 feet to a ledge with a few trees, then climb up and right about 40 feet. 7. Climb up, then move right past a tiny tree to a fingertip traverse right and easy friction to the top. You can also traverse out right a bit higher (5.3) or climb the crack directly over the roofs (5.7). Pro: to 3 inches. FA: Jim Smith and Arthur Johnson, August 1937.

58. **Maiden to Fool's Rush (Variation)** 5.5 From right side of the large ledge atop the 2nd pitch, follow cracks and flakes up for 2 pitches, joining *Fool's Rush* at the 4th belay.

59. **Zeno's Paradox** 5.10d ★ Start at the large ledge atop the 2nd pitch of *White Maiden* (can be reached from a number of routes on the buttress). Climb up the 3rd pitch of *White Maiden* a short distance, then face-climb left, below and past a left-facing corner, to another left-facing corner/crack. Follow the crack and face climbing to join *Illegitimate* at the end of the 2nd pitch. Pro: to 4 inches. FA: Spencer Lennard and Chris Robbins, 1978.

60. **Warm Fuzzies** 5.10b/c ★ This is the first left-facing corner system to the right of *Zeno's Paradox*. FA: Rick Linski, Diane Linski, and Bob Sachs.

WHITE MAIDEN'S APRON

The following two routes are located on the skirt or slab just right of the start of *White Maiden's Walkaway*, on the left flank of the lower Maiden Buttress.

61. **Iron Maiden** 5.11d ★ Slab to roofs on apron's left flank. Optional pro: 0.4-inch TCU. Rap 80 feet from a tree. FA: Bob Gaines and Charlie Peterson, July 1990.

62. **Maiden Heaven** 5.10c ★ Face to arete (7 bolts) starting behind a large tree, joining *Iron Maiden* at the top. FA: Bob Gaines and Charlie Peterson, July 1990.

LOWER MAIDEN BUTTRESS

The very toe of the Maiden Buttress is actually split into a number of subsidiary sub-buttresses, and the following climbs are found here. The trail from Lunch Rock passes directly along the toe of the Maiden Buttress.

WHITE MAIDEN'S APRON

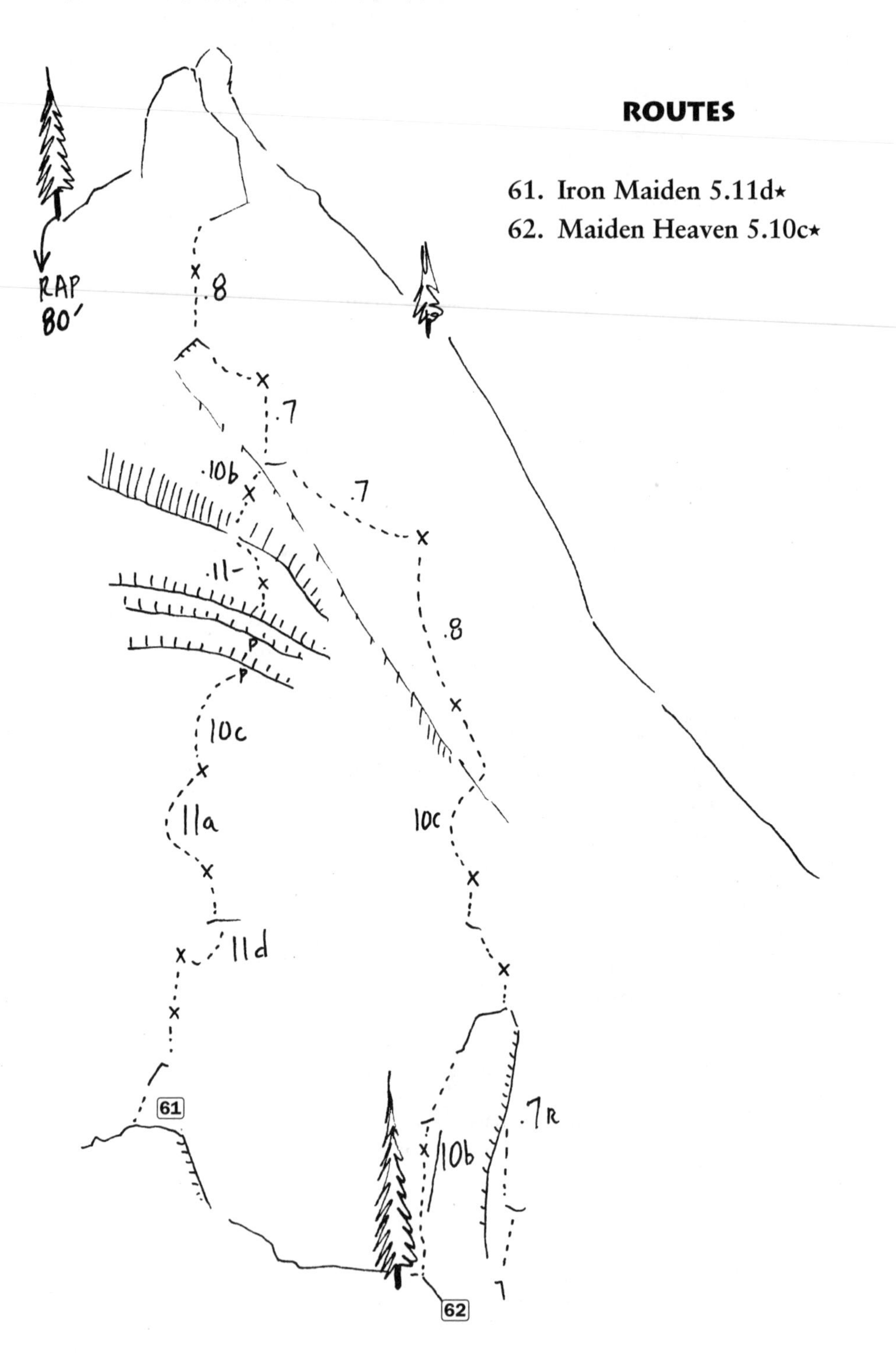

ROUTES

61. Iron Maiden 5.11d★
62. Maiden Heaven 5.10c★

63. **Heimlich Maneuver** 5.10d On the small central buttress climb the left face up to and over a small roof. FA: Todd Battey, Dave Evans, Margy Floyd, and Paul Binding, August 1990.
64. **Chronic Dislocater** 5.11a/b Face right of *Heimlich Maneuver,* with several bolts. FA: Dave Evans and Todd Battey, August 1990.
65. **Bodacious** 5.10c/d Face of separate block up and right from the proceeding routes. FA: Todd Battey, Dave Evans, and Margy Floyd, August 1990.
66. **The 5.7 Arete** 5.10b R ★ Obvious arete on the lower right side of the Maiden Buttress (the lower left skyline when viewed from Lunch Rock) Pro: to 2 inches. FA: Dave Evans, Charles Cole, Todd Gordon and Margy Floyd, 1986.

MAIDEN BUTTRESS RIGHT SIDE

The following routes begin along the right-hand side of the Maiden Buttress, which is easily visible from Lunch Rock. The approach to some of these routes may require scrambling (class 4) up a wide gully directly below the West Face Bulge.

67. **Zuma** 5.12a ★ The steep crack system on the lower right side of the Maiden Buttress, visible from Lunch Rock. Scramble up (class 4) to a sling belay at the base of the wall. Traverse left, then climb up over a bulge, to the bizarre crux. Rap 80 feet. Pro: thin nuts, good range of TCUs and CDs from .4 to 2.5 inches. FA: Bob Gaines and Charlie Peterson, August 1990.
68. **Stinger** 5.11d ★ Begin about 50 feet up the gully from *Zuma.* 2 bolts protect the overhanging bulge to a thin crack with 2 fixed pins. 2-bolt rap anchor, 80 feet. Pro: medium nuts, 0.4-inch TCUs, CDs to 2 inches. FA: Bob Gaines and Dave Mayville, August 1993.
69. **One Nut Willie** 5.11d ★ After you place the first nut your partner may be thinking "Will he go for it?" Start about 50 feet uphill from *Stinger* at the base of a deep chimney leading to the crest of the lower Maiden Buttress. This is also the starting point for *Looking Backward.* An overhanging lieback (11d) leads to stemming (11b) past 2 bolts. Move right (11-) at the top of the corner to a 3rd bolt; the face and mantle (10b) above is a wee bit scary. 2-bolt rap, 80 feet. Pro: to 2 inches. FA: Bob Gaines and Dave Mayville, July 1993.
70. **Looking Backward** 5.10a Start out of a deep recess on the right side of the Maiden Buttress; face climbing to a thin crack and thin corner leads to a wide flare. Ends atop 2nd pitch of *White Maiden.* Pro: to 3 inches. FA: Randy Vogel and Randy Grandstaff, 1979.

MAIDEN BUTTRESS LOWER RIGHT SIDE

ROUTES

67. Zuma 5.12a★
68. Stinger 5.11d★
69. One Nut Willie 5.11d★

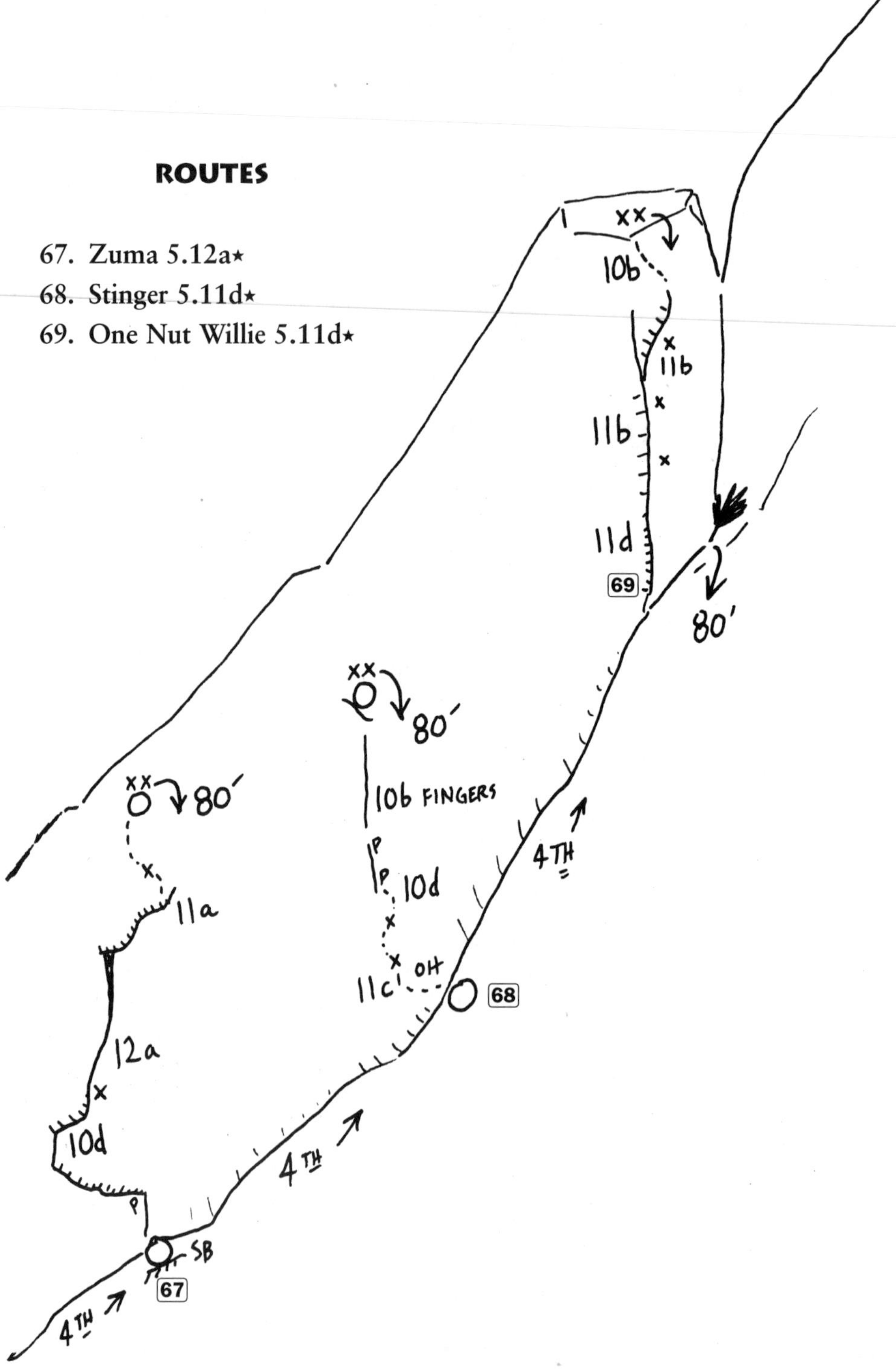

71. **It's a Bummer Please** 5.9 Often mistaken for *Fools Rush,* this one-pitch route is located a short distance left of the *Fools Rush* gully. Climb the prominent right-facing corner (which widens to form a shallow chimney), or better yet, the thin crack just right. Cross the roof (5.9) and move up and left to the top of the second pitch of *White Maiden.* Pro: thin to 2 inches. FA: Craig Fry, Dave Evans, and Jim Angione, 1981.
72. **Fools Rush** 5.6 This route follows a corner system in the chute or gully on the right side of the Maiden Buttress. Follow the main corner system for several progressively difficult pitches until an overhang in the corner is encountered. Pass this on the right and belay at a nice ledge a bit higher. Move up and left, then back into the main corner. Join *White Maiden's Walkaway* for its last pitch. Pro: to 3 inches. FA: Omar Conger, Barbara Lilley, and Don Rappolee, 1959.

WEST FACE BULGE ROUTES

This section of Tahquitz Rock features the large, bulging headwall on the west face of Tahquitz Rock. This bald-looking feature hosts several excellent routes, including Southern California's finest route, *The Vampire* (5.11a). This area includes routes on the steep rock just to the left and is bordered on the right by a large break in the rock that runs diagonally up and right (*The Trough* 5.4). From Lunch Rock head straight up to the base of the rock (near *Angel's Fright*) traverse left along the base to the *Trough* gully.

Routes 73 (*The Step*) through 76 (*Super Pooper*) start from a large ledge (From Bad Traverse Ledge, a.k.a. FBT Ledge) located above and to the left of *The Trough.* From Bad Traverse Ledge is best reached by climbing *From Bad Traverse,* a relatively easy traverse/ledge system beginning near the top of the first pitch of *The Trough.* Easy climbing (5.0) up and left leads to a ledge with trees. Continue up and left (5.6) on a blocky ramp to a ledge with mountain mahogany bushes. To approach Routes 78 (*The Flakes*) through 87 (*The Bat*), take a short crack/corner system (5.7) directly above this point to reach a large, flat ledge (Vampire Ledge). From Bad Traverse Ledge is reached by continuing (5.6) up and left from the mountain mahogany to reach a series of bushy ledges below the prominent roof of *Le Toit.*

The Lower Bulge Routes lie on the section of rock below From Bad Traverse Ledge. From Lunch Rock, the Lower Bulge is approached by heading left about 50 yards, then scrambling (class 3 and 4) up the wide gully and slabs which lies between the Maiden Buttress and *The Trough.*

Descent from the top is down the *Friction Route* (see p. 39).

WEST FACE BULGE
Summit
Blocks
To Friction Route
descent
81
86
79
81
85
West
Face
Bulge
76
81
73
100
Lower Bulge routes

UPPER BULGE ROUTES

73. **The Step** 5.10a ★★ Start from the upper left side of FBT Ledge, climbing a crack system just left of the obvious large roof of *Le Toit.* From the end of the 3rd pitch you can either go right and finish up last bit of *Super Pooper* (better), or escape left and finish up *White Maiden's Walkaway.* Pro: Small to 2.5 inches. FA: Royal Robbins and Jerry Gallwas, 1957. FFA: Royal Robbins and TM Herbert.

74. **Le Toit** 5.12a R ★★★ This route surmounts the large roof above FBT Ledge. 1. Start to the right, climbing face moves to an unprotected (5.8 R/X) mantle, then past a bolt (10+) to an arch that leads to a 2-bolt belay below the intimidating roof. 2. Jam over the roof (12-) and face climb up to a 2-bolt hanging belay. 3. Up and right, following an arch, until you can climb straight up, joining *Super Pooper* a bit higher. Pro: several thin to 2.5 inches. FA: (A3) TM Herbert, Tom Frost, and Yvon Chouinard, March 1960. FFA: John Long and Rick Accomazzo, 1973.

75. **Le Toitlette** 5.11c ★ Begin just right of *Le Toit.* Climb the face past two bolts to an easier line through the roofs to join *Super Pooper* at its first belay stance. Pro: thin to 2 inches. FA: Charles Cole and Craig Fry, August 1985.

76. **Super Pooper** 5.10a ★★★ A beautiful, soaring line up the distinct cleft forming the left margin of the West Face Bulge. From FBT Ledge, climb up and right up easy ledges to establish a belay (class 4). 1. A long crux pitch leads to a good ledge. 2. Thin finger cracks on the left wall to a small belay stance. 3. A long pitch liebacks the corner, around a small overhang, then moves up and right to turn the summit overhangs. Pro: thin to 3 inches. FA: Chuck Wilts, Don Wilson, John and Ruth Mendenhall, September 1952. FFA: Bob Kamps and Mark Powell, 1967.

77. **The Price of Fear** 5.10c ★★ Airy, with spectacular location. From the beginning of the lieback on pitch 3 of *Super Pooper,* traverse up and right on a green face to a thin crack just left of the lip of a huge arch. (This can also be approached from the last belay on The Flakes.) Follow the thin crack to bolts that protect face climbing to the top. FA: Milo Prodanovich and Steve McKinny, 1969. FFA: Tobin Sorenson and Matt Cox, 1972.

78. **The Flakes** 5.11c ★★★ (with *Price of Fear* finish) Begin off the left side of the Vampire Ledge. 1. Take the thin crack up to and over a small roof, to a belay at a bush. 2. Diagonal left up a flake system left of the main corner, to the large ledge that extends left to *Super Pooper.* 3. Surmount a flake, then a bouldery move (.11+, height dependent) over a bulge to flake system that leads to a ledge at the base of the huge arch. 4. For a

UPPER BULGE ROUTES

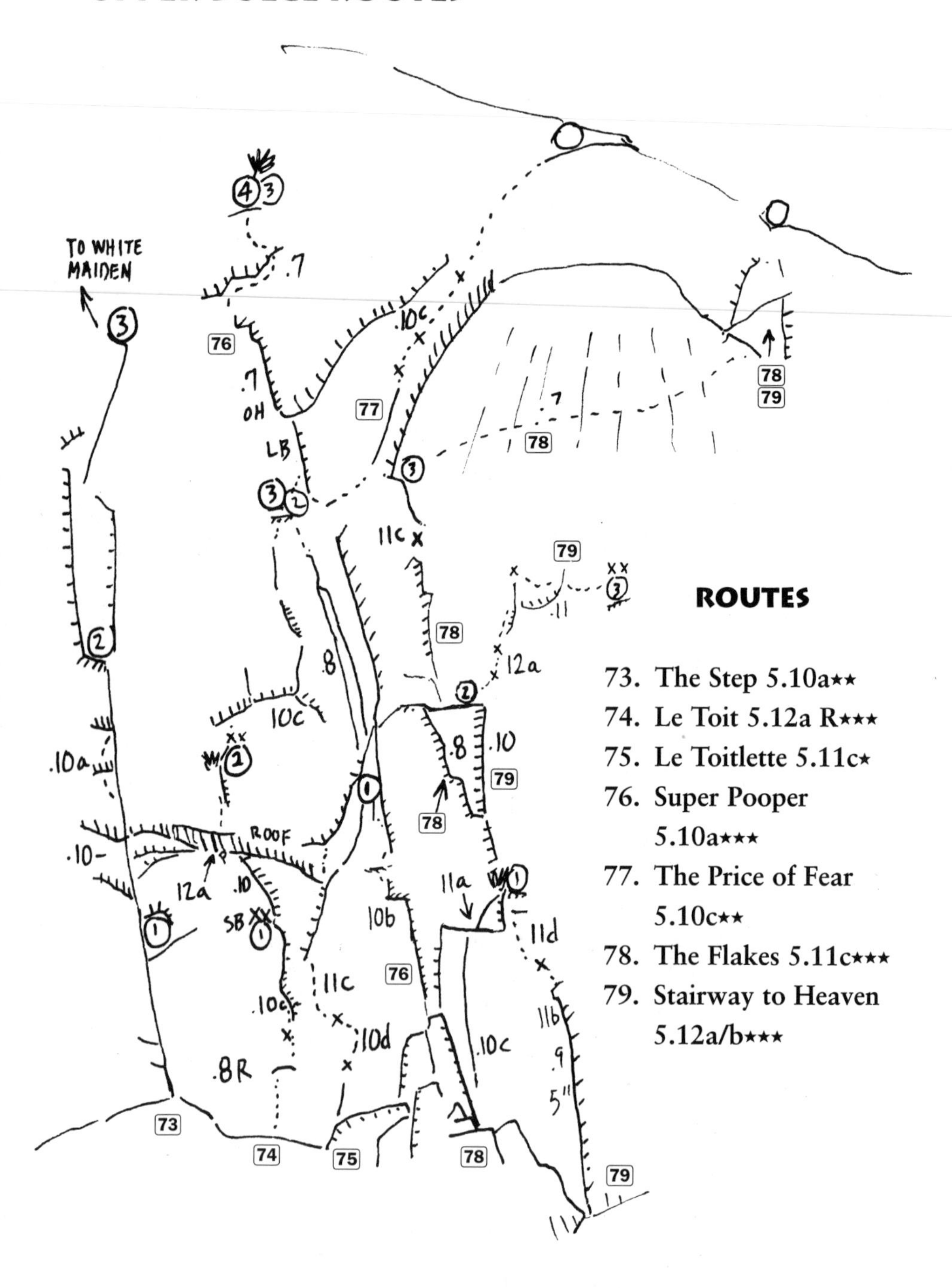

UPPER BULGE

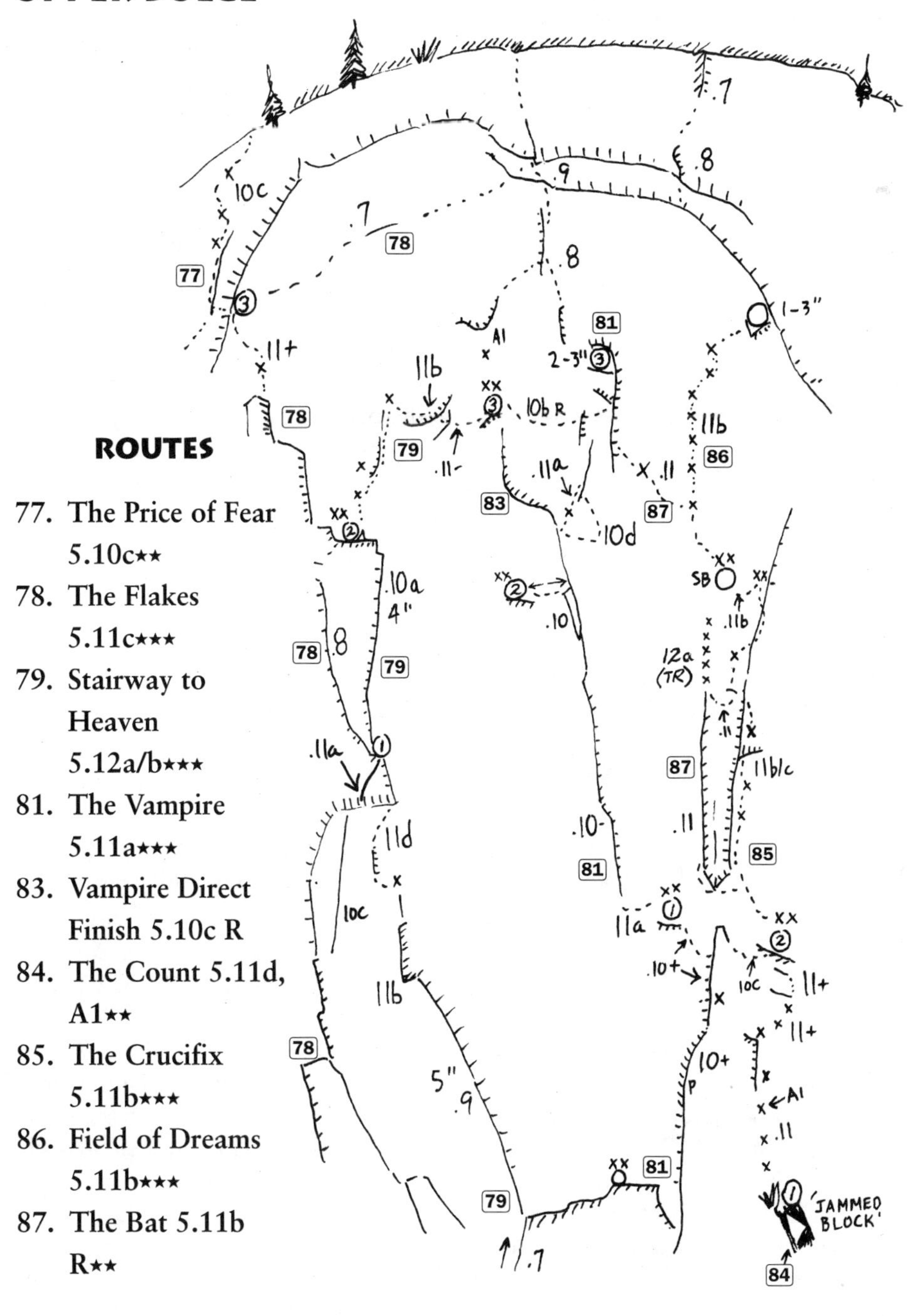

ROUTES

77. The Price of Fear 5.10c★★
78. The Flakes 5.11c★★★
79. Stairway to Heaven 5.12a/b★★★
81. The Vampire 5.11a★★★
83. Vampire Direct Finish 5.10c R
84. The Count 5.11d, A1★★
85. The Crucifix 5.11b★★★
86. Field of Dreams 5.11b★★★
87. The Bat 5.11b R★★

great direct finish, move left and climb *The Price of Fear* to the top. The original finish diagonals 80 feet right on exposed 5.7 friction, then climbs a weakness in the arch (5.9) to the top. FA: Royal Robbins and Don Wilson, July 1953. FFA: John Long, Tobin Sorenson, Richard Harrison, and Bill Antel, 1973.

79. **Stairway to Heaven** 5.12a/b ★★★ The first pitch is exceptionally demanding, although the third pitch is technically the crux. Begin at the left side of the Vampire Ledge. 1. Lieback and stem up the dihedral past a bolt, then left and up (crux), sharing *The Flakes* belay. 2. Straight up the right-facing corner (10-) to the large ledge. 3. Up and right past 2 bolts (clipping these is difficult unless aid is employed) to an arch (5.12), up to a bolt, then traverse 30 feet right (med. stopper) (11b) to a 2-bolt belay. 4. Move down and right (5.10 R) to join *Vampire* (the original route used aid from a bolt above the belay to reach 5.9 face climbing). Pro: to 4.5 inches. FA: (5.9, A4) Dave Black, Dave Hamburg, and Mike Graber, September 1973. FFA: John Long and Bob Gaines, July 1984.

80. **Happy Hooker** 5.10, A4- ★★ An exhilarating excursion up the center of the West Face Bulge. As "Big Wall" as Tahquitz gets. 1. Begin at the 2-bolt belay at Vampire Ledge. After some pins, aid an expanding flake (#1 Camalot, TCUs) to a bolt, tension-traverse left, then aid up to a hanging belay. 2. Hook moves and bathooks past 4 bolts, ending with a few free moves to the *Vampire* belay. 3. Reach left to a bolt, tension-traverse left (or 5.12) to a 5.10 face traverse to a narrow ledge with a two-bolt stance. 4. Bolts and hooks, then face-climb up to the *Stairway to Heaven* belay. (This pitch is one of Tahquitz's last great remaining free climbing challenges.) 5. A bolt and nut for aid lead to a 5.9 finish. Rack: assorted hooks, bathooks (2 Black Diamond talons), TCUs, #1 Camalot, knifeblades, lost arrows, small angles. FA: Bob Gaines and Mike Borello, July 1994.

81. **The Vampire** 5.11a ★★★ A fantastic line that achieves magnificent position, perhaps Tahquitz's finest route. 1. From the right side of Vampire Ledge, climb down slightly to reach a hand crack (the "Bat Crack"). Belay at triple bolts that protect the crux of the second pitch. 2. A delicate traverse left leads to a spectacular thin flake system; lieback this, then step down left to a hanging belay. 3. Move back right to the flake, then past a bolt up a thin crack (11-), belaying higher at a small arch. The crux section can be avoided by moving down and right from the bolt, then back up and left to join the thin crack (10+) 4. Climb up and over the headwall (5.9) to the top. Pro: small wires, many cams to 3 inches. FA: (5.9, A3) Royal Robbins and Dave Rearick, June 1959. FFA: John Long, Rick Accomazzo, Mike Graham, and Bill Antel, 1973.

HAPPY HOOKER

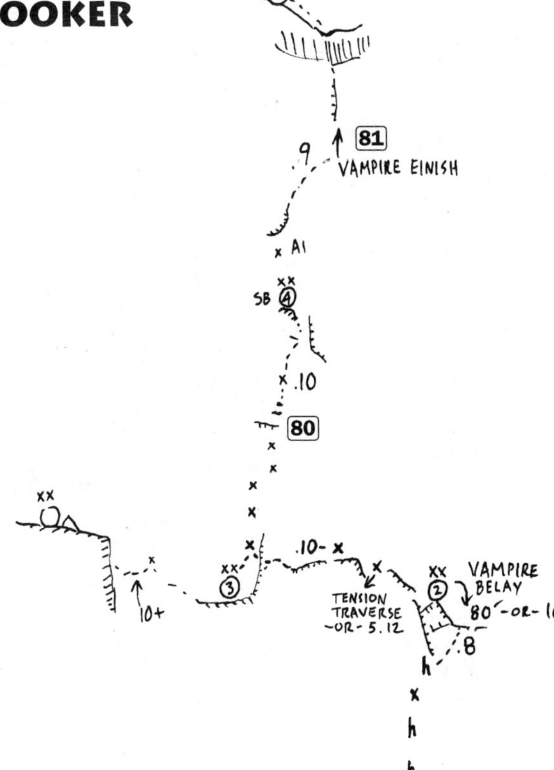

ROUTES

80. Happy Hooker 5.10, A4★★
81. The Vampire 5.11a★★

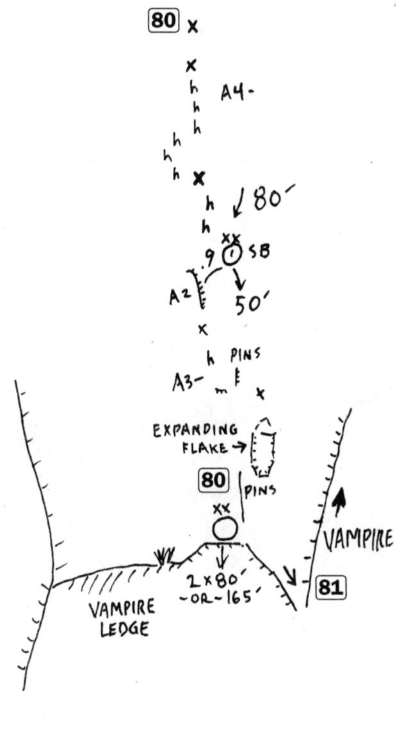

Clark Jacobs on The Vampire *(5.11)*. PHOTO BY GREG COLEMAN

82. **Vampire Direct Start** 5.10d Start at *From Bad Traverse* and climb directly up to The Bat Crack. FA: unknown.
83. **Vampire Direct Finish** 5.10c R On 3rd pitch, instead of climbing the thin crack above the bolt, undercling and lieback left on a very thin flake to the belay on *Stairway to Heaven.* FA: Tim Sorenson, 1970s.
84. **The Count** 5.11d, A1 ★★ 1. From the base of the *Vampire Direct Start* (Route 82) climb grungy rock up and right to a belay at a jammed block. 2. Fantastic face climbing up and right to the arete. A single point of aid was used at the third bolt. 7 bolts plus a 0.4- or 0.5-inch TCU above the last bolt. Pro: to 2 inches. FA: Scott Cosgrove, Bob Gaines, and Dave Mayville, August 1993.
85. **The Crucifix** 5.11b ★★★ At the top of *Vampire*'s first pitch (The Bat Crack, 11a) move down and right (10c) to a small, flat ledge with 2 bolts. *The Bat* (Route 87) traverses around the corner to the left. *The Crucifix* climbs the obvious dihedral directly above the belay ledge, joining *The Bat* near the top of the pitch. Both *The Bat* and *The Crucifix* are roughly the same difficulty, but *The Crucifix* has far better protection. Either way, the entire route involves three stellar 5.11 pitches. Pro: thin nuts, TCUs, 6 bolts. FA: (A2) Unknown. FFA: Bob Gaines and Tommy Romero, August 1995.
86. **Field of Dreams** 5.11b ★★★ Combine *The Vampire's* Bat Crack with *Crucifix* to the *Field of Dreams* finish for a Tahquitz classic. From the hanging belay on *The Bat,* move left to the *Bat's* first bolt, then instead of continuing left, climb straight up a beautiful slab past 6 more bolts to a belay at the arch on the right (1- to 3-inch CDs). A 5.8 pitch (you are now on *Upper Royal's Arch*) takes you up and over the overhang to the top. FA: Bob Gaines and Charlie Peterson, August 1996.
87. **The Bat** 5.11b R ★★ 1. Start per *The Vampire.* At the top of The Bat Crack, traverse down and right to a nice, flat belay ledge with 2 bolts. 2. Don't ascend the dihedral above, but traverse around the corner to the left and lieback a steep crack to an old bolt ladder, clip the first bolt, then traverse out right and up past two bolts, then move left (11b) to a two-bolt belay. 3. Diagonal left up a ramp past two bolts (11a), join *The Vampire* briefly at a slim, left-facing corner, then climb out right to a sling belay. The last pitch climbs over the headwall. Pro: several to 3 inches. FA: with bolt ladder (5.7, A2) Don Wilson, Jerry Gallwas, and Chuck Wilts, 1960 (they pendulumed right from the top of the bolt ladder). FFA of dihedral to bolt ladder: Tobin Sorenson, 1973. FA of complete route: Bob Gaines and Yvonne Gaines, September 1987. FFA of dihedral and bolt ladder: Matt Bebe and Ian Katz, 5.12a (TR), July 2000.

LOWER BULGE BUTTRESS

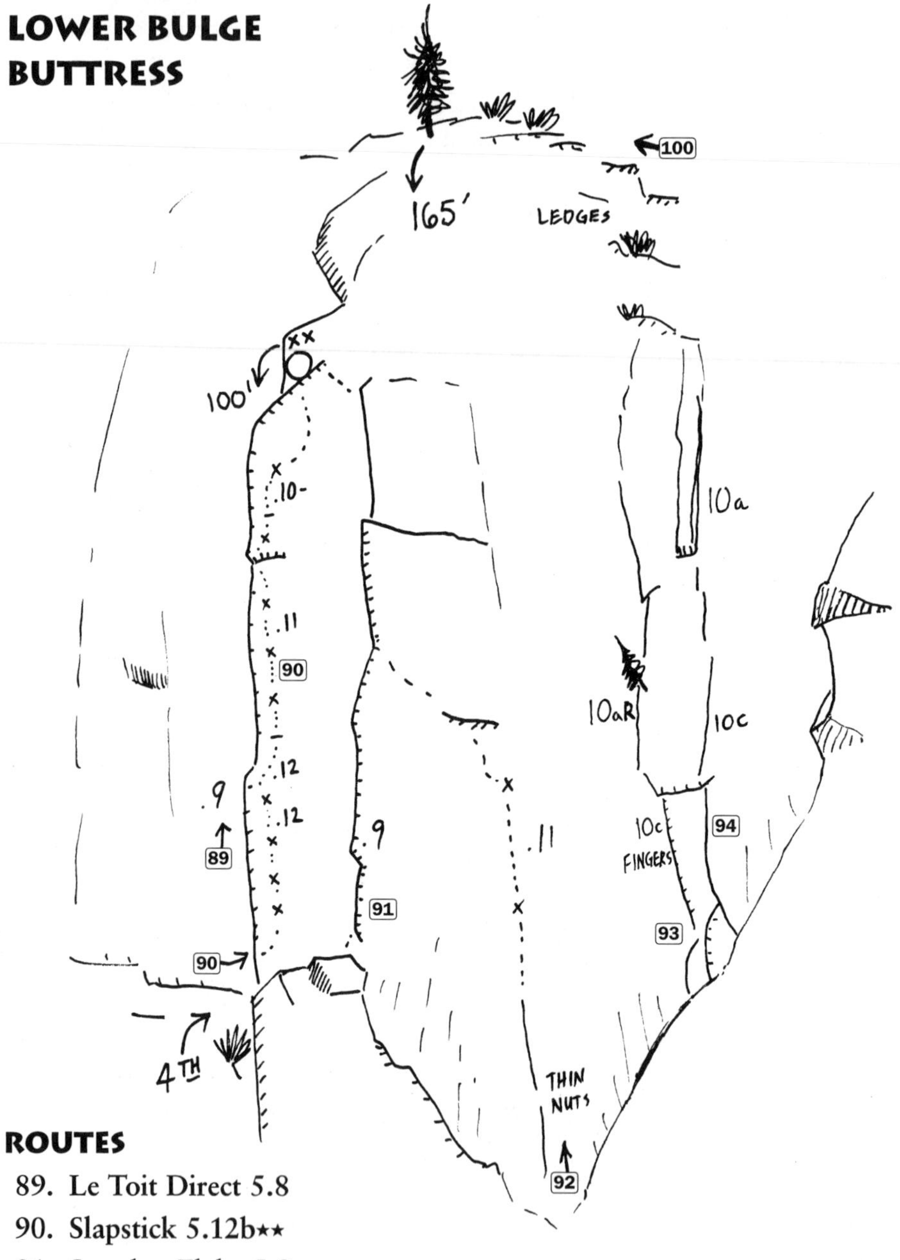

ROUTES

89. Le Toit Direct 5.8
90. Slapstick 5.12b★★
91. Standup Flake 5.9★
92. Cause for Alarm 5.11b★
93. Man Bites Dog 5.10c R★
94. Dog Bites Man 5.10c
100. From Bad Traverse 5.6

88. **The Pharaoh** 5.12b ★ Start near the trees at the beginning of *From Bad Traverse*. This is the awkward, arching, sustained thin crack on the right side of the face below Vampire Ledge. Pro: many thin to 3.5 inches. FA: Lynn Hill and John Long, 1983.

LOWER BULGE BUTTRESS

The Lower Bulge Routes lie on the section of rock below From Bad Traverse Ledge (FBT Ledge). From Lunch Rock, the Lower Bulge is approached by heading left about 50 yards, then scrambling up the (class 3 and 4) wide gully and slabs between the Maiden Buttress and *The Trough*.

89. **Le Toit Direct** 5.8 A great direct start up the left-facing corner directly below *Le Toit* and just left of *Slapstick*. FA: Unknown.
90. **Slapstick** 5.12b ★★ The steep, rounded arete just right of Route 89. 10 bolts. 100-foot rappel. FA: Dave Mayville, May 1999.
91. **Standup Flake** 5.9 ★ The flake/crack just right of *Slapstick*. Pro: to 3 inches. FA: Unknown.
92. **Cause for Alarm** 5.11b ★ Left of *Man Bites Dog*, a thin crack leads to a face with 3 bolts, then traverse left to *Standup Flake*. Pro: very thin to 3 inches. FA: Dave Evans and Jim Angione, June 1989.
93. **Man Bites Dog** 5.10c R ★ The left-hand crack that leads past a small pine on the right side of the buttress. Pro: #1 stopper to 2.5 inches. FA: Charles Cole, Randy Vogel, and Paul Schweizer, June 1985.
94. **Dog Bites Man** 5.10c The crack to the right. Pro: small to 3 inches. FA: Charles Cole, Dave Evans, and Craig Fry, July 1985.

ROYAL'S ARCHES

This section of rock lies directly right of the Upper Bulge and above the lower section of *The Trough*. Routes 95 and 96 start from the bottom of *From Bad Traverse* (Route 100). Routes 97, 98, and 99 start from Pine Tree Ledge, a large ledge (with pine tree) found three pitches up *The Trough* (Route 101). Pine Tree Ledge can also be reached via Routes 105 through 112.

95. **Chin Strap Crack** 5.10c R Start near the trees at the beginning of *From Bad Traverse*. Climb to the top of a big, loose flake, clip 2 poor bolts, then downclimb 20 feet and lieback up the wide crack to a belay shared with *Passover* and *Lower Royal's Arch*. Pro: to 5 inches. FA: Charlie Raymond and Lee Harrell, June 1966.
96. **The Passover** 5.10d Begin at *From Bad Traverse* about 40 feet left of *The Trough*. 1. Up to a belay directly below the prominent overhang of *Lower Royal's Arch*. 2. Climb the slab below the roof past two bolts,

ROYAL'S ARCHES

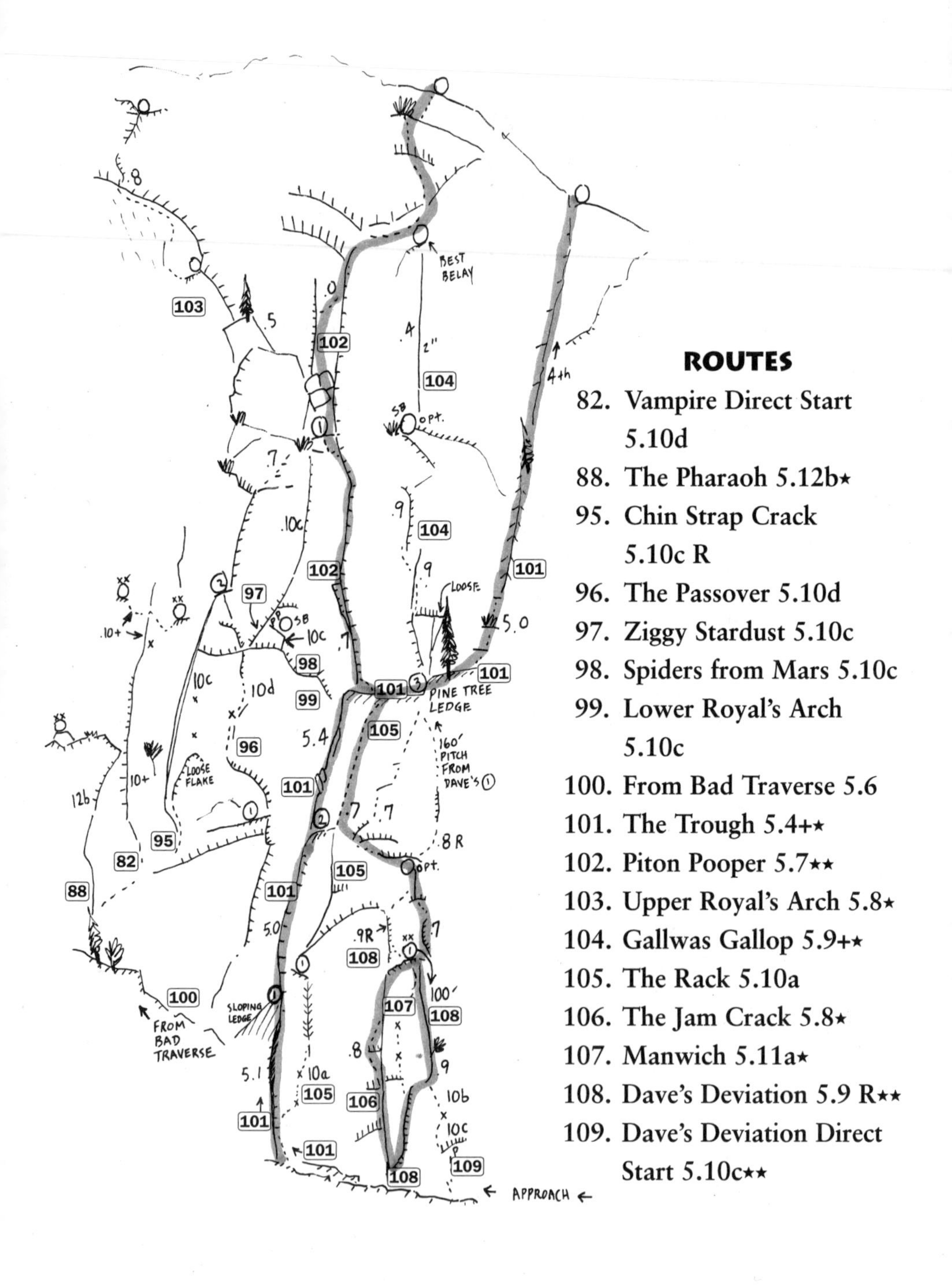

ROUTES

82. Vampire Direct Start 5.10d
88. The Pharaoh 5.12b★
95. Chin Strap Crack 5.10c R
96. The Passover 5.10d
97. Ziggy Stardust 5.10c
98. Spiders from Mars 5.10c
99. Lower Royal's Arch 5.10c
100. From Bad Traverse 5.6
101. The Trough 5.4+★
102. Piton Pooper 5.7★★
103. Upper Royal's Arch 5.8★
104. Gallwas Gallop 5.9+★
105. The Rack 5.10a
106. The Jam Crack 5.8★
107. Manwich 5.11a★
108. Dave's Deviation 5.9 R★★
109. Dave's Deviation Direct Start 5.10c★★

then "passover" the roofs to a belay about 15 feet higher on the left. 3. Climb up and right to join *Piton Pooper.* FA: Bob Kamps, Roy Coats, and Tom Higgins, June, 1964; FFA: Rick Accomazzo and Tobin Sorenson, 1973.

97. **Ziggy Stardust** 5.10c Start at Pine Tree Ledge (see *The Trough*), traverse left under the arch, then pull directly over the arching roof crack, eventually joining *Piton Pooper.* Pro: to 2.5 inches. FA: Peter Wilkening and Jim Wilson, 1975.
98. **Spiders from Mars** 5.10c Go over the overhang a short distance to the right of *Ziggy Stardust,* then up left to rejoin that route. FA: John Yablonski and Greg Theil, 1978.
99. **Lower Royal's Arch** 5.10d Start at Pine Tree Ledge (see *The Trough*), traverse left under the arch, then up and left to the belay ledge on *Chin Strap Crack.* Follow that route above. FA: (A2) Royal Robbins, Don Wilson, and Chuck Wilts, May 1952. FFA: Rick Accomazzo and Tobin Sorenson, 1973.
100. **From Bad Traverse** 5.6 This relatively easy traverse/ledge system begins partway up the 1st pitch of *The Trough.* Easy climbing (5.0) up and left leads to a ledge with trees. Continue left up a blocky ramp, past a ledge with mountain mahogany bushes, to a few 5.6 moves up and left to From Bad Traverse Ledge (FBT Ledge). One can continue left to join *White Maiden's Walkaway.* This route is most commonly used as an approach to West Face Bulge routes (see page 75). FA: Bob Brinton and H. Fuller, September 1939.

THE WEST FACE

This section of rock is bordered on the left side by the large break in the rock that runs diagonally up and right (*The Trough,* 5.4) and on the right by the enormous arete of *The Edge.* This section of rock lies directly above the vicinity of Lunch Rock. The routes on this section of rock seem to share (converge upon) several final pitches leading to the top. Routes tend to end on The Pine Tree Ledge or Lunch Ledge (a ledge with a solitary pine several hundred feet directly above Lunch Rock).

Descent is usually via the *Friction Route* (see page 39), although very skilled climbers sometimes downclimb *The Trough* (5.4). It is also possible to rappel from Lunch Ledge via several pine trees (single rope will suffice, but two ropes recommended). Numerous rappel routes are also possible from bolt anchors and are noted in the route descriptions and topos.

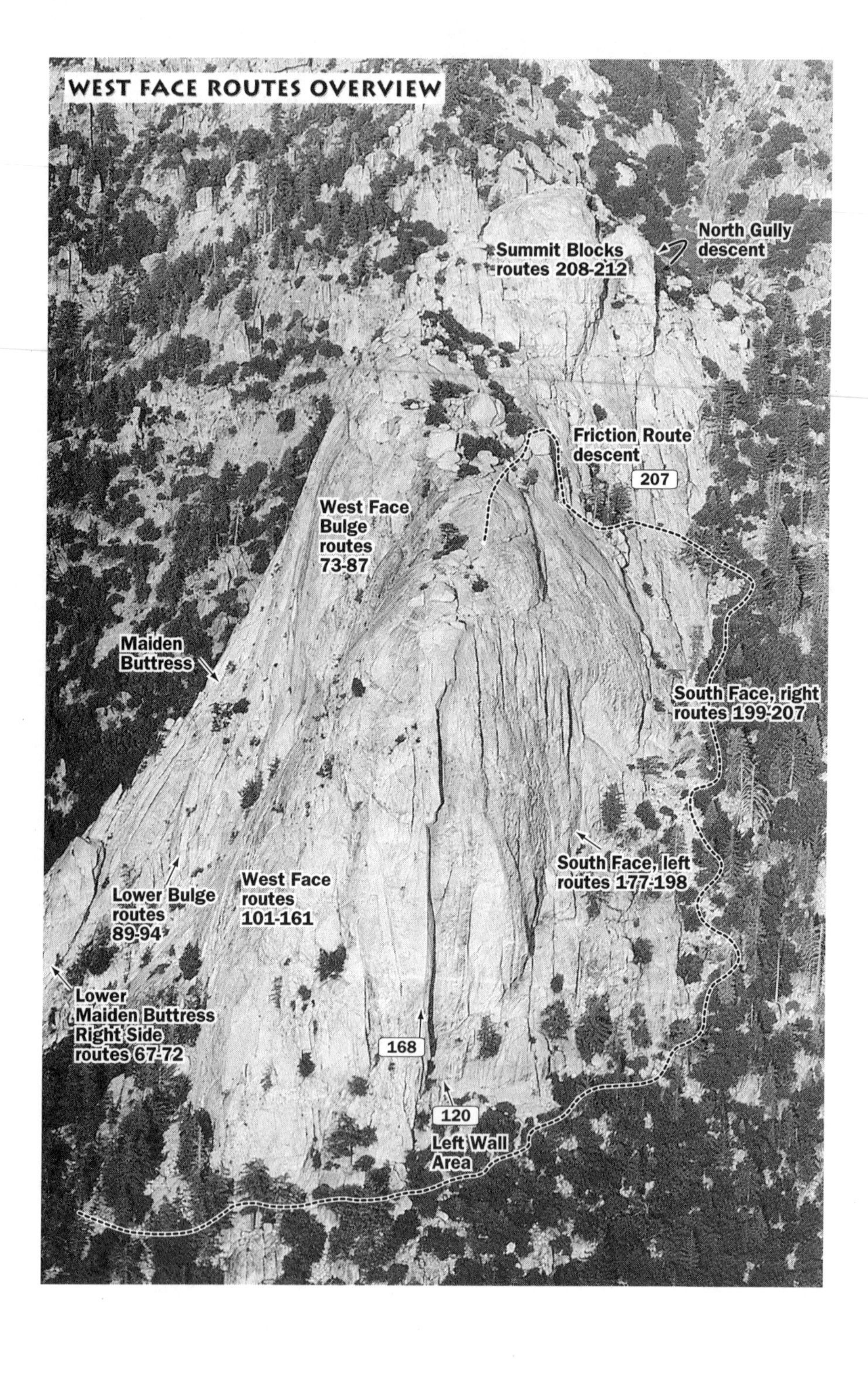
WEST FACE ROUTES OVERVIEW
Summit Blocks routes 208-212
North Gully descent
Friction Route descent
207
West Face Bulge routes 73-87
Maiden Buttress
South Face, right routes 199-207
South Face, left routes 177-198
Lower Bulge routes 89-94
West Face routes 101-161
Lower Maiden Buttress Right Side routes 67-72
168
120
Left Wall Area

WEST FACE LEFT SIDE ("THE TROUGH" TO "HUMAN FRIGHT")

From Lunch Rock head straight up to the base of the rock (near *Angel's Fright/Human Fright*) then traverse right or left along the base. Routes 102 through 104 begin from Pine Tree Ledge, (located 3 pitches up *The Trough*). Routes 105 through 113 end on Pine Tree Ledge.

101. **The Trough** 5.4 ★★ The first route on Tahquitz, also the easiest route up the cliff and a good introduction to multipitch climbing. The best approach is from Lunch Rock. Hike straight up to the base of the cliff to the start of *Angel's Fright* (the first pitch is a prominent vertical chimney crack), then scramble left (tunneling under a chockstone and squeezing through a short chimney) and walk left across a broad ledge (past the start of *Dave's Deviation*) to a prominent break in the cliff. 1. Rope up here and climb a low angle jamcrack that widens before ending at a wide, sloping ledge. 2. Up the obvious chute to a belay at a small ledge on the right. 3. Continue up the corner system, traversing right to large Pine Tree Ledge. Several other climbs either end or start at this ledge. 4. A short, steep face (5.0) is encountered, then 4th class up and right to the top. Pro: to 3 inches. FA: Jim Smith, Bob Brinton, and Z. Jasaitis, August 1936.

102. **Piton Pooper** 5.7+ ★ From the extreme left end of Pine Tree Ledge on *The Trough*, lieback the steep, classic dihedral to a belay ledge about 80

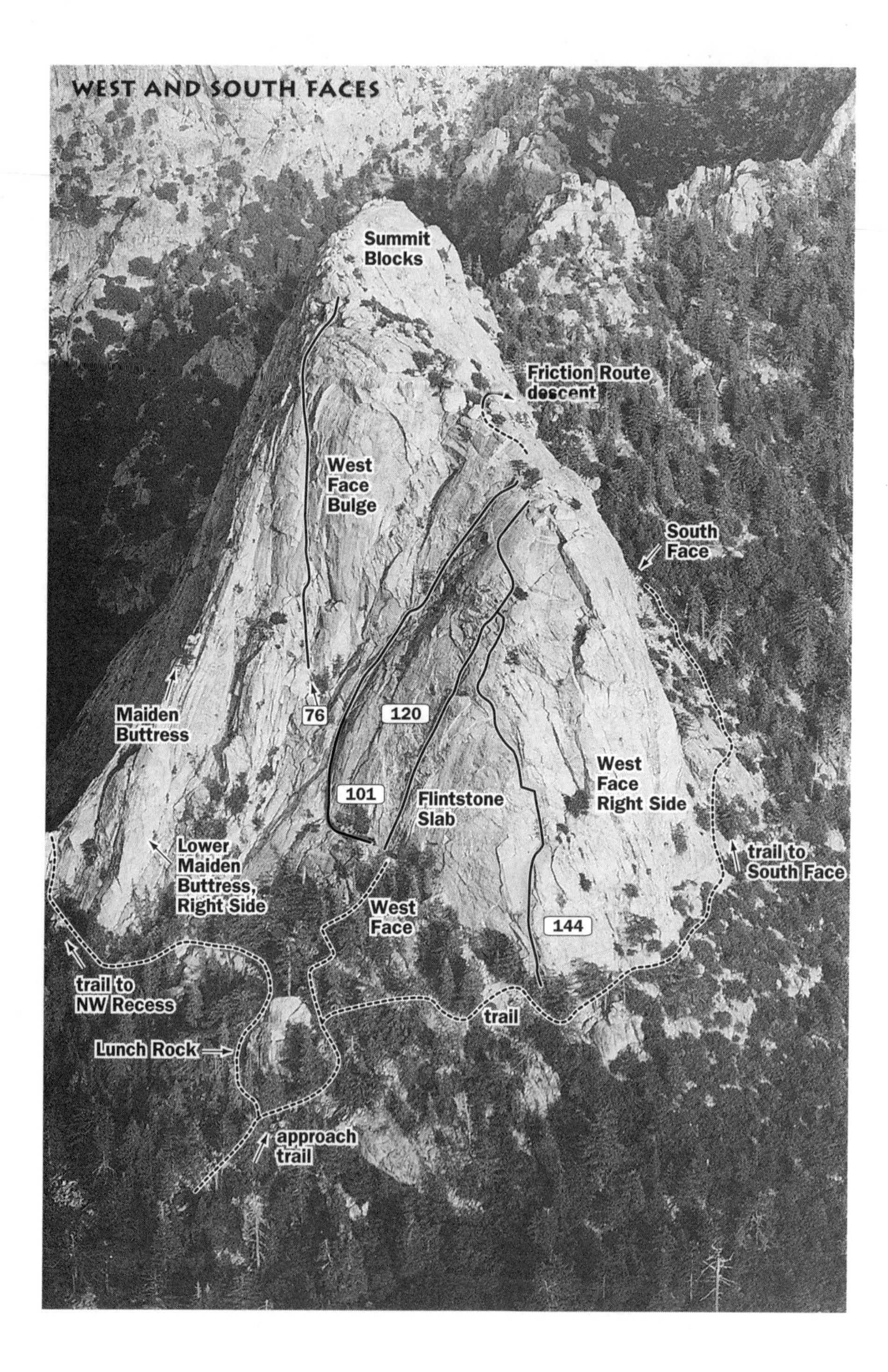
WEST AND SOUTH FACES
Summit Blocks
Friction Route descent
West Face Bulge
South Face
Maiden Buttress
76
120
101
Flintstone Slab
West Face Right Side
Lower Maiden Buttress, Right Side
trail to South Face
West Face
144
trail to NW Recess
trail
Lunch Rock
approach trail

feet higher. The final pitch climbs up and exits right from a deep trough. Pro: thin to 2 inches. FA: (A2) Bob Brinton and Andy Johnson, September 1936. FFA: Chuck Wilts, Ellen Wilts, and Spencer Austin, 1949.

103. **Upper Royal's Arch** 5.8 ★ This route provides a more interesting finish to *Piton Pooper,* as well as *Chin Strap Crack, The Passover, Lower Royal's Arch* and *Ziggy Stardust.* After the first pitch of *Piton Pooper,* you may want to move the belay up and left. Lots of exposure! This route is reportedly much more difficult (5.10) if you follow the crack in the arch exclusively; look for face moves out left. Pro: thin to 2 inches. FA: Royal Robbins, Jerry Gallwas, and Chuck Wilts, 1953.

104. **Gallwas Gallop** 5.9+ ★ From Pine Tree Ledge, start just left of the tree. 1. Climb a discontinuous flake system up the vertical face for about 60 feet, then move up and right to a belay. 2. Up a straight-in crack then exit up and right via *Piton Pooper.* Pro: thin to 2.5 inches. FA: Jerry Gallwas, Chuck Wilts, and Royal Robbins, 1953.

105. **The Rack** 5.10a 1. Start up *The Trough* and after about 30 feet, climb the face immediately to the right past 2 bolts to a crack system. 2. Lieback around a small roof, then up a corner to a belay ledge on the left. 3. Step right and climb a slab to Pine Tree Ledge. Pro: thin to 2 inches. FA: Bob Kamps, Mark Powell, and Beverly Powell, 1961.

106. **The Jam Crack** 5.8 ★ 1. Start just to the right of *The Trough* in a small corner/crack system. 2. Climb the lieback flake on the right to a belay beneath some arches. 3. Traverse left about 30 feet, then move back right and over some overlaps (sketchy pro here) directly up to Pine Tree Ledge. Pro: thin to 2.5 inches. FA: Royal Robbins and Don Wilson, September 1959.

107. **Manwich** 5.11a ★ Climb the first 20 feet of *Dave's Deviation,* then climb the narrow face above past 2 bolts, moving right at the top to join *Dave's Deviation* just below the ledge. FA: Terry Ayers, Craig Fry, and Jack Marshall, June 1986.

108. **Dave's Deviation** 5.9 R ★★ 1. Start as for *The Jam Crack,* but lieback a flake on the right up to a classic straight-in finger crack with a mountain mahogany bush growing out of it. This might be the best 5.9 finger crack pitch in Idyllwild, ending at a tiny ledge with a bolt anchor. (90-foot rappel.) 2. Move left and up a thin (5.9 R) corner, then face-climb up right to a belay shared with *The Jam Crack.* 3. Climb out the right side of an arch, then straight up (5.8 R) to Pine Tree Ledge. Most parties do only the well-protected first pitch and continue up *The Jam Crack.* Pro: thin to 2 inches. FA: Tom Frost and Royal Robbins, 1960.

109. **Dave's Deviation Direct Start** 5.10c ★★ A more challenging start to a great pitch. Begin 20 feet right of the regular route and climb directly past a fixed pin and bolt to the start of the straight-in finger crack. FA: Charlie Peterson and Bob Gaines, August 1994.

SCARFACE SLAB AREA

This is the steep, triangular slab located about 50 feet up and left from the start of *Angel's Fright* (Route 120). Routes 110 through 113 share a common 2-bolt belay/rappel anchor at the top of the slab. An 80-foot rappel reaches the base. This anchor can also be reached by climbing the first two pitches of the *Frightful Variation to the Trough* (Route 116, 5.2).

110. **Poker Face** 5.12a (or 5.8) ★ You can bluff your way through this one by moving left at the first bolt for a 5.8 pitch. Start about 30 feet left of *Scarface,* at a crack that veers sharply left about 30 feet up. Climb the crack (5.8) and the face above (12a) past 2 bolts. (80-foot rappel.) Pro: a few CDs to 2 inches. FA: Bob Gaines and Dave Mayville, July 1993.

111. **Scar Face** 5.11d ★★ An amazing 4-bolt route up the center of the slab 40 feet right of *Dave's Deviation,* ending at a ledge on *Frightful Variation to the Trough.* 80-foot rappel from bolts. FA: Charles Cole and Bob Gaines, August 1985.

112. **Devil's Delight** 5.10b R ★ Start 50 left of *Angel's Fright.* 1. Climb the crack behind a pine, move left, up past a bolt (10a) to a ledge with 2 bolts. 2. 40 feet up a steep flake system. 3. Up past 2 bolts, over a small overhang, then traverse 15 feet right to a thin, vertical crack with poor protection, past a bolt to a belay a bit higher. 4. Climb up, then traverse left across an easy slab, then down to Pine Tree Ledge. Pro: many thin (RPs or equivalent) to 3 inches. FA: Mark and Beverly Powell, August 1966.

113. **Cutter** 5.11b/c ★ An elegant crux. Begin a few feet right of *Devil's Delight,* up an easy corner until you can move out right to a bolt. A direct start (5.10 R) is also possible. FA: Bob Gaines and Dave Mayville, August 1993.

114. **The Blank** 5.10a ★★ 1. Climb the short, left-facing dihedral 20 feet left of *Angel's Fright* to the ledge. 2. Up the face and over the left side of the roof to a crack leading to a ledge below a right-slanting dihedral. 3. Up the dihedral to a bushy ledge on the right. 4. Step up and right, then left into a lieback leading to a bolt and a face traverse left, finally up to ledges. Go right to Lunch Ledge. Pro: to 4 inches, incl. several 3-inch and 4-inch. FA: Royal Robbins and Jerry Gallwas, May 1954. FFA: Tom Frost and Bob Kamps, 1960.

WEST FACE SCARFACE SLAB

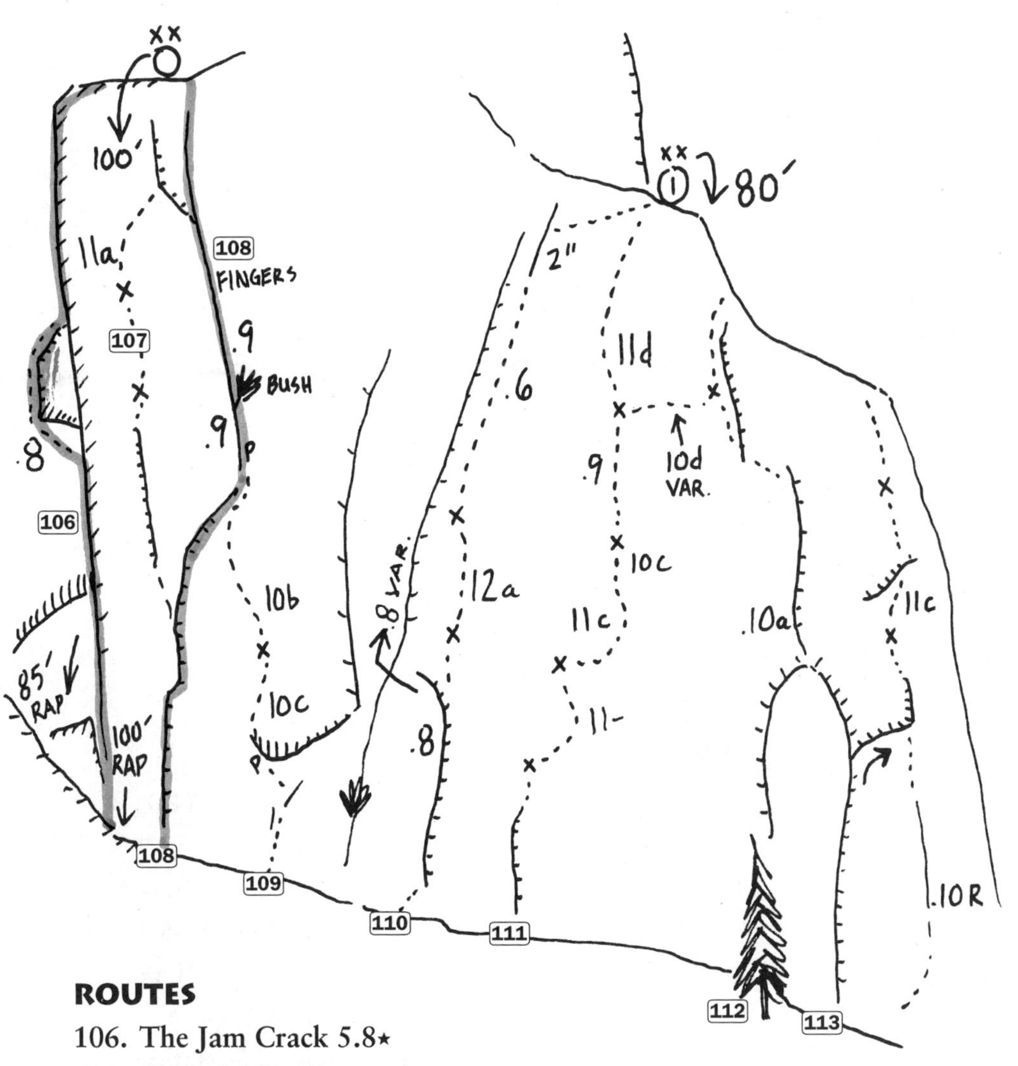

ROUTES

106. The Jam Crack 5.8★
107. Manwich 5.11a★
108. Dave's Deviation 5.9 R★★
109. Dave's Deviation Direct Start 5.10c★★
110. Poker Face 5.12a (or 5.8)★
111. Scar Face 5.11d★★
112. Devil's Delight 5.10b R★
113. Cutter 5.11b/c★

WEST FACE, LEFT SIDE

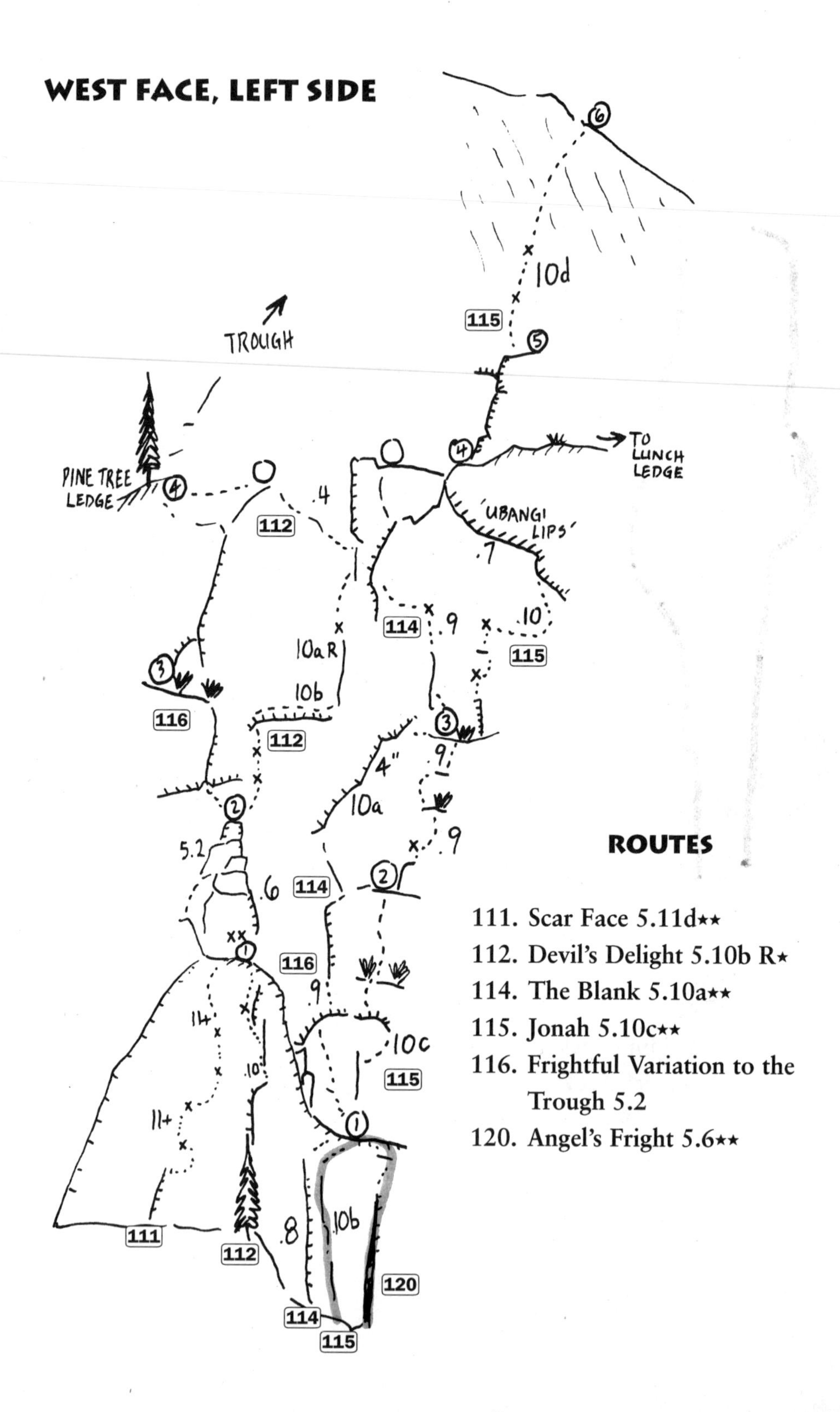

ROUTES

111. Scar Face 5.11d★★
112. Devil's Delight 5.10b R★
114. The Blank 5.10a★★
115. Jonah 5.10c★★
116. Frightful Variation to the Trough 5.2
120. Angel's Fright 5.6★★

Kris Solem on the last pitch of Jonah *(5.10d), Tahquitz.* PHOTO BY KEVIN POWELL

115. **Jonah** 5.10c ★★ 1. The very thin crack just right of *The Blank*. 2. A tricky headwall directly above the ledge, then up to a belay shared with *The Blank*. 3. Up the face past a bolt and up to a sloping ledge with bushes. 4. Up past 2 bolts, traverse 20 feet straight right then up to and left under a gaping flake known as The Ubangi Lips and up to a ledge. 5. Short, easy pitch to a higher belay. 6. Thin edges past 2 bolts (10+) leads to a friction slab finish. FA: Tom Higgins, Roy Coats, and M. Cohen, August 1964.

116. **Frightful Variation to the Trough** 5.2 1. The first chimney pitch of *Angel's Fright*. 2. Climb the chimney/crack above the far left side of the ledge (beware of huge, loose flakes) up to a good belay. 3 and 4. From the left end of this ledge follow the obvious flake/ramp system that leads up to Pine Tree Ledge on *The Trough*. FA: Chuck Wilts and Jim Gorin, September 1944.

LUNCH ROCK

This is the 60-foot high rock located about 150 feet directly below the West Face. The Lunch Rock Trail leads directly to this rock.

117. **Lunch Rock Chimney Route** 5.7 This is the crack system on the main (west) face, seen directly above the approach trail. FA: Unknown.

118. **Chongo Arete** 5.11 (TR) This route climbs the short, steep northwest corner (the far left side as you are walking up to Lunch Rock). It once had bolts but they're gone now. FA: Chongo brothers, circa 1993.

119. **Freelove** 5.11b Climb the flake system to a headwall with several bolts. FA: Bart Barry, et al., 1993.

WEST FACE CENTER

From Lunch Rock walk directly up to the base of the rock. *Angel's Fright* will be recognized by a narrow chimney leading about 40 feet up to a bushy ledge.

120. **Angel's Fright** 5.6 ★★ The obvious crack and left-facing corner system almost directly above Lunch Rock. 1. A short, tight chimney to a bushy ledge. 2. Head up and right and then back left, up (5.6) steep face climbing to reach a good ledge at the base of the right-tending crack/corner system marking this route. 3. Up the corner past a 5.4 overhang, to a nice ledge above a pine tree (Lunch Ledge). 5. From the right end of Lunch Ledge, climb up past several bushy ledges for about 60 feet, tiptoe left across a slim ledge, then up past a bolt on smooth friction to the top (160 feet). A good variation (5.6) heads straight up a thin lieback flake above the last bush. Another variation (5.1) moves up and right to

FLINTSTONE SLAB—WEST FACE CENTER

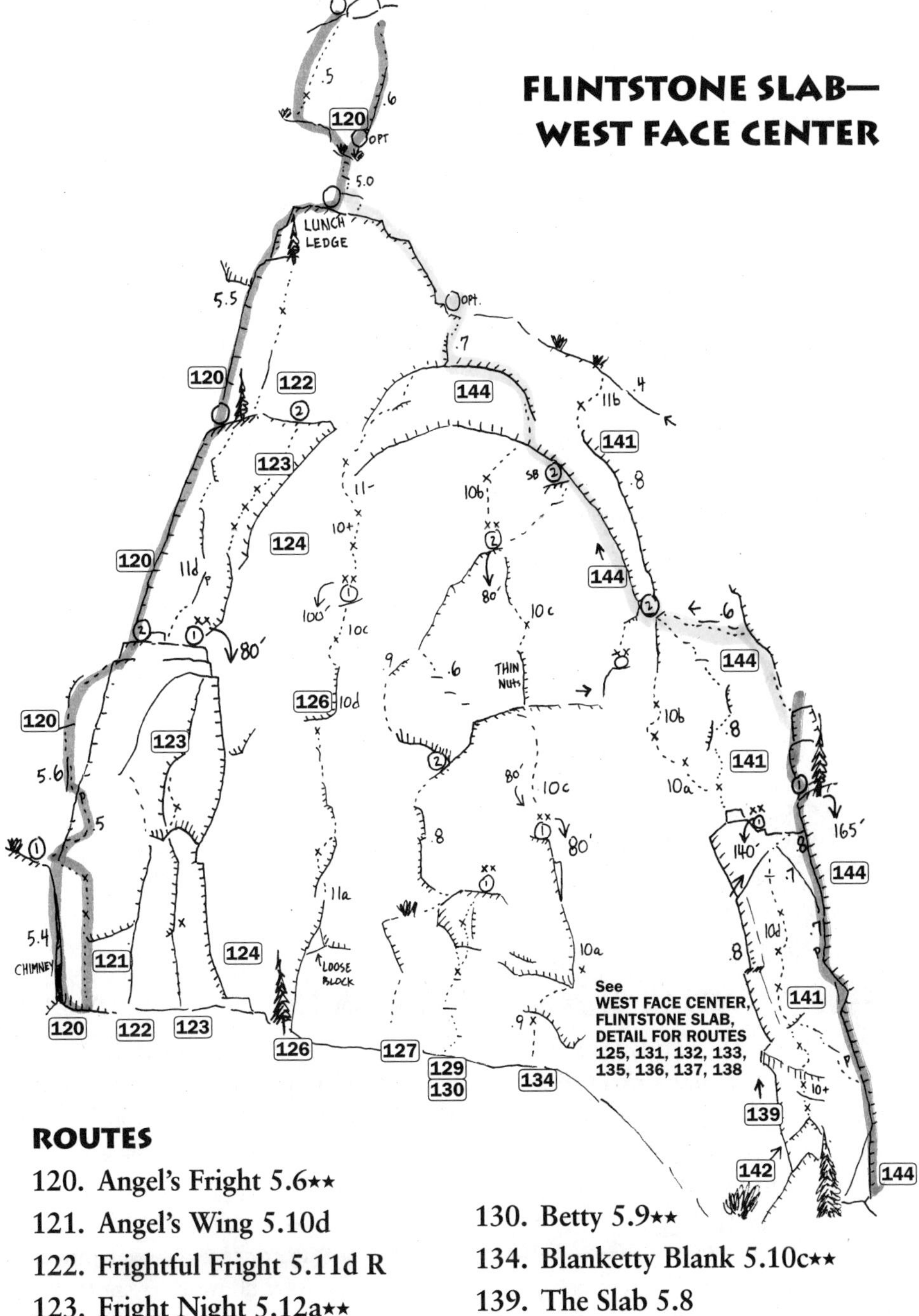

ROUTES

120. Angel's Fright 5.6★★
121. Angel's Wing 5.10d
122. Frightful Fright 5.11d R
123. Fright Night 5.12a★★
124. Human Fright 5.10a★★
126. Fred 5.11a★★★
127. Switchbacks 5.8 R★★
129. Switchbacks Direct Start 5.8
130. Betty 5.9★★
134. Blanketty Blank 5.10c★★
139. The Slab 5.8
141. Crimes of Passion 5.11b★
142. Crimes of Passion Direct Start 5.10d★★
144. Fingertrip 5.7★★★

a short headwall and the top. Pro: to 2.5 inches. FA: Jim Smith and William Rice, September 1936.

121. **Angel's Wing** 5.10d This is a 3-bolt face variation beginning just right of the *Angel's Fright* first pitch chimney. FA: Troy Mayr and Charles Cole, 1987.

122. **Frightful Fright** 5.11d R Between *Angel's Fright* and *Human Fright.* Begin just left of *Fright Night.* 1. Up a right-facing corner to a ramp in the center of the slab to a good ledge. 2. Climb unprotected 5.10 face to reach an ultra-thin crack with a fixed pin, then up and left and up to a belay ledge. 3. Unprotected 5.10 off the ledge to easier face past a bolt up to Lunch Ledge. Pro: many thin to 2 inches. FA: (A2) Royal Robbins and Don Wilson, July 1953. FFA: John Long and Mike Lechlinski, 1978.

123. **Fright Night** 5.12a ★★ The first pitch climbs the first right-facing dihedral to the left of *Human Fright.* The crux (protected by a bolt) involves wild pinching and liebacking on the arete of an arching dihedral above a small roof. Pitch 2. Follow *Human Fright,* but exit left over the corner to face protected by 4 bolts. Pro: small to 1.5 inches. FA: Charles Cole and Troy Mayr, August 1988 (Pitch 1) and October 1991 (Pitch 2).

124. **Human Fright** 5.10a ★★ Start almost directly above Lunch Rock. 1. A clean crack in a right-facing corner up to the right side of huge flakes/cracks. 2-bolt anchor (80 feet). 2. Up easy ground to the huge, right-facing dihedral, then face climb up to Lunch Ledge. Pro: thin to 3 inches. FA: John Mendenhall and Royal Robbins, June 1952. FFA: Bob Kamps, 1963.

FLINTSTONE SLAB—WEST FACE

This high-angle slab is located on the West Face of the rock, directly above Lunch Rock, framed by *Human Fright* (Route 124) on the left and *The Slab* (Route 139) on the right. The rock consisits of high quality, wonderfully featured granite, reminiscent of the North Apron of Yosemite's Middle Cathedral Rock. Consult the topo and individual route descriptions for the numerous rappel descents from bolt anchors.

125. **Mr. Slate** 5.10d R ★★ A bit contrived, yet fine rock and novel moves make this a highly recommended outing. Begin by climbing a short distance up the *Human Fright* dihedral, then traverse right to the first bolt. After clipping the first bolt it is advisable to climb back and remove the pro from *Human Fright* to prevent rope drag higher. Rap 120 feet, or, with one rope, rap to the *Human Fright* anchor, then 80 feet to the deck. Pro: a few 2–3-inch CDs. FA: (TR variation to *Fred*) Clark Jacobs,

FLINTSTONE SLAB—WEST FACE

ROUTES

123. Fright Night 5.12a★★
124. Human Fright 5.10a★★
125. Mr. Slate 5.10d R★★
126. Fred 5.11a★★★
127. Switchbacks 5.8 R★
128. Bam Bam 5.9
129. Switchbacks Direct Start 5.8
130. Betty 5.9+★
131. Barney 5.11a
132. Dino 5.10c
133. The Quarry 5.11c★★ or 5.10d★★
134. Blanketty Blank 5.10c★★
135. Blanketty Blank Direct Start 5.10d
136. Wilma 5.11c R★
137. Pebbles 5.11c★★
138. Bedrock 5.11a★★★

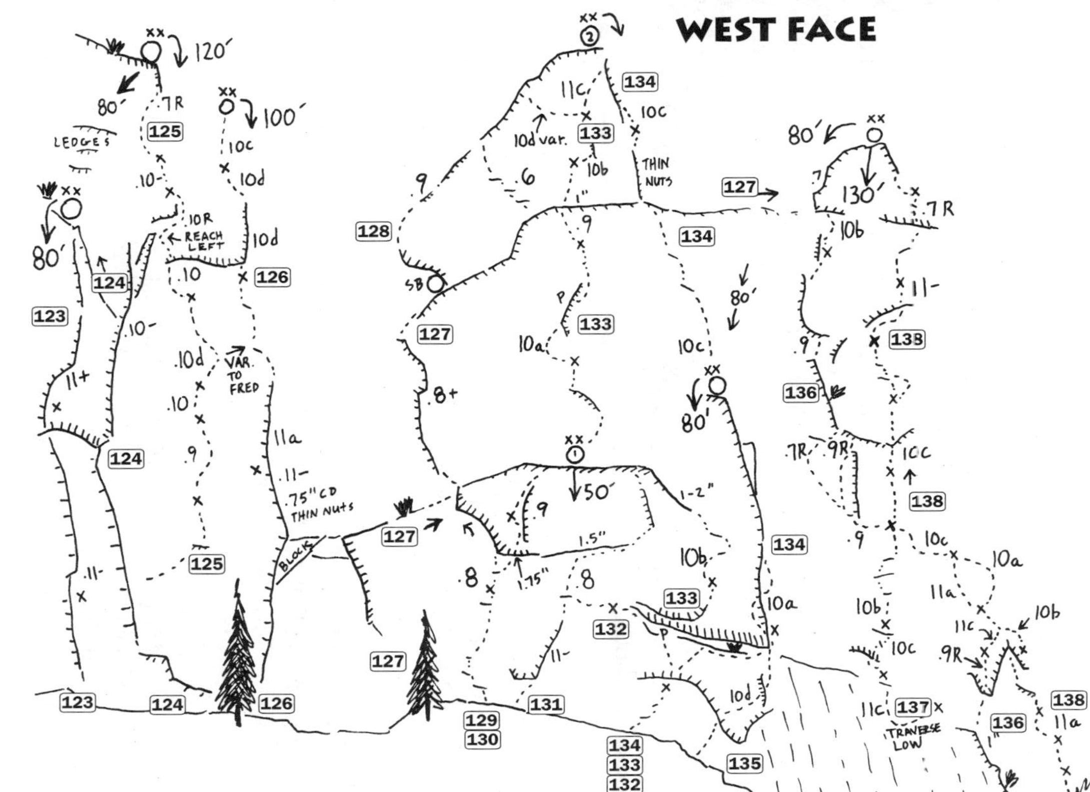

December 1994. FA: Complete pitch, Bob Gaines and Charlie Peterson, August 1996.

126. **Fred** 5.11a ★★★ 1. Start just right of a large pine growing at the base, almost directly above Lunch Rock. Many climbers rap off after the first pitch (100 feet). 2. Climb up past 3 bolts, then diagonal right to join *Fingertrip* over the arch and up to Lunch Ledge. Pro: thin to 1-inch. FA: Charles Cole and Randy Vogel, 1981.

127. **Switchbacks** 5.8 R ★ Begin just right of *Fred.* 1. Climb up to a ledge with a small oak; traverse the face to the right then up to a belay beneath a small arch. 2. Climb up and right to a ledge and traverse far right to the bolted belay on *Wilma* (take care to protect the last climber BEFORE the traverse). 3. Face climb up to join *Fingertrip.* FA: Jerry Gallwas and Barbara Lilley, July 1953.

128. **Bam Bam** 5.9 From the first belay, undercling left out the arch, then face climb back up and right to the bolted belay on *Blanketty Blank.* FA: Bob Gaines and Art Thoelke, June 1987.

129. **Switchbacks Direct Start** 5.8 Climb the face 20 feet right of Route 127 past one bolt, then left up a crack to the first belay. FA: Dave Rearick, 1958.

130. **Betty** 5.9+ ★ A short and fun pitch. From the bolt on *Switchbacks Direct,* continue straight up past another bolt (5.9+) to a two-bolt anchor at a small ledge. FA: Yvonne Gaines, July 4, 1994.

131. **Barney** 5.11a (TR) Toprope the curving, thin flake just right of *Betty.* FA: Bob Gaines, July 4, 1994.

132. **Dino** 5.10c From the first bolt at the start of *Blanketty Blank* move up left to a fixed pin, then traverse straight left past a bolt (10c) to easier climbing. Pro: CDs 0.75- to 1.5- inch. FA: Bob Gaines and Bob Carmichael, July 1994.

133. **The Quarry** 5.11c ★★ or 5.10d ★★ A classic two-pitch face with good pro at the hard bits. At the last bolt you can traverse left for an easier (5.10d) finish. 1. From the first bolt on *Blanketty Blank* move up and left to a fixed pin, then climb over a bulge to a bolt. 5.10 face climbing takes you to the 2-bolt belay at a small ledge. 2. Wander more or less straight up the face above, with the crux at the very top, above the last bolt, to the 2-bolt anchor shared with *Blanketty Blank.* Two 80-foot rappels to the ground (or one 165 feet). Pro: several CDs from 0.75- to 1.5-inch and one 3-inch. FA: Bob Gaines and Mike Borrello, October 1993.

134. **Blanketty Blank** 5.10c ★★ From Lunch Rock walk directly up to the base, then head down and right for about 40 feet. A bolt beneath a small arch above a smooth face marks the start. Two 80-foot rappels or one

160-foot rappel are possible from top of second pitch. Third pitch leads to Lunch Ledge. Pro: several thin to 1- inch. FA: Tom Frost and Harry Daley, June 1959. FFA: Bob Kamps and Tom Higgins, 1963. FA: 3rd Pitch, John Long and others, 1977. FA: 2nd Pitch Direct, Randy Vogel and Paul Schweizer, 1984.

135. **Blanketty Blank Direct Start** 5.10d This more challenging start begins about 15 feet downhill and right of *Blanketty Blank* and climbs up, then right, past a small flake to join *Blanketty Blank* just before its right-facing dihedral. Pro: thin nuts, CDs 0.75- to 1- inch. FA: Bob Gaines and Bob Carmichael, July 1994.

136. **Wilma** 5.11c R ★ Start 40 feet downhill and right of *Blanketty Blank* and 50 feet left of *Fingertrip*. Poorly protected climbing (5.9 R/X) is encountered getting to the first bolt. Rap 80 feet to the *Blanketty Blank* anchor or continue right to join *Fingertrip*. Pro: several thin to 1.5-inch. FA: Randy Vogel, Charles Cole, and Rob Raker, 1983.

137. **Pebbles** 5.11c ★★ Clip the first bolt on Wilma, downclimb about ten feet, then traverse left and up to the crux. Pro: thin to 1.5-inch. FA: Bob Gaines, August 1994.

138. **Bedrock** 5.11a ★★★ 160 feet of beautiful sustained face climbing with many cruxes. Begin about 30 feet uphill and right of *Wilma,* where a large oak tree grows close to the wall. Thin edging (11-) leads past 3 bolts on a slab to an overlapping arch. At the 4th bolt move up left to join *Wilma* for its leftward traverse, then at the 7th bolt climb straight up, where 5 more bolts protect interesting face climbing up to the 2-bolt belay shared with *Wilma*. Bring some slings; beware rope drag. With one rope you can rap 80 feet to the *Blanketty Blank* anchor, then less than 80 feet to the ground. Pro: 12 quickdraws, slings. FA: Bob Gaines, Todd Gordon, and Charlie Peterson, August 1997.

WEST FACE—RIGHT SIDE ("THE SLAB" TO "THE EDGE")

From Lunch Rock head right along a trail until it meets the base of the rock. Routes 139 (*The Slab*) through 144 (*Fingertrip*) are found in this vicinity. The remaining routes are found up and right from this point. *The Edge* (Route 160) climbs the sharply defined arete on the extreme right side of the West Face.

139. **The Slab** 5.8 Often mistaken for *Fingertrip* (Route 144) this route climbs the left-facing dihedral up the left side of the prominent, white exfoliation slab plainly visible from Lunch Rock. Near the top, exit right up the handcrack that diagonals right on the outside face of the slab.

WEST FACE—RIGHT SIDE DETAIL

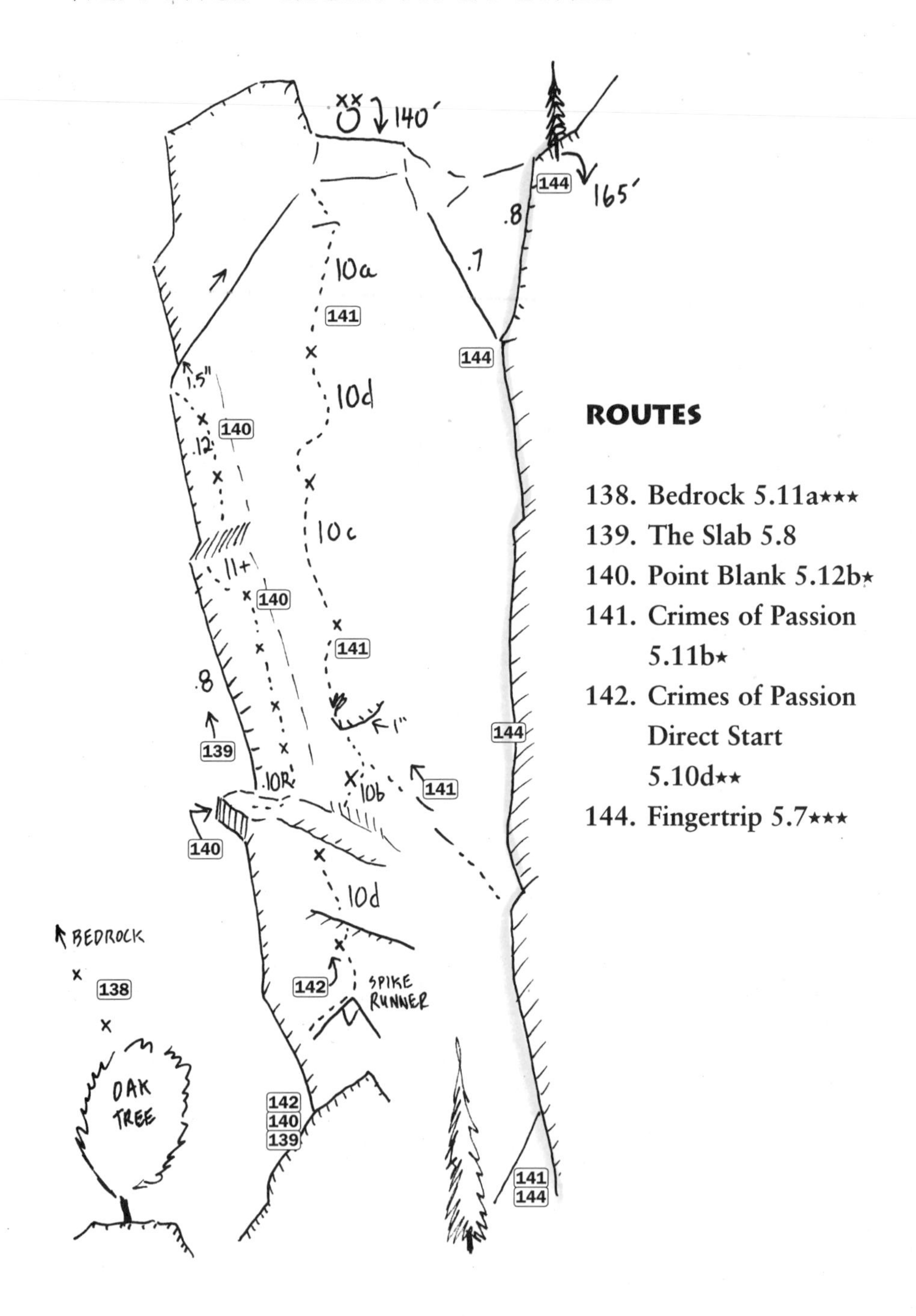

ROUTES

138. Bedrock 5.11a★★★
139. The Slab 5.8
140. Point Blank 5.12b★
141. Crimes of Passion 5.11b★
142. Crimes of Passion Direct Start 5.10d★★
144. Fingertrip 5.7★★★

Pro: to 3 inches. FA: Harry Daley and D. McCelland, August 1958. FFA: Bob Kamps and TM Herbert, 1963.

140. **Point Blank** 5.12b ★ Unique climbing up the blunt arete right of the *The Slab*. Begin by climbing about 40 feet up the slab, then make a delicate step out right (5.10 R) to the bolts on the "arete." Pro: to 3 inches. FA: Bob Gaines, May 1998.

141. **Crimes of Passion** 5.11b ★ 1. Begin by climbing the first 40 feet of *Fingertrip,* then move out left and climb a clean, white slab with 3 bolts (10+) up to a narrow ledge with a two-bolt anchor. 2. From the highest ledge on the left, climb up past a bolt (5.9) (*Ten Years After* moves left at this point), then continue straight up via thin flakes to a belay at the base of the *Fingertrip* arch. 3. Lieback the left-facing corner just right of and above the arch of *Fingertrip* to a bolt that protects a short blank section (11-) up to the *Fingertip Traverse*'s namesake leftward traverse. Pro: to 4 inches. FA: Bob Gaines and Yvonne Gaines, August 1987.

142. **Crimes of Passion Direct Start** 5.10d ★★ This is a direct start to the first pitch, consisting of two difficult mantleshelves, both protected by bolts, leading directly up to the 3-bolt slab. FA: Bob Gaines and Charlie Peterson, August 1997.

143. **Ten Years After** 5.10b ★ From the belay bolt at the top of *Crimes of Passion*'s first pitch, climb up and left (*Crimes of Passion* goes straight up after the first bolt) past 3 bolts, then back right to a fourth bolt and the crux (10b) joining *Fingertrip* or *Crimes of Passion* to finish. FA: Bob Gaines and Charlie Peterson, August 1997.

144. **Fingertrip** 5.7 ★★★ From Lunch Rock, head right along a trail until it meets the base of the rock. The first pitch starts in a shallow, red-stained corner directly behind a huge pine tree. 1. Classic liebacking and stemming up the corner to a small ledge with a large pine tree (165 feet). 2. Up past blocks to face climbing for about 40 feet, then traverse up and left around the corner and up to a semi-hanging belay under the arch. 3. Undercling 30 feet left, then surmount the overhang at the apex of the arch; 5.0 climbing leads to Lunch Ledge. Pro: to 2.5 inches. FA: Chuck Wilts, Don Gillespie, and Jerry Rosenblatt, September 1946.

145. **Toe Tip** 5.9 This obscure route ascends the face between *Fingertrip* and *Shit for Brains* to The Jungle Ledge, then continues between *Fingertip Traverse* and *Fingergrip* for another pitch. FA: Mark and Beverly Powell, 1966.

146. **Shit for Brains** 5.10b Just a short distance right of where the trail going right from Lunch Rock first touches the base of the rock, several bolts will be seen on the slab above. Climb past these to a ledge with a pine tree (165 feet). FA: Mark Powell, 1966.

WEST FACE—RIGHT SIDE

ROUTES

139. The Slab 5.8
141. Crimes of Passion 5.11b★
142. Crimes of Passion Direct Start 5.10d★★
143. Ten Years After 5.10b★
144. Fingertrip 5.7★★★
145. Toe Tip 5.9
146. Shit for Brains 5.10b
147. Fingertip Traverse 5.3★★
148. Fingergrip 5.8★
150. El Camino Real 5.10a★★
151. Pigs in Bondage 5.10a
152. Des Equis 5.11a
153. Coffin Nail 5.8★
154. On the Road 5.10c★
155. Jensen's Jaunt 5.6★

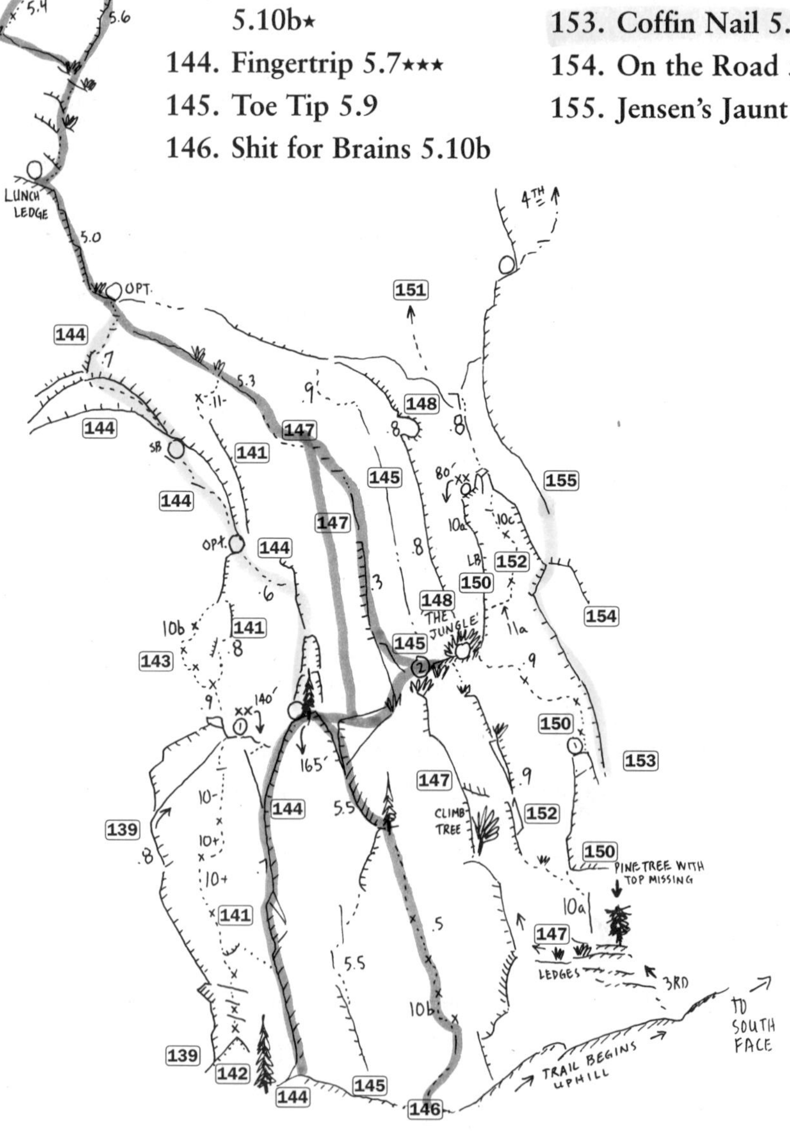

147. **Fingertip Traverse** 5.3 ★★ From Lunch Rock follow the trail to the right, until it reaches the base of the rock (*Fingertrip* starts here) then walk right to just past the point where the trail begins going uphill. Look for a pine tree with its top missing. From a bushy ledge left of the pine tree, scramble (class 3) up a gully to an oak tree beneath an overhang. 1. Climb the tree, then step left around the corner then up to a large, bushy ledge known as The Jungle Ledge. 2. Lieback a brief, right-facing corner, then face climb up and left to the infamous "fingertip traverse," which leads diagonally left on an exposed crack to 5.0 face climbing up to Lunch Ledge. Follow *Angel's Fright* above Lunch Ledge. Pro: to 2.5 inches. FA: Jim Smith, Bob Brinton, Arthur Johnson, and William Rice, September 1936.

148. **Fingergrip** 5.8 ★ From The Jungle Ledge on *Fingertip Traverse* climb the huge left-facing dihedral capped by a cavelike flake. Lieback around this, then traverse left over to Lunch Ledge. Pro: thin to 3.5 inches. FA: Ray Van Aken, Ivan Weeks, and Curt Kreiser, June 1947.

149. **Angle Iron Traverse** 5.7 1. From The Jungle Ledge climb the initial lieback on *Fingertip Traverse,* then move right, crossing the *Fingergrip Corner* at a fixed pin (5.7), continuing up and right to the belay on *El Camino Real.* 2. Climb up and right to meet *Jensen's Jaunt.* Pro: thin to 2 inches. FA: Ray Van Aken and George Harr, July 1948.

150. **El Camino Real** 5.10a ★★ The third pitch is one of the rock's classic liebacks. Walk about 40 feet right of *Fingertip Traverse,* then 3rd class up to a large pine tree. 1. A bouldery start just left of an incipient crack leads to a small overlap and crack/flake; belay at a block. 2. Climb past 2 bolts, then make a long friction traverse left past another bolt to a belay at Jungle Ledge. 3. Lieback the classic left-facing dihedral on the right to a ledge with bolts. (80-foot rappel to Jungle Ledge) 4. Climb 5.8 cracks up and left, then traverse right to join *Jensen's Jaunt.* Pro: several thin to 2 inches. FA: Royal Robbins, Harry Daley, and Janie Taylor, November 1961.

151. **Pigs in Bondage** 5.10a This is a direct finish to *El Camino Real;* from the top of pitch 3, head up and left then straight up (5.10-) past a bolt. Pro: thin to 2 inches. FA: Jack Roberts and John Allen, 1985.

152. **Dos Equis** 5.11a 1. Start up *El Camino Real.* At the overlap move up and left to a crack system, then up an awkward corner past several blocks to a belay just below Jungle Ledge. 2. A short pitch up to Jungle Ledge. 3. Climb the initial 15 feet of the *El Camino Real* lieback, make an extended reach out right, and climb past 2 bolts to the *El Camino Real* belay. Follow *El Camino Real* to top. Pro: several thin to 2 inches. FA: Bob Gaines and Ann Albert, June 1986.

153. **Coffin Nail** 5.8 ★ Start a few feet right of *El Camino Real* and ascend class 3 rock to a belay at the base of a clean, right-facing dihedral. Lieback this, and where the corner arches right, handjam a vertical crack that takes you up to *Jensen's Jaunt*. Pro: thin to 2.5 inches. FA: Unknown.

154. **On the Road** 5.10c ★ Begin with the initial section of *Jensen's Jaunt,* then climb up and left to a crack system and follow this to a belay at the base of a classic, left-facing dihedral facing *Coffin Nail*. Lieback this to eventually connect with *Jensen's Jaunt*. Pro: Several thin to 2 inches. FA: Unknown.

155. **Jensen's Jaunt** 5.6 ★ This route starts at the southwest "toe" of the rock, just left of the sharp edge of the West Face. 1. Head up easy, blocky rock until a prominent crack can be reached. 2. Continue up the corner until just below the roofs. 3. An awkward offwidth crack leads around the left side of the overhangs, then up the corner to a ledge. 4. From here you can continue up the corner system, or climb out right onto the West Buttress and up slabs to the top. Pro: to 3 inches. FA: Carl Jensen, Jim Smith, and Don McDonald, August 1938.

156. **Traitor Horn** 5.8 ★★ One of the early classics, with a spectacular, exposed crux. Start on *Jensen's Jaunt,* climbing that route for nearly 2 pitches until you can head right below the headwall to a protruding horn of rock. This proves to be the "traitor horn" as the "true horn" will now be seen farther up and right. Continue traversing to a small niche and belay. 3. Climb up and over to, and then onto, the "true horn," belay a bit higher. 4. A long pitch up low-angle slabs. Pro: thin to 2.5 inches. FA: Jim Smith, Arthur Johnson, and M. Holton, August 1938. FFA: Roy Gorin and William Shand, 1941.

157. **The Hangover** 5.12c From the second belay of *Jensen's Jaunt,* this route takes on the massive overhang above and to the right, at a bolt and fixed pin. A huge dynamic move is required. FA: (A3) Royal Robbins, Jerry Gallwas, Frank Martin, and Mike Sherrick, August 1954. FFA: John Long, Rick Accomazzo, Rob Muir, and Mike Lechlinski, 1978.

158. **Pearly Gate** 5.9 From the 2nd belay on *Traitor Horn,* climb through the left side of the alcove: a short, slightly overhanging, 4-inch lieback crack. Pro: several large to 4 inches. FA: Dave Rearick and Bob Kamps, 1969.

159. **Last Judgment** 5.11b R From the first pitch of *Jensen's Jaunt,* climb up and right past a set of double bolts to another set of double bolts (shared with *The Edge*), traverse up and left to a thin crack (with a bush), which is followed to the belay on *Traitor Horn*. Pro: many thin to 2 inches, may require thin pitons. FA: (5.10, A3) Tom Higgins and Ivan Couch, September 1964. FFA: Fred Zeil, Eric Erickson, and Frank Noble, 1976.

WEST FACE—RIGHT SIDE

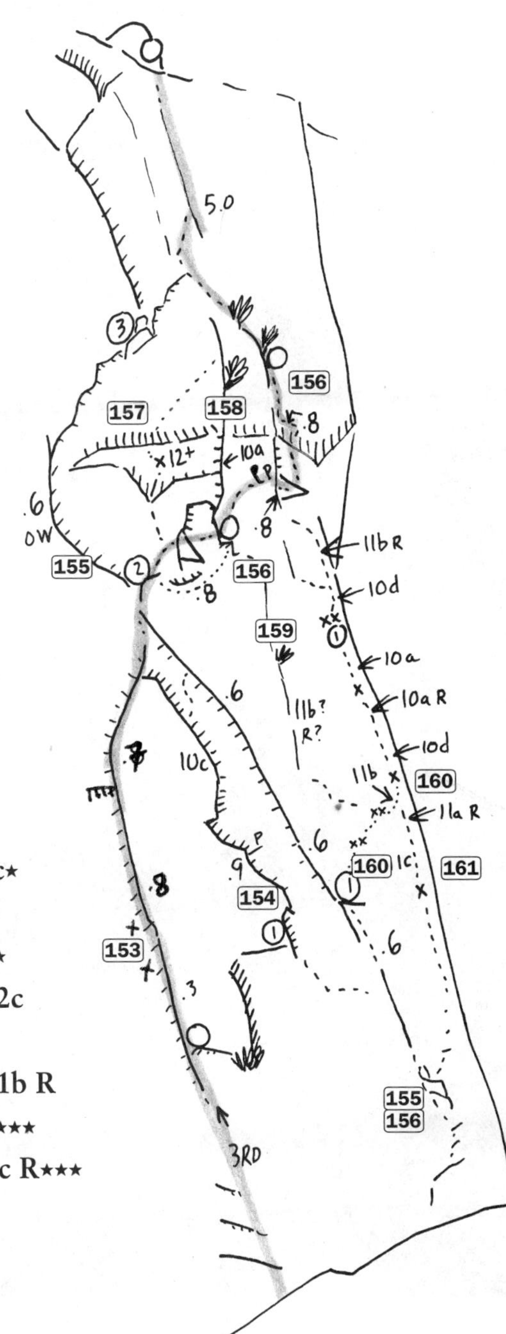

ROUTES

153. Coffin Nail 5.8★
154. On the Road 5.10c★
155. Jensen's Jaunt 5.6★
156. Traitor Horn 5.8★★
157. The Hangover 5.12c
158. Pearly Gate 5.9
159. Last Judgment 5.11b R
160. The Edge 5.11a R★★★
161. Turbo Flange 5.11c R★★★

Darrell Hensel on The Edge *(5.11), Tahquitz.* PHOTO BY KEVIN POWELL

160. **The Edge** 5.11a R ★★★ An awesome line visible from downtown Idyllwild. A serious and committing undertaking. Start as for *Jensen's Jaunt.* After the first pitch, head out right to the "edge", which is followed for two pitches. Finish on *Traitor Horn* or *Pearly Gate.* Pro: thin to 2 inches. FA: Tobin Sorenson and Gib Lewis, 1976.

161. **Turbo Flange** 5.11c R ★★★ Even more serious than *The Edge,* this route climbs the entire arete from the base, joining *The Edge* where it traverses out from *Jensen's Jaunt.* Pro: a #3 Camalot is useful before the first bolt. FA: John Long and Dwight Brooks, 1984.

SOUTH FACE AREA

This section of the guide covers all the routes to the right of, and including *The Open Book. The Open Book* is the huge dihedral forming the southwest corner of Tahquitz: the single most prominent feature on the rock. To approach the South Face area, walk right from Lunch Rock on the rough trail that runs along the base of the rock. Approach for routes on the south side of the Summit Block requires one to walk past the Friction Route Descent Area then scramble up slabs (class 3-4) to the base. See Tahquitz Approach Overview Map.

Descent for South Face routes is usually via the *Friction Route.* A rappel descent can be made with two 165-foot rappels beginning from bolts near the top of *The Open Book* (Route168) to the bolt anchor on *Green Arch* (Route 174).

For routes lying on the south face of the Summit Blocks, an easy scramble down to the notch between Tahquitz and the mountainside above will give access to a trail running down the south side of the rock.

OPEN BOOK AREA

The following routes lie within the huge dihedral formed by *The Open Book.*

LEFT WALL AREA

The steep wall forming the base of the left side of *The Open Book* features vertical and overhanging face climbs on extraordinary rock.

162. **Bibliography** 5.10b R ★ Begin about 50 feet downhill and left of *The Open Book.* Reach left to a flake, stem up the shallow, difficult-to-protect corner (10-), exit left to an arete, then up easier (5.8), run-out face to a 2-bolt belay at a nice ledge. Pro: thin nuts and CDs to 1- inch. FA: Bob Gaines, John Rosholt, Sheryl Basye, and Mark Hoffman, June 1994.

SOUTH FACE
Friction descent route
165'
186
192
196
168
181
165'
168
181
186
173
168
174
160
161
Left Wall Area routes 162-167
trail

Schatzi Sovich on the second pitch of The Open Book *(5.9), Tahquitz.* PHOTO BY KEVIN POWELL

SOUTH FACE—LEFT WALL AREA

ROUTES

162. Bibliography 5.10b R★
163. The Glossary 5.11b★
164. The Bookend 5.11a★★
165. Hedgehog 5.11c★
166. The Hedge 5.10d★
167. Bookworm 5.12c★★
168. The Open Book 5.9★★★

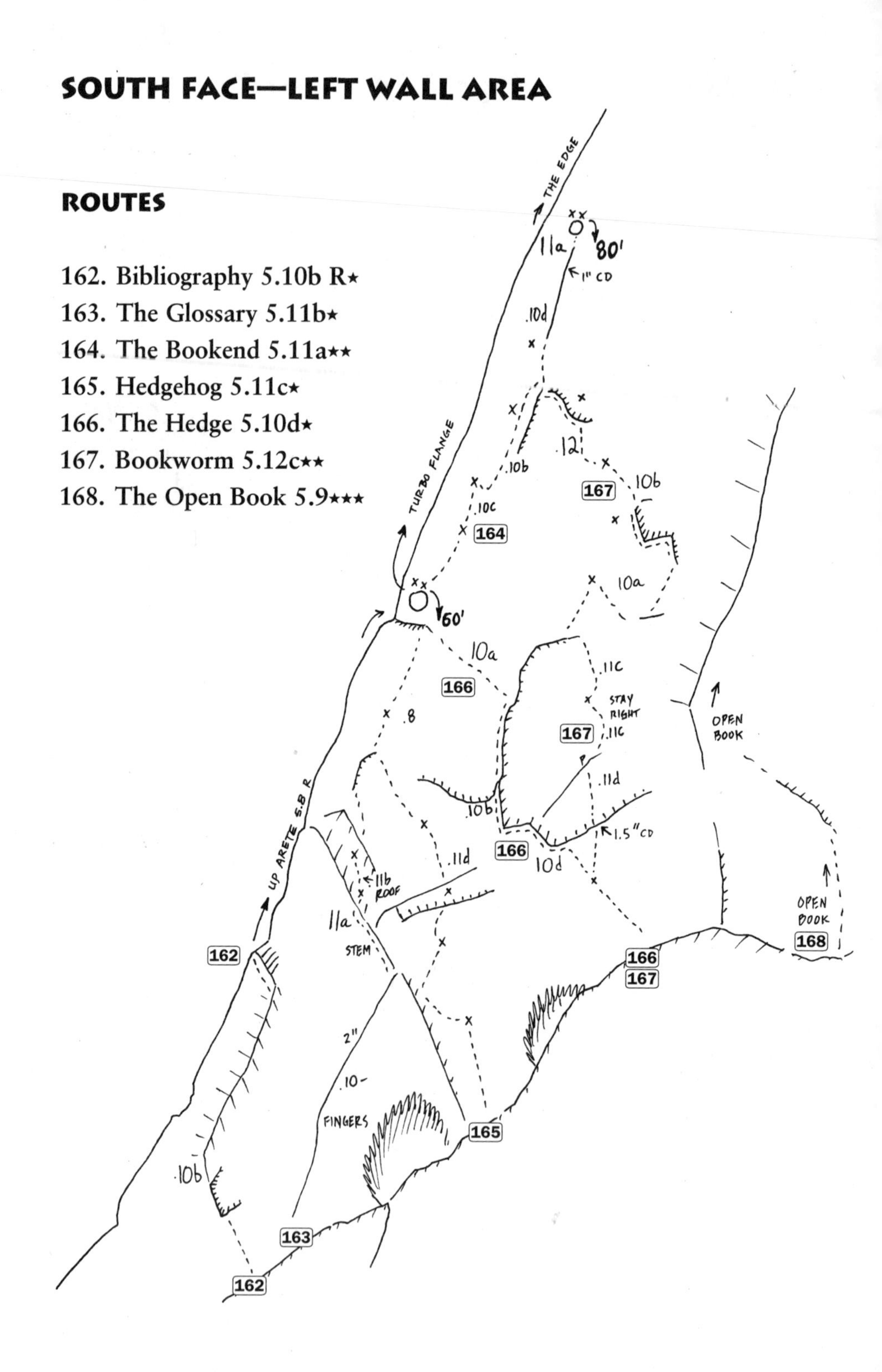

163. **The Glossary** 5.11b ★ Jam the left-slanting crack just right of *Bibliography*, stem a short way up the smooth dihedral, then pull over the roof to the right. FA: Bob Gaines, Mark Hoffman, and John Rosholt, June 1994.

164. **The Bookend** 5.11a ★★ This pitch is located just right of the arete of *Turbo Flange*. From the shared two-bolt belay, climb up and right past 4 bolts to a thin crack. A 1-inch CD is needed to protect the final step-up to the belay. Pro: 1- inch CD. FA: Bob Gaines and Charlie Peterson, July 1994.

165. **Hedgehog** 5.11c ★ The steep wall between *The Glossary* and *The Hedge*. A small overhang is the crux. FA: Bob Gaines and John Rosholt, June 1994.

166. **The Hedge** 5.10d ★ Steep and solid. Start about 30 feet downhill and left of *The Open Book*. A bolt protects the crux reach left (10d) to a flake: undercling left, lieback about 20 feet higher, then traverse left (10a) across the face to a two-bolt belay stance. Pro: nuts and CDs 0.5- to 1.5-inch. FA: Gib Lewis and Charles Cole, 1983.

167. **Bookworm** 5.12c ★★ Start with the initial bolt of *The Hedge* and climb directly over the small roof (11d, 1.5-inch CD) to a fixed pin. From here a bolt protects a technical, thin-edge section (11+, stay right) to a small ledge. 5 more bolts protect intricate face moves on the gently overhanging wall. A 1-inch CD is needed in the thin crack above the last bolt. FA: Bob Gaines, July 1994. The second ascent was made by Kevin Thaw and Bill Leventhal in 1996, who confirmed the rating.

168. **The Open Book** 5.9 ★★★ This route climbs the huge, right-facing dihedral that forms the boundary between the West Buttress and the South Face. America's first 5.9. 1. Face climb up a slight overhang to the right of the crack (5.8), then move left to the main crack. The crux is jamming/liebacking at the top of the first pitch. Belay in an alcove. 2. Stem and lieback the widening crack in the awesome dihedral (5.9, 3- to 4-inch CDs are useful), then move right, under a big overhang, to a belay at a small ledge a bit higher (2- to 3-inch CDs). 3. An easy lieback leads to an overhang. Move right across a smooth slab (5.6 R) to a short chimney and an easy ramp to the top. Pro: thin to 4 inches, including several 3 to 4 inches.) FA: (5.8 A2, using 2 x 4 wooden pitons!) John Mendenhall and Harry Sutherland, September 1947. FFA: Royal Robbins and Don Wilson, 1952.

169. **Turn the Page** 5.10b ★ This short but dramatic pitch connects *The Open Book* with *The Edge*. Begin at the belay atop *The Open Book*'s first pitch, then tiptoe up and left out the left wall past one bolt to *The Edge* belay. FA: Bob Gaines and Mike Borrello, October 1993.

SOUTH FACE—OPEN BOOK AREA

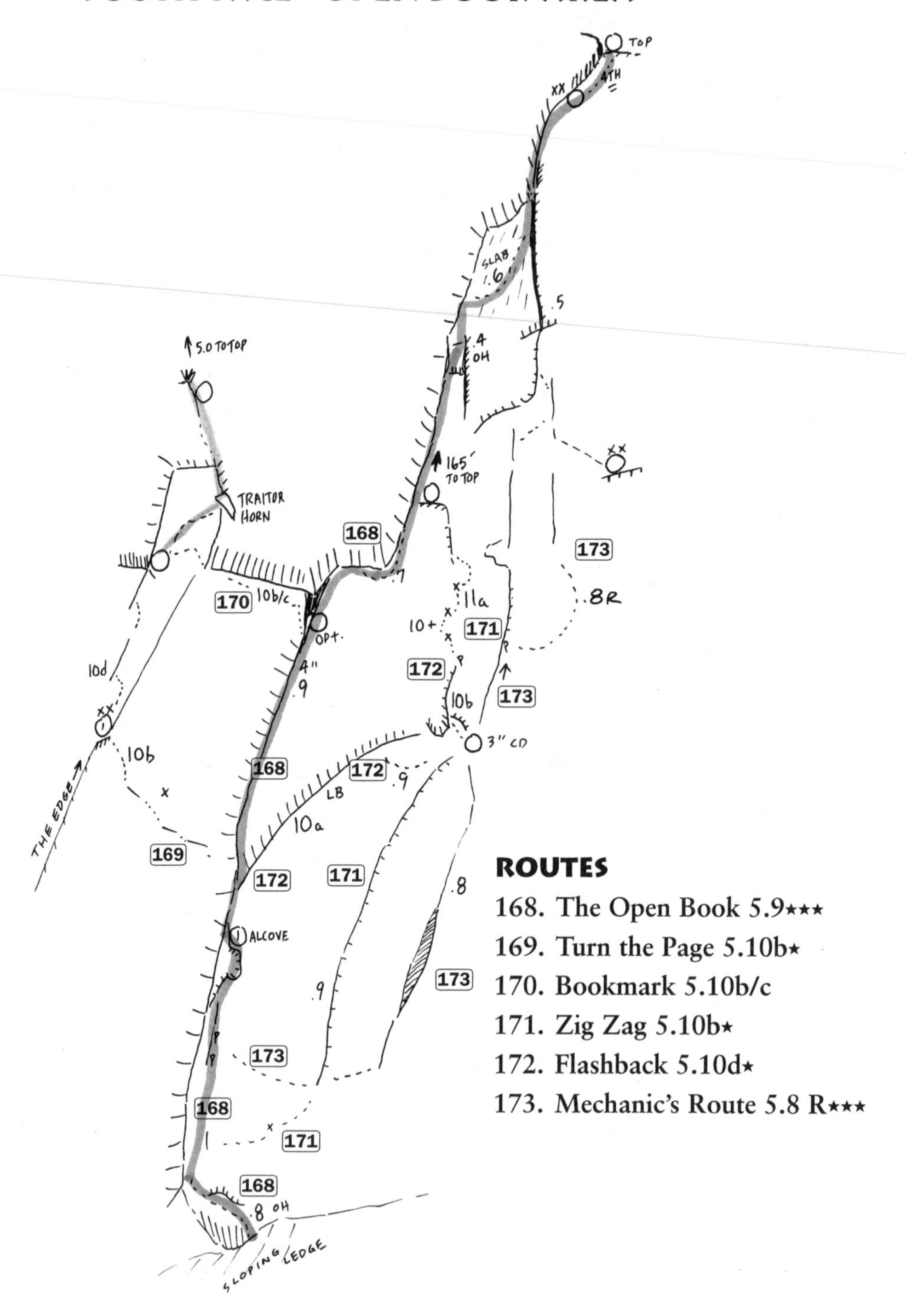

ROUTES

168. The Open Book 5.9★★★
169. Turn the Page 5.10b★
170. Bookmark 5.10b/c
171. Zig Zag 5.10b★
172. Flashback 5.10d★
173. Mechanic's Route 5.8 R★★★

170. **Bookmark** 5.10b/c This variation connects *The Open Book* with the *Traitor Horn* route. Climb up to the big overhang on the second pitch of *The Open Book* (4-inch CDs), then traverse straight left under the big roof. Belay in the alcove for *Traitor Horn.* Pro: medium nuts, CDs .75-inch to 4- inch. FA: Bob Gaines and Charlie Peterson, July 1994.

171. **Zig Zag** 5.10b ⋆ 1. Climb the initial overhang of *The Open Book,* traverse right to a bolt, then straight up to a strenuous lieback just left of *Mechanic's Route.* Where this crack touches *Mechanic's Route,* move left at an obvious horn. 2. Continue up the crack system between *The Open Book* and *Mechanic's Route,* then either move left to finish on *The Open Book* or traverse right to finish up *Mechanic's Route.* FA: TM Herbert and Mark Powell, 1961. FFA: Mark Powell and Bob Kamps, 1967.

172. **Flashback** 5.10d ⋆ This two-pitch alternative begins after the first pitch of *Open Book.* 1. Lieback the obvious arch that curves up and right (5.10-), then move right on face moves up to the belay shared with *Zig Zag* and *Mechanic's Route.* 2. Mantle the overhanging block on the left (10-, 4-inch CD), to a thin corner (0.4-inch CD, #3 RP), step up to a fixed pin, then face climb past 3 bolts (10+) to a belay on *The Open Book* (2- to 3-inch CDs). Pro: many thin to 4- inch. FA: Bob Gaines and Tommy Romero, August 1995.

173. **Mechanic's Route** 5.8 R ⋆⋆⋆ Imagine yourself tied into a manila rope and shod in sneakers on the crux run-out—pretty bold stuff for 1937!

SOUTH FACE—OPEN BOOK AREA

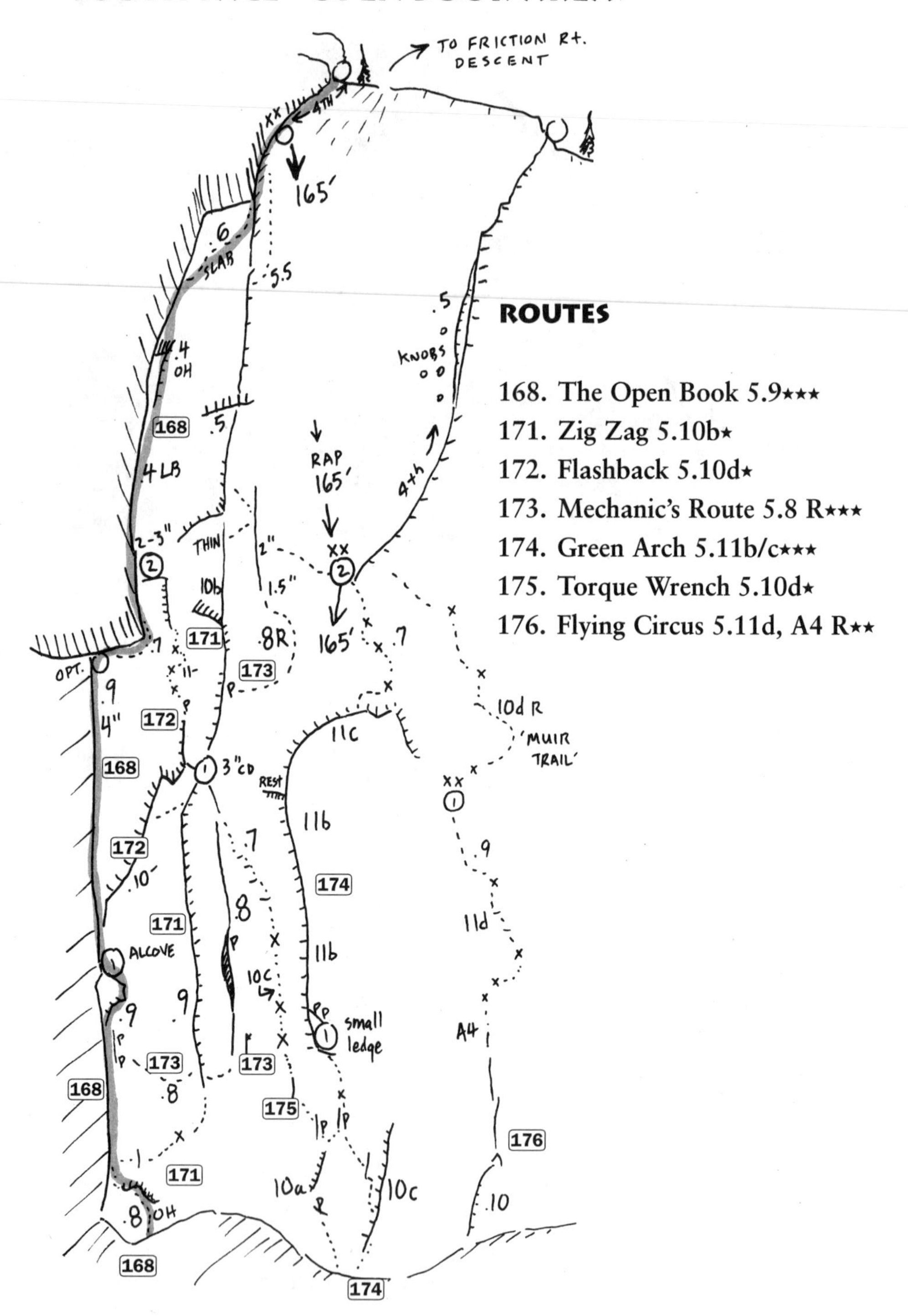

ROUTES

168. The Open Book 5.9★★★
171. Zig Zag 5.10b★
172. Flashback 5.10d★
173. Mechanic's Route 5.8 R★★★
174. Green Arch 5.11b/c★★★
175. Torque Wrench 5.10d★
176. Flying Circus 5.11d, A4 R★★

1. Climb 40 feet up *The Open Book,* clip a fixed pin, then traverse 20 feet right to an easy crack that widens into a chimney; belay just above it. 2. Climb about 30 feet up a crack, then move up and right via large solution pockets (crux, 5.8 R) and diagonal back left to a 5.6 crack. From here you can traverse right to the two-bolt belay on *Green Arch.* A bolt was added on the fifth ascent to protect this section, but subsequently broke in a fall; concensus is that it should not be replaced. 3. A 5.5 pitch leads to the top. Pro: thin to 3 inches. FA: Dick Jones and Glen Dawson, October 1937.

174. **Green Arch** 5.11b/c ★★★ The aesthetic, curving dihedral just right of *Mechanic's Route.* 1. There are 2 variations (both 5.10) to gain the ledge at the base of the arch: one starts 25 feet right of *The Open Book* at a large horn and the other starts about 15 feet farther right. 2. Incredible stemming (5.11) up the dihedral (usually with many fixed pins) leads to a possible rest spot on the left before the arch curves right. Where the arch becomes horizontal, climb up over it (5.11) to less steep face climbing past 3 bolts to a two-bolt belay ledge. 4. A 5.5 pitch leads to the top. Pro: many thin to 1.5-inch. (Variation: From a point below where the arch curves right, it is possible to climb out left and over to *Mechanic's Route* (5.7).) FA: (with 5.7 variation and A2) Don Wilson and R. Smith, 1953. FA: (5.8, A2, complete arch) Mark and Beverly Powell, 1964. FFA: Rick Accomazzo, John Long, and Tobin Sorenson, 1975.

175. **Torque Wrench** 5.10d ★ From the first pitch of *Green Arch,* instead of moving right up to the belay niche, continue more or less straight up past 3 bolts (10+) to easier (5.8) knob climbing to the belay on *Mechanic's Route.* Pro: to 3 inches. FA: Kevin Powell and Darrel Hensel, July 1993.

176. **Flying Circus** 5.11d, A4 R ★★ 1. Begin about 30 feet right of *Green Arch.* A lieback leads to aid climbing with hooks, rurps, and 2 aid bolts, then face climbing past 2 bolts up to two-bolt belay. 2. The infamous "Muir Trail," with an unprotected 5.10d move almost 20 feet above the belay. Join *Green Arch.* Pro: Bring copperheads, rurps, several hooks. FA: Rick Accomazzo, Rob Muir, and Charles Cole, August 1978.

SOUTH FACE LEFT

The following climbs lie on the steep south face of Tahquitz Rock, to the right and around the corner from the huge dihedral of *The Open Book.*

177. **New Wave** 5.12a R/X ★ This pitch begins per *Unchaste* to the right of the roofs below *Flying Circus* and traverses diagonally up and left to the *Flying Circus* belay. Groundfall potential at the crux after the first bolt. Pro: 3 bolts, thin to medium. FA: Gib Lewis and Charles Cole, 1983.

SOUTH FACE—LEFT

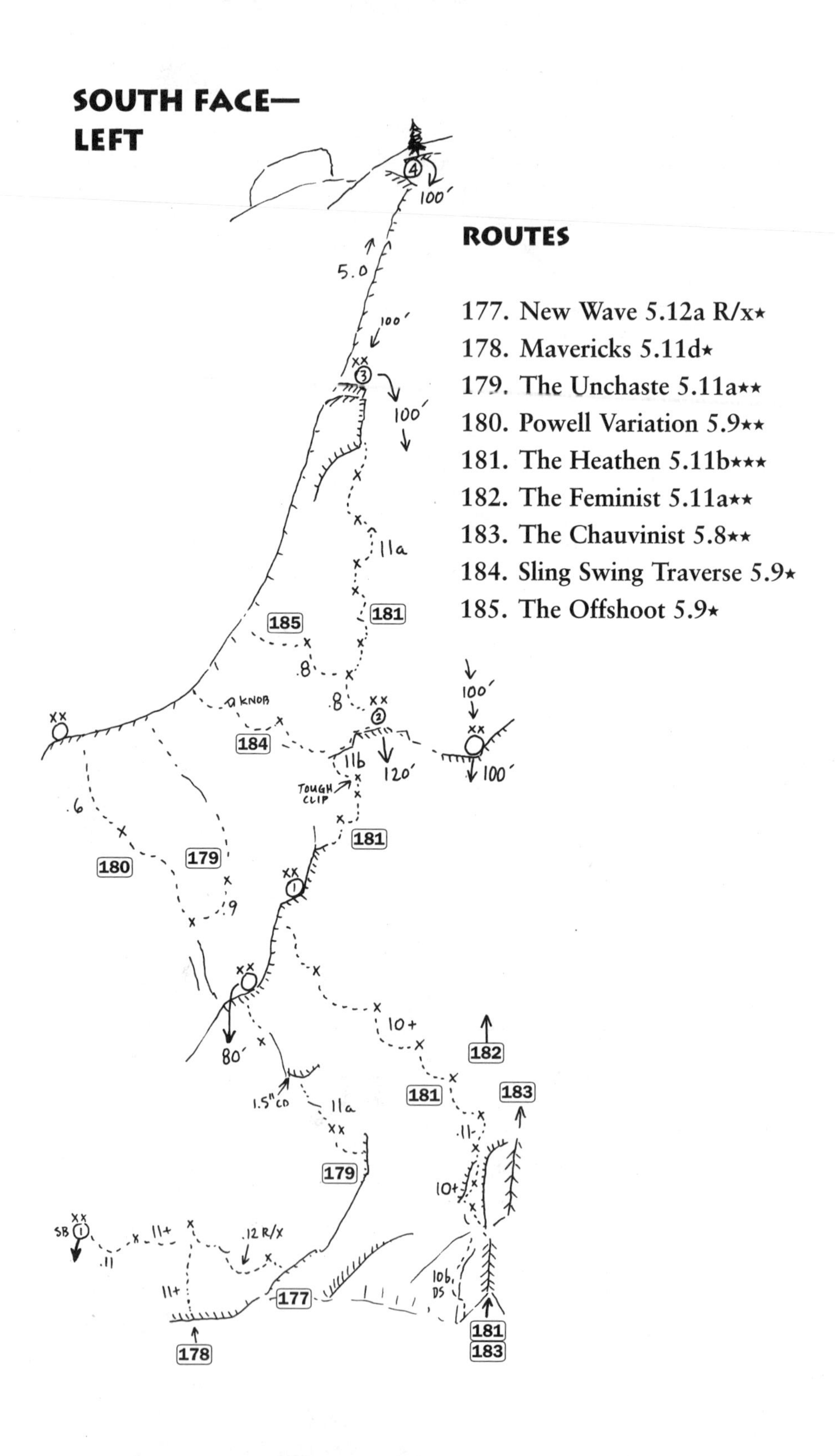

ROUTES

177. New Wave 5.12a R/x★
178. Mavericks 5.11d★
179. The Unchaste 5.11a★★
180. Powell Variation 5.9★★
181. The Heathen 5.11b★★★
182. The Feminist 5.11a★★
183. The Chauvinist 5.8★★
184. Sling Swing Traverse 5.9★
185. The Offshoot 5.9★

SOUTH FACE
192
196
196
181
186
179
198

178. **Mavericks** 5.11d (TR) ★ A direct start to *New Wave*. FA: Dave Mayville and Bob Gaines, July 1999.

179. **The Unchaste** 5.11a ★★ This improbable route climbs the steep, intimidating face left of the *Ski Tracks*. 1. Begin in a right-slanting crack, then move left to two bolts, one being very difficult to clip. Up past one more bolt (and 1.5-inch pro) up to a nice belay stance at two bolts. 2. Traverse left to a crack, then up to a shallow "bowl" with a bolt. Traverse right and up to another bolt, then up and left to the belay ledge on *Green Arch*. Pro: to 3 inches. FA: (5.9, A3) Royal Robbins and Mike Sherrick, September, 1957. FFA: Tobin Sorenson and Gib Lewis, 1974.

180. **Powell Variation** 5.9 ★★ From the first bolt on the second pitch traverse up and left to another bolt, then up to the *Green Arch* ledge/bolt anchor. FA: Mark and Beverly Powell, October 1964.

181. **The Heathen** 5.11b ★★★ 1. Begin with the start of *The Chauvinist* in a short dihedral. From here 8 bolts protect face climbing up, then left, to a belay at a small stance above *The Unchaste*. 2. A short steep headwall with 3 bolts (11b/c, the third bolt is a tough clip) to a two-bolt stance. 3. Move left to a bolt shared with *The Offshoot,* then straight up the steep slab past 5 more bolts (11-) and up to a big ledge with a two-bolt anchor. Two 100-foot rappels from here reach the ground, or climb an easy (5.0) pitch up the corner to the top. Pro: to 2 inches. FA Pitches 1 and 2: Bob Gaines and Dave Mayville, July 1999. FA: Pitches 3 and 4: Bob Gaines and Charlie Peterson, August 1999.

182. **The Feminist** 5.11a (TR) ★★ Climb the first section of *The Heathen,* but instead of traversing left, climb the steep "moguls" directly up to the bolt belay for *The Chavaunist*. FA: Bob Gaines, July 1999.

183. **The Chauvinist** 5.8 ★★ 1. Start below *Left Ski Track* in a short dihedral, then climb straight up past a steep, flared crack to easy face climbing just left of *Left Ski Track,* sharing its belay. 2. Up to a pin, then open face climbing past 3 bolts to a class 4 crack that leads to the top. Pro: to 2.5 inches. FA: Mark Powell, T. Rygg, and Roy Coats, January 1964.

184. **Sling Swing Traverse** 5.9 ★ An obscure traversing pitch beginning at the first belay on *The Chauvinist* and traversing left past one bolt to the easy top pitch of *Mechanic's Route* (or vice versa; 5.10a). FA: Chuck and Ellen Wilts and John Moore, September 1951.

185. **The Offshoot** 5.9 ★ Start across (left) on *Sling Swing Traverse*. About 25 feet across, at the 2-bolt anchor for *The Heathen,* climb up and left to the first bolt on *The Heathen*'s third pitch, then traverse left past another bolt to a low-angle corner. FA: Mark Powell, T. Rygg, and Roy Coats, January 1964.

SOUTH FACE—CENTER

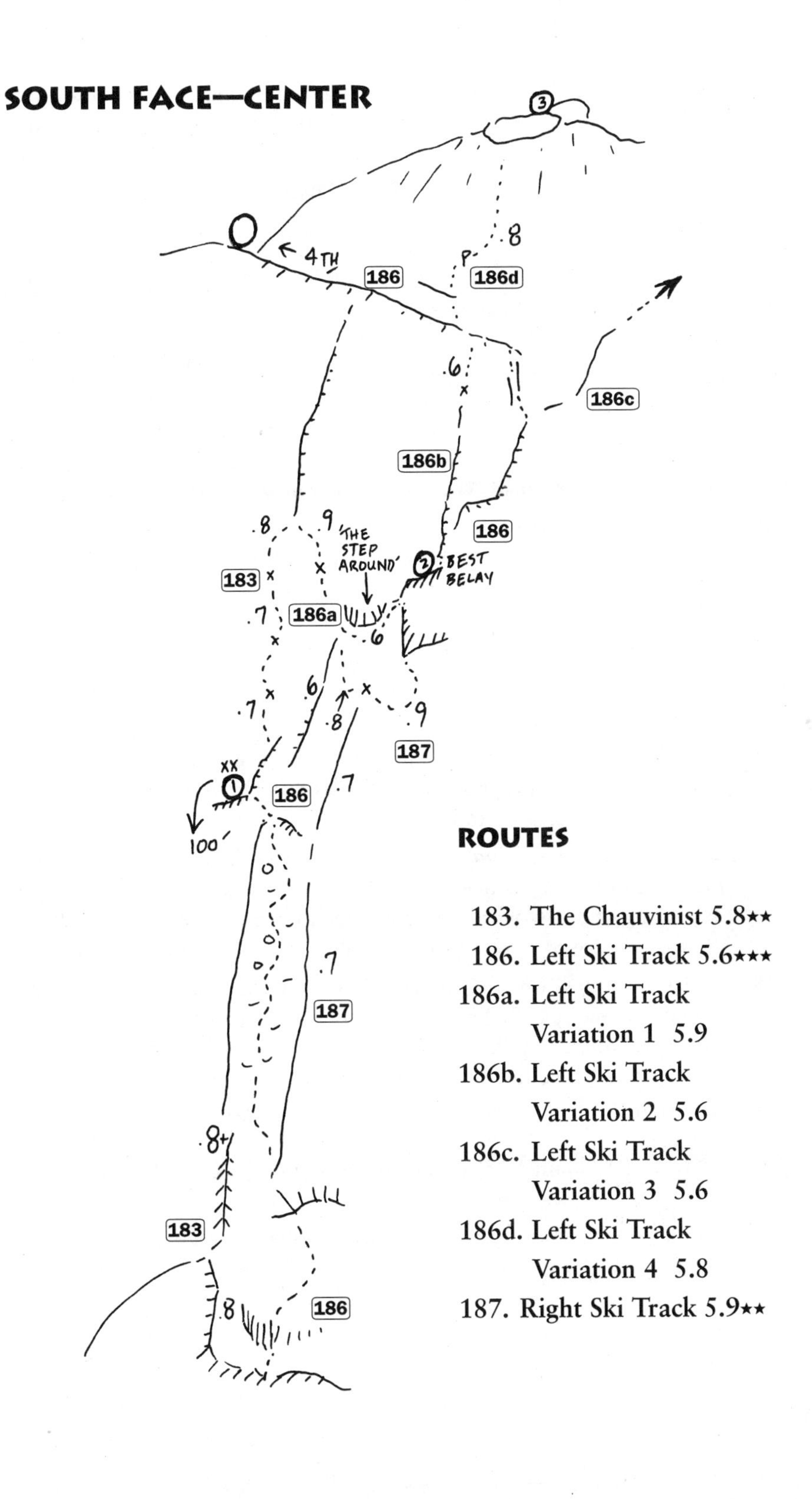

ROUTES

183. The Chauvinist 5.8★★
186. Left Ski Track 5.6★★★
186a. Left Ski Track Variation 1 5.9
186b. Left Ski Track Variation 2 5.6
186c. Left Ski Track Variation 3 5.6
186d. Left Ski Track Variation 4 5.8
187. Right Ski Track 5.9★★

186. **Left Ski Track** 5.6 ★★★ This route is located about 200 feet right and around the corner from *The Open Book*. Two parallel, right-curving cracks in the middle of the South Face will be seen. 1. Start beneath the right-hand crack, climb up onto a sloping platform then climb a short crack leading to the face between the "ski tracks" on unbelievably good jugs up to a two-bolt belay on a small ledge on the left (100 feet). (*Sling Swing Traverse* starts here.) 2. Climb the left "ski track" crack to its end at a small ledge with a fixed pin (Var. 1); the classic "step-around" move takes you around the corner to the right to a series of ledges; belay on the first good ledge (Var. 2). 3. The original route climbs a crack system up and right past a series of ledges. At the third ledge above the belay (Var. 3); move left up an 8-foot vertical wall with double cracks to a class 4 ledge that leads straight left to the top. Pro: to 2.5-inch. FA: Chuck Wilts and Ray Van Aken, September 1947.

186a. **Left Ski Track Variation 1** Face variation 5.9 At the small ledge at the end of the crack (2nd pitch), climb up and left past a bolt (5.9) to a crack system leading to the top.

186b. **Left Ski Track Variation 2** Arête finish 5.6 From the first ledge after the step-across: on the 2nd pitch climb straight up an arête/crack that blanks into a slab with a bolt that leads to the fourth-class ledge. From here traverse straight left to the top.

186c. **Left Ski Track Variation 3** Slab finish 5.6 From the last ledge on the 3rd pitch move out right up a 5.6 crack until it ends, then traverse right across the slab and up to the top.

186d. **Left Ski Track Variation 4** Direct finish 5.8 Perhaps the most aesthetic way to do the *Ski Tracks* is variation 2 with a direct finish. At the beginning of the leftward traverse at the fourth class ledge, climb directly over a bulge to a fixed pin, with delicate friction moves to the top.

187. **Right Ski Track** 5.9 ★★ 1. Start below the right crack, up it to a belay about 100 feet up. 2. Jam up to a bolt at the end of the crack where two variations are possible: (a) move up and left (5.9) to join *Left Ski Track* at the ledge just before the "step-around," or (b) traverse down and right (5.9) then climb up through a squeeze chimney to the first ledge on pitch 2 of *Left Ski Track*. Pro: to 2.5 inches. FA: (a) George Harr and William Dixon, September 1957. (b) Dave Rearick, Mark and Beverly Powell, 1961.

188. **South Face** 5.11a R ★ This is the first bolted face climb immediately right of the *Ski Tracks;* start around the corner and up from the *Ski Tracks,* moving over a small headwall. Route ends at a two-bolt belay/rappel stance. FA: Don Bedford, Dan Haughelstine, and Johnathon Spurgin, November 1987.

SOUTH FACE—CENTER

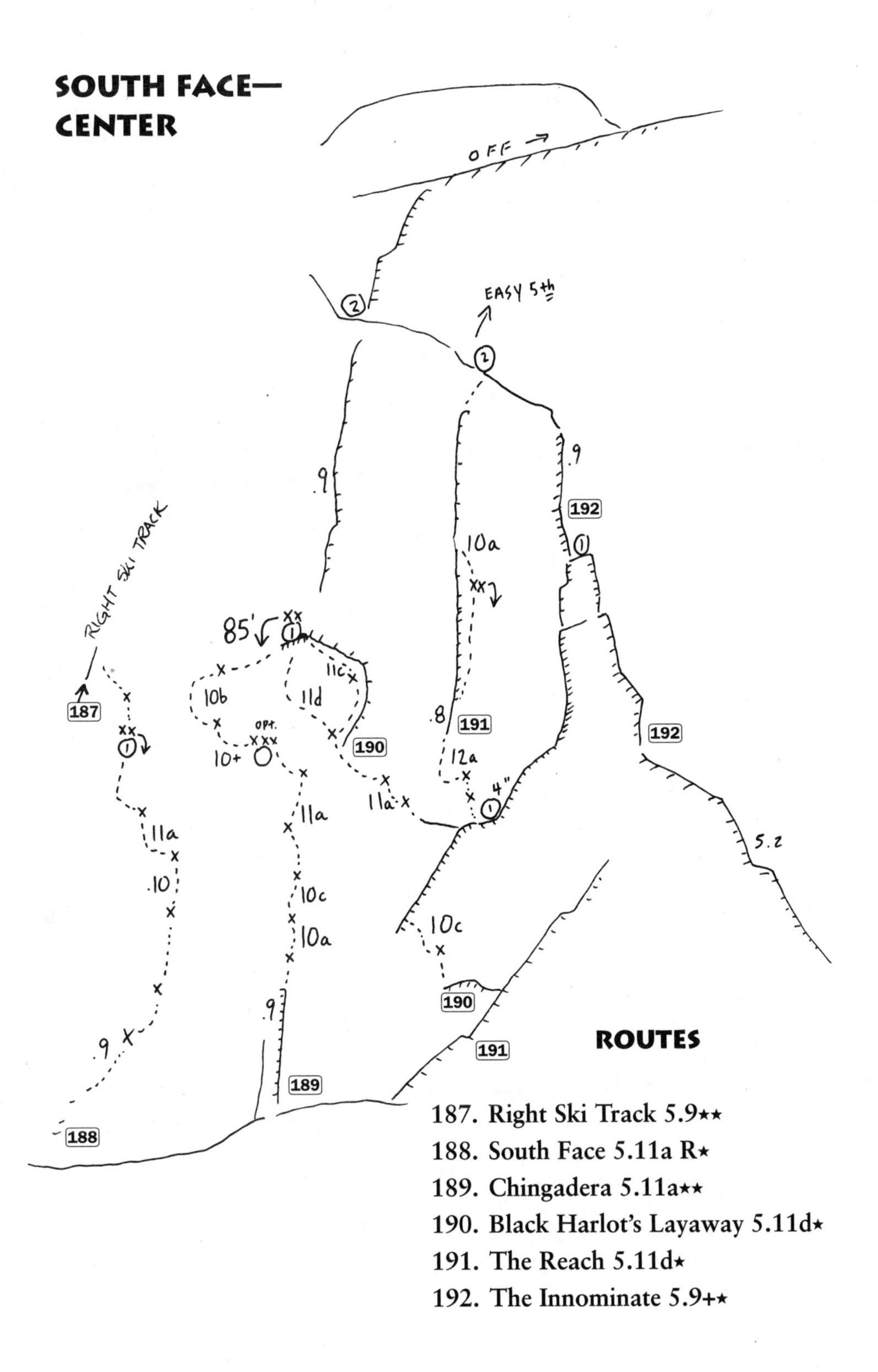

ROUTES

187. Right Ski Track 5.9★★
188. South Face 5.11a R★
189. Chingadera 5.11a★★
190. Black Harlot's Layaway 5.11d★
191. The Reach 5.11d★
192. The Innominate 5.9+★

189. **Chingadera** 5.11a ★★ One the country's hardest face pitches when first done in 1967. Start up and right of the *South Face* and climb a steep crack to reach a series of bolts. Can be done as one pitch; however, rope drag can be problem. 85-foot rappel. Pro: thin to 1.5-inch. FA: Bob Kamps and Mark Powell, February 1967.

190. **Black Harlot's Layaway** 5.11d ★ 1. Climb the first pitch of *The Reach*. 2. Traverse left past 2 bolts (11a) to the base of an arch, where two more bolts protect crux moves (11c/d) leading left to the belay ledge shared with *Chingadera*. 3. A 5.9 pitch up the crack system leads to the ledge at the top of *The Reach* and *The Innominate*. Pro: to 2 inches. FA: Mark and Beverly Powell, and Bob Kamps, September 1968. FFA: Tobin Sorenson, John Bachar, and Gib Lewis, 1974.

191. **The Reach** 5.11d ★ 1. Up the ramp right of *Chingadera,* traverse left past a bolt, then up another ramp to a belay. 2. Steep, thin (and height-dependent) moves past two bolts to a dihedral with a bolt anchor. Rappel from here, or continue (5.10-) to the top. Pro: thin to 2- inch. FA: Mike Sherrick and Royal Robbins, September 1956. FFA: Eric Erickson, John Long, and Rick Accomazzo, 1978.

192. **The Innominate** 5.9+ ★ This route climbs the long, left-slanting crack system that forms an overhanging dihedral near the top. Begin about 50 feet right of *The Reach*. Pro: to 3 inches. FA: (A2) Chuck Wilts and Gary Bloom, August 1947. FFA: Royal Robbins and Jerry Gallwas, 1957.

SOUTH FACE—RIGHT SIDE

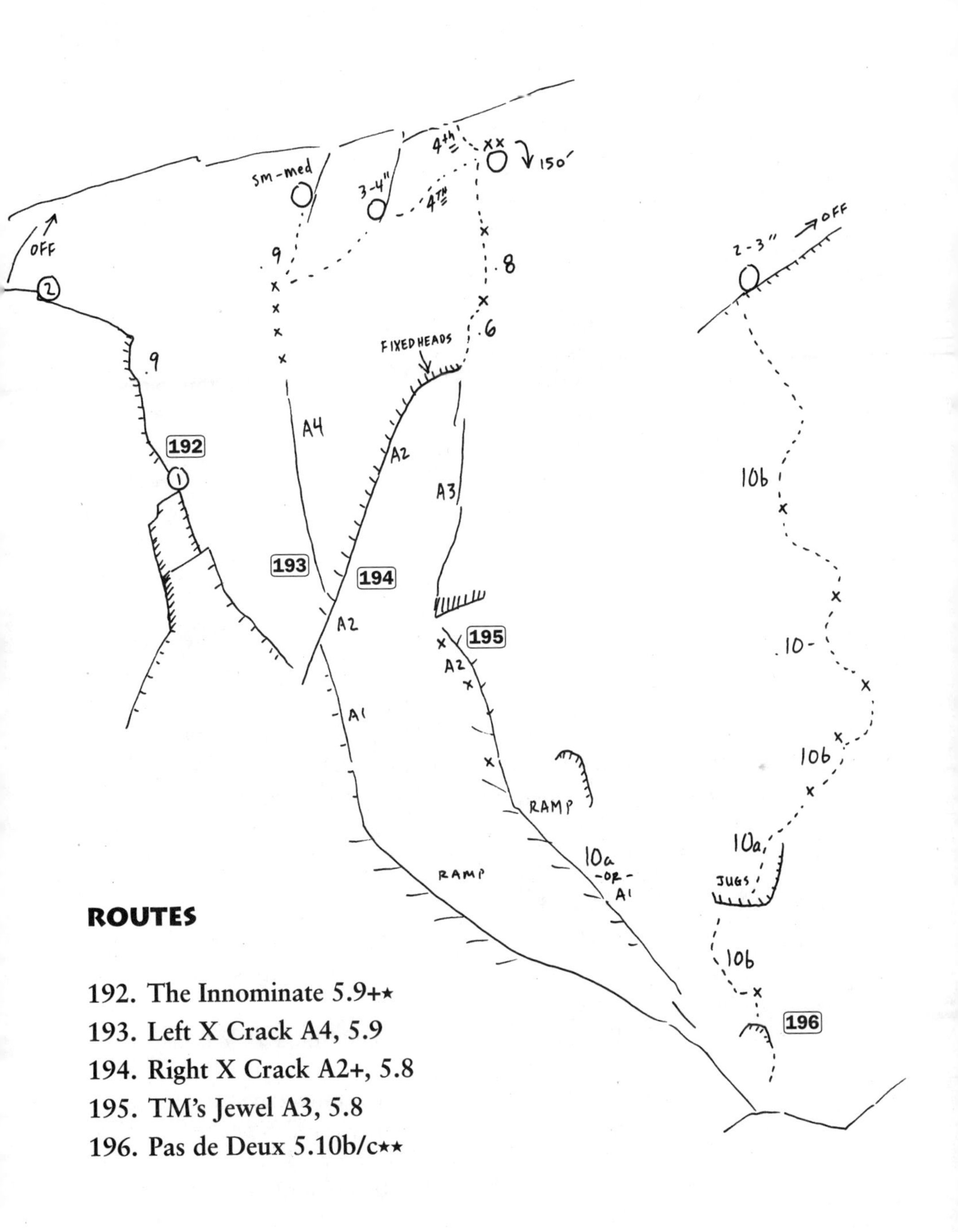

ROUTES

192. The Innominate 5.9+★
193. Left X Crack A4, 5.9
194. Right X Crack A2+, 5.8
195. TM's Jewel A3, 5.8
196. Pas de Deux 5.10b/c★★

193. **Left X Crack** A4, 5.9 Above the ramp on *The Innominate* is a steep headwall with two cracks that intersect to form an X. The upper left branch is A4. At the top of the crack a bolt protects 5.9 slab climbing to a ledge. Pro: copperheads, rurps, pitons, etc. FA: Jack Roberts, et al., 1978.

194. **Right X Crack** A2+, 5.8 Aid the upper right branch of the X crack to its end, then face climb up past 2 bolts to a two-bolt belay. Can be done clean if fixed heads are in place. Pro: thin to 2 inches including pins and copperheads. FA: Mark Powell, Frank DeSaussure, and Gary Hemming, February 1965.

195. **TM's Jewel** A3, 5.8 Begin at the base of the *Pas de Deux* buttress and free-climb the ramp just right of *The Innominate* to a bolt. A bit higher, 3 aid bolts give access to a 30-foot vertical seam. Nail this, then free climb past 2 bolts to a two-bolt belay. Pro: rurps, breaks, thin pitons to 0.5 inches, copperheads, hooks, nuts, and CDs to 2.5 inches. FA: Mark Powell and Don Lauria, June 1965.

196. **Pas de Deux** 5.10b/c ★★ An sustained pitch up the striking buttress near the right side of the South Face. Begin at a tree just right of *The Innominate* ramp with a difficult mantle up to a bolt. Traverse left, then pull over a small roof, up past 5 more bolts to a belay ledge. Pro: thin cams to 3-inch. FA: Gib Lewis and Tobin Sorenson, May 1974.

197. **Pas de Deux Variation (Original Route)** 5.10a/b Start up *Daley's Direct.* After about 20 feet, traverse up and left, past two bolts, to join *Faux Pas.* FA: Tom Higgins and Tom Cochrane, 1964.

198. **Faux Pas** 5.10c ★ Begin just left of *Daley's Direct* and climb a short, steep headwall past two bolts to easier (5.9) slab climbing. Pro: medium nuts, 2- to 3-inch CDs. FA: Bob Gaines and Charlie Peterson, August 1996.

SOUTH FACE RIGHT

The following routes lie on the smaller and generally lower-angle face to the right and around the corner from the *Pas de Deux* Buttress and the large dihedral formed by *The Innominate.*

199. **Daley's Direct** 5.6 R Begin about 50 feet uphill from *Pas de Deux* by traversing left on a bushy ledge to a squat, stunted sugar pine. Climb the improbable bulge above (unprotected except for the first ten feet), traverse right to a bolt, then up to a belay ledge. The slab pitch above (5.5) is unprotected, or one can traverse right to *Baby's Butt* for an easier finish. A more logical route is to climb directly up to *Orange Peel* and finish on that route. FA: Yvon Chouinard and Harry Daley, October 1965.

SOUTH FACE RIGHT

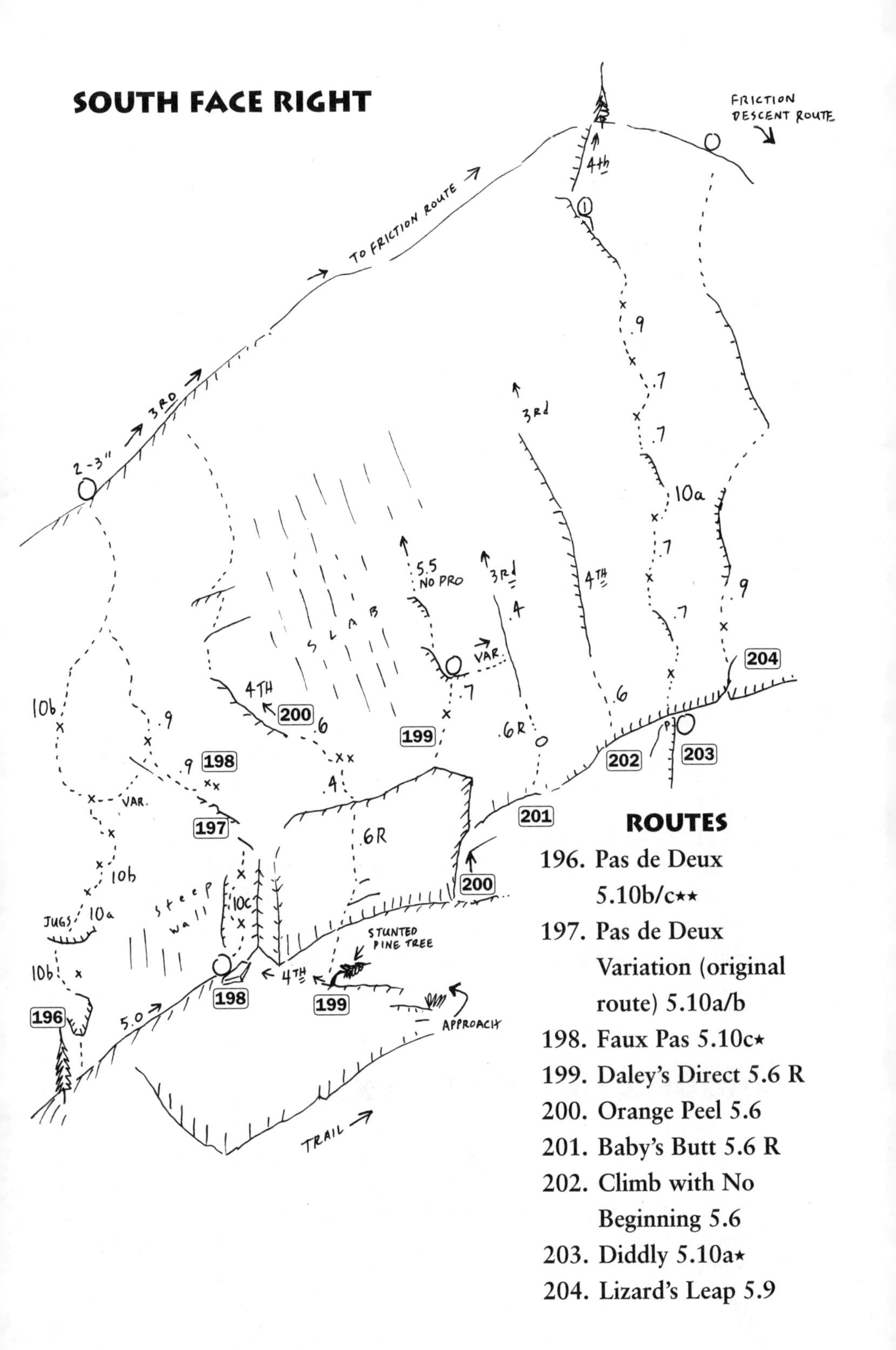

ROUTES

196. Pas de Deux 5.10b/c★★
197. Pas de Deux Variation (original route) 5.10a/b
198. Faux Pas 5.10c★
199. Daley's Direct 5.6 R
200. Orange Peel 5.6
201. Baby's Butt 5.6 R
202. Climb with No Beginning 5.6
203. Diddly 5.10a★
204. Lizard's Leap 5.9

200. **Orange Peel** 5.6 Begin just right of *Daley's Direct* and climb the right side of the block. Traverse left to the "Orange Peel," a prominent orange flake with a bolt. A delicate (5.6) step off the flake leads to a 4th-class slab finish. FA: Chuck and Ellen Wilts, 1951.
201. **Baby's Butt** 5.6 R Start just left of *Climb with No Beginning* and friction up rock "as white and smooth as a baby's butt," up to a red solution pocket. A thin crack 20 feet higher leads toward the top. Pro: to 2 inches. FA: Yvon Chouinard, et al., March 1960.
202. **Climb with No Beginning** 5.6 Move over the wall at a short, slanting overhang to reach the very prominent low-angle gully (class 4). Pro: to 2 inches. FA: Chuck Wilts, Robert Cosgrove, G. Ham, and Ray Van Aken, May 1950.
203. **Diddly** 5.10a ★ Just right of the *Climb with No Beginning* is this smooth slab pitch protected by 6 bolts. Pro: to 3 inches. FA: Mark Powell and Bob Kamps, January 1967.
204. **Lizard's Leap** 5.9 Start a few feet right of *Diddly* and cross the overhang at a right-slanting crack. 5.9 face climbing above a bolt eases to a run-out 5.6 slab finish. FA: Royal Robbins and Harry Daley, November 1961.
205. **Fitschen's Folly** 5.6 This silly route immortalizes Joe Fitschen's 200-foot slab-splashing fall after he got off-route on the *Friction Route* descent. Begin up the left-hand gully just right of the previous climbs; 5 feet left of a block wedged beneath an overhang, traverse left up to a tiny ledge. Move back right and up to a belay ledge. The *Friction Route* is up and right. Pro: to 2 inches. FA: Don Wilson and Mark Powell, December, 1954.
206. **The False Fitchen's Folly** 5.6 Start partway up the right-hand slabs of the *Friction Route,* near a large bush (this is right of the big tree). Climb up a ramp past blocks, eventually traversing left to reach a small, left-facing corner. Pro: thin to 2 inches. FA: Unknown.
207. **Friction Route** Class 4 The most commonly used means of descent off the rock. See description page 39. FA: Jim Smith and Mary Jane Edwards, 1936.

TAHQUITZ SUMMIT BLOCK

Above and right of the *Friction Route* and the main South Face of Tahquitz are the summit blocks of Tahquitz Rock. A few routes have been done on the south and southeast sides of the Summit Blocks. Approach via the *Friction Route* or along the upper south side of the rock. Descend the east side of the rock to a notch, go right to get to the South Face; go left to descend the North Gully (only if you want to go to the North Face).

SUMMIT BLOCK

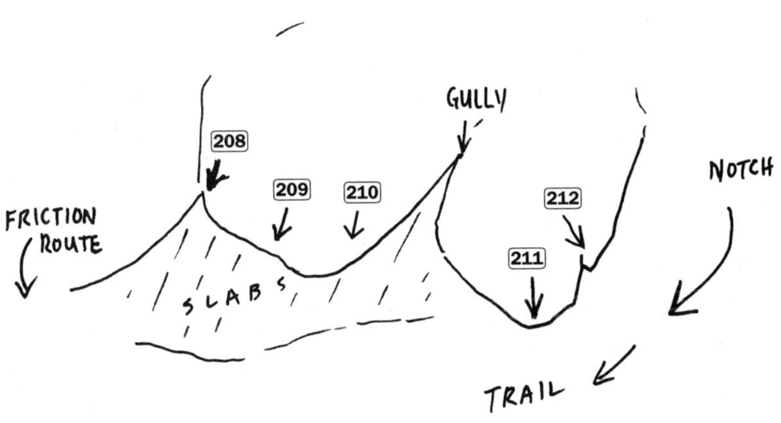

SUMMIT BLOCK

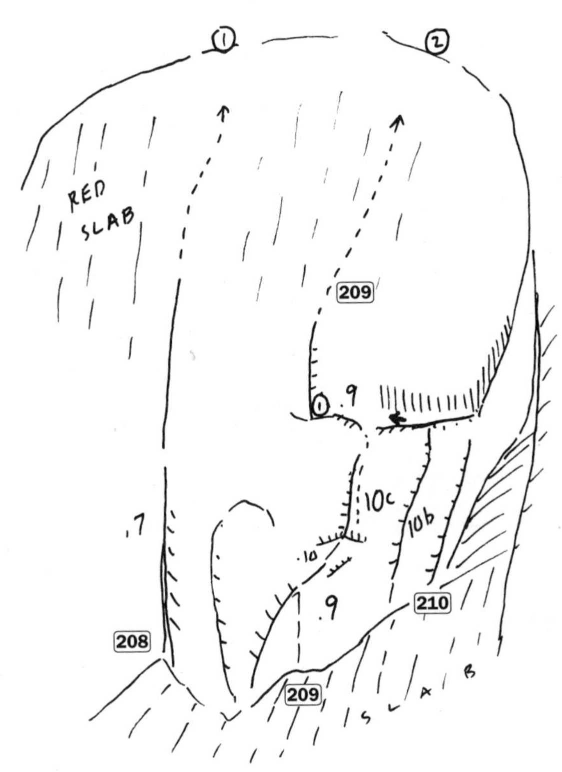

ROUTES

208. Red Rock Route 5.7★
209. Big Daddy 5.10c★
210. Big Momma 5.10b★
211. Little Momma 5.11c
212. Upsidedown Cake 5.10b

SUMMIT BLOCK

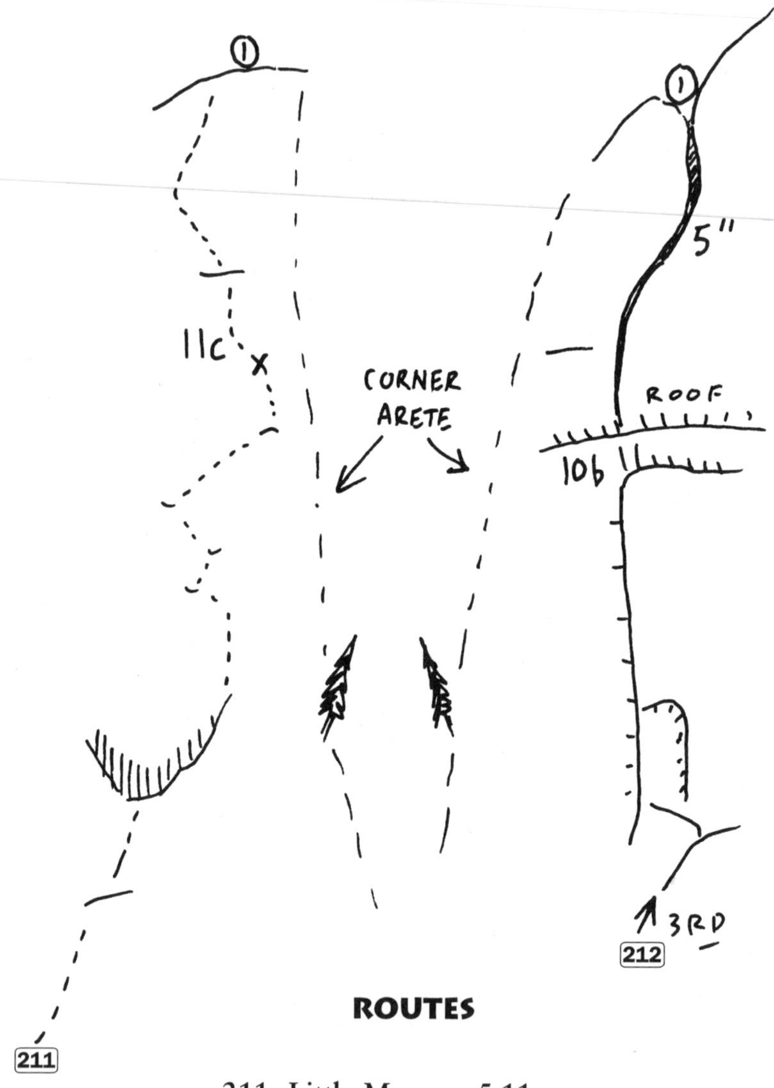

ROUTES

211. Little Momma 5.11c
212. Upsidedown Cake 5.10b

208. **Red Rock Route** 5.7 ★ This route is up the left summit block located above and to the right of the *Friction Route.* Climb the discontinuous crack system with red-colored rock on the left side of the face. Can be done in one long pitch with a 60 meter rope (200 feet). Pro: to 3 inches. FA: Don Wilson and Gary Hemming, August 1953.

209. **Big Daddy** 5.10c ★ 30 feet right of the *Red Rock Route,* make a difficult step-around to reach a crack leading over a roof. 20 feet above the overhang, move up and left to a belay ledge. Follow a crack that peters out to a slab finish. Pro: to 4 inches. FA: Yvon Chouinard and TM Herbert, May 1959. FFA: Tom Frost and Royal Robbins.

210. **Big Momma** 5.10b ★ Climb the right-facing corner to the right of the regular route. At the horizontal break, traverse left to join *Big Daddy.* Pro: to 3.5 inches. FA: Rob Raker and Darrell Hensel, 1987.

211. **Little Momma** 5.11c This route is on the right (east) summit block when viewed from the vicinity of the *Friction Route,* separated from the left summit block by a deep gully. Begin left of an arete and climb a slanting, awkward crack up a headwall, then face-climb up to a bolt that protects a thin, blank section to easier climbing and the top of the block. Pro: thin to 2-inch. FA: Chuck Wilts and D. McClelland, 1961. FFA: John Long and Rick Accomazzo, 1974.

212. **Upsidedown Cake** 5.10b Around the corner to the right of *Little Momma* is a crack system that shoots up through a 5-foot roof. The crack widens to 5 inches above the overhang. Pro: to 5 inches. FA: Tom Higgins and Bob Kamps, July 1966.

Suicide Rock

APPROACH INFORMATION

For approaches to particular routes or sections of the rocks, see the text.

The approach to Suicide tends to be less steep than at Tahquitz. The first part of the trail is maintained and easy, but the upper part of the trail is not maintained. Use care to hike along only the established trail, and don't forge new paths. This will help avoid unnecessary soil erosion. If you are in poor physical condition, plan on taking extra time to get to the base of the rock.

The trail to Suicide begins almost directly across Fern Valley Road from the first large water tanks encountered on the way to Humber Park (a small building is located in front). This is about 0.25 mile before you get to Humber Park. Park along Fern Valley Road (avoid areas signed No Parking) or along a side road (running south) just below the water tanks. Walk down the hillside along the trail, cross the creek (often dry in late summer/fall), then head right on a paved road (Forest Haven Drive). Follow Forest Haven Drive, keeping straight, past a left-hand split (private residence). Eventually, the road becomes dirt and then ends. At this point a climber's trail heads off left, contouring the hillside. A short distance later the trail is unmaintained and steepens considerably. This trail eventually leads to the base of Suicide Rock near The Buttress of Cracks and The Weeping Wall. Plan on about 30 minutes or more for the approach. See Suicide Rock Overview Map.

WINTER SLAB

This 80-foot face is located at the extreme western boundary of Suicide Rock, several hundred feet left (west) of Arpa Carpa Cliff. The easiest approach is from the top of the rock. Either climb a route to the summit or from the base of the Weeping Wall head right for about 175 yards (past the North Face) then left up a trail to the summit. From the summit, head southwest, down a slope to the right (west) of the cliff. At the bottom of the slope, the Winter Slab will be found to your right (west).

1. **Winter Heat** 5.9 The finger crack and face on the left side of the face. FA: Robin and Scott Erler, December 1987.
2. **Winter Flake** 5.11b R This route follows a flake on the right side of Winter Slab, then up the face past a bolt. FA: Scott and Robin Erler, December 1987.

SUICIDE ROCK OVERVIEW MAP

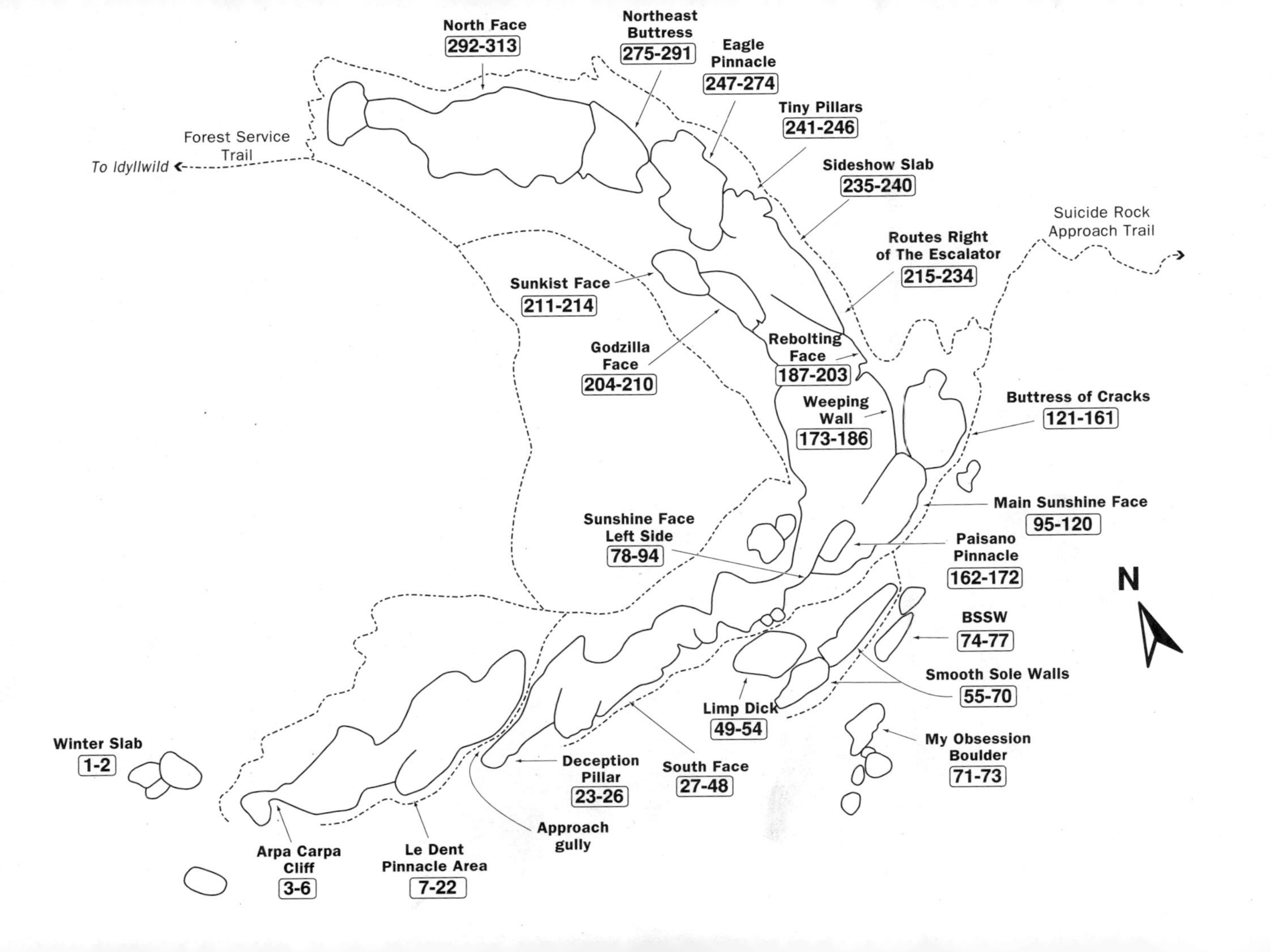

SUICIDE ROCK OVERVIEW

ARPA CARPA CLIFF

The easiest approach is from the top of the rock. Either climb a route to the summit, or from the base of the Weeping Wall head right for about 175 yards (past the North Face) then left up a trail to the summit. From the summit, head southwest, down a slope to the right (west) of the cliff. At the bottom of the slope, the Arpa Carpa Cliff will be found to your left (east). Alternatively, you can reach the cliff by a rather hard to find trail in the forest leading several hundred yards west (left) from the South Face (this approach is only recommended if you are already at the South Face). See Suicide Rock Overview Map.

3. **Arpa Carpa** 5.10a R ★ For the first pitch, climb the left-facing dihedral on the left (5.10a), or the right-facing corner on the right (5.9) to a belay ledge. The second pitch climbs the slab above past one bolt (5.10a). Pro: small to 1.5 inches. FA: Phil Warrender, Jim Wilson, Tobin Sorenson, and Paul Cowan, May 1973.
4. **Wild Women** 5.11c ★★ 3 bolts to 2-bolt anchor, just left of *Wild Gazongas*. FA: Scott and Robin Erler, December 1987
5. **Wild West** 5.12a (TR) ★ Climb past 4 bolts directly up to *Wild Women* belay. FA: Scott Erler, May 1988. First lead: Darell Hensel, 1997.
6. **Wild Gazongas** 5.10c R ★ 1. Climb the twin vertical cracks on the right side of the face to a belay ledge. 2. Up and left to a 3-bolt face. Pro: Many small to 2 inches. FA: Rick Accomazzo, Richard Harrison, and John Long, July 1973.

ARPA CARPA CLIFF

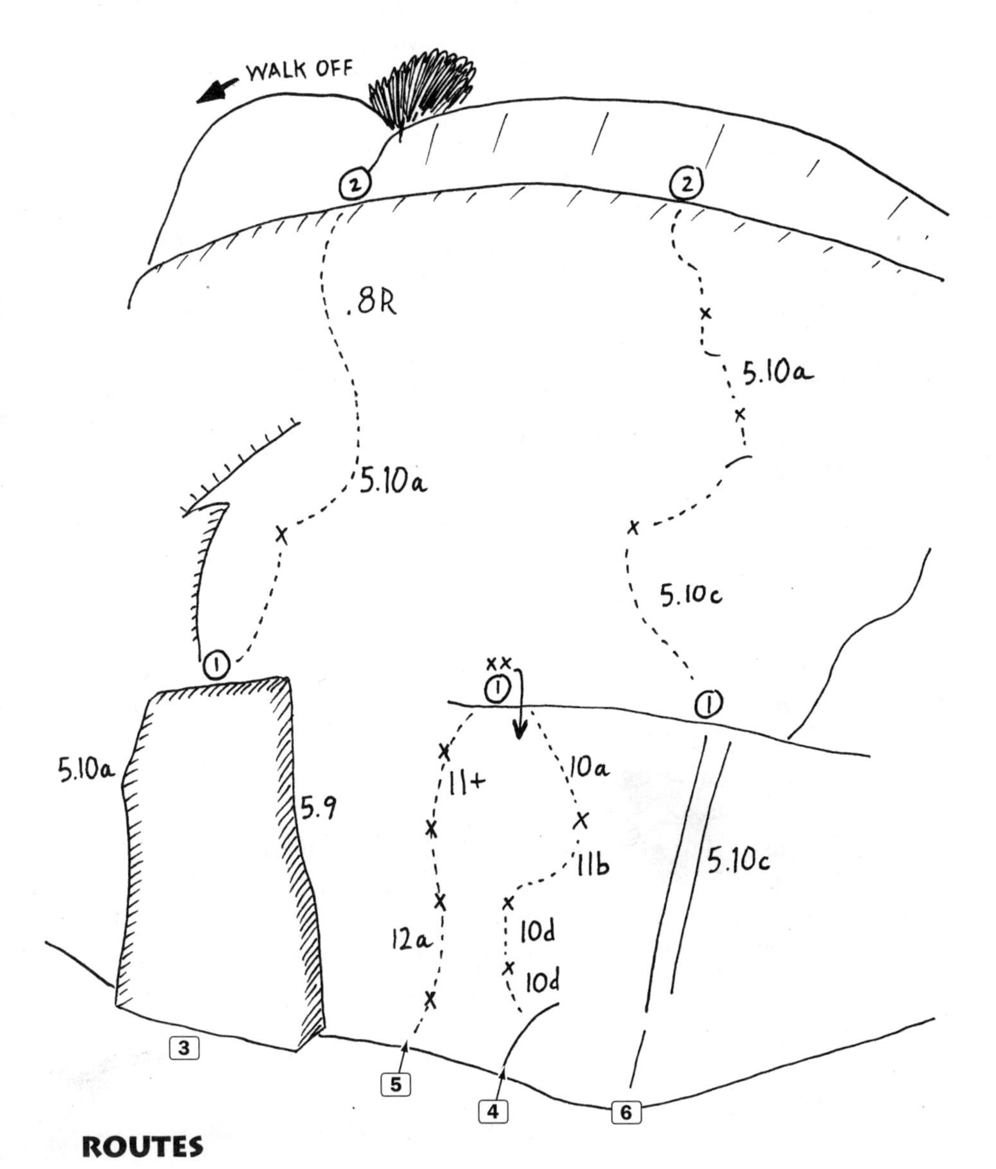

ROUTES

3. Arpa Carpa 5.10a R★
4. Wild Women 5.11c★★
5. Wild West 5.12a★
6. Wild Gazongas 5.10c R★

LE DENT PINNACLE AREA

This is a complex area with a long approach. The best (easiest) approach is from the top of the rock. Descend a steep gully that drops down just west of the top of the South Face, on the west side of the Deception Pillar Buttress. This involves a short bit of easy 5th-class downclimbing, tunneling under some chockstones.

Alternatively, from the vicinity of South Face, hike west (left) several hundred yards, dropping down to avoid the Deception Pillar Buttress, then contour back up to the cliff (this approach is only recommended if you are already at the South Face). The large detached pillar on the left side (facing the cliff) of the gully is the Le Dent Pillar. See Suicide Rock Overview Map.

7. **Floating Log** 5.11c ★ The 3-bolt face climb up the slab left of *Munge Dihedral.* Pro: to 2 inches. FA: Jonny Woodward and Darrell Hensel, August 1986.
8. **Munge Dihedral** 5.10a ★★ The obvious hand-and-fist jam crack in the large, left-facing corner left of the *Le Dent Pillar.* Pro: to 4 inches. FA: Tom Higgins and Pat Ament, mid-1960s.
9. **Forest Lawn** A2 ★ One of Suicide's last remaining aid climbs, this is the thin, overhanging crack on the right side of the *Munge Dihedral.* Pro: knifeblades, lost arrows, nuts, and CDs to 2 inches. FA: Phil Warrender, Jim Wilson, and Tobin Sorenson, May 1973.
10. **Root Canal** 5.7 R ★ Climb the chimney system formed by the left side of the Le Dent Pillar. From the top of the pillar, a 5.6 step-across, then an unprotected slab lead to the top. Pro: small to 4-inch. FA: Ivan Couch and Mike Dent, 1970.
11. **South Arete** 5.11d ★★ The impressive 6-bolt face climb on the steep left wall of the pillar. The first ascent was done on the lead by Tom Gilge with only 3 bolts; the other bolts added later by less bold climbers. 100-foot rappel from horn. FA: Tom Gilje and Scott Erler, January 1988.
12. **Le Petite Gratton** 5.11c R ★ This route works the right edge of the *Le Dent Pillar*. Rap 80 feet from a horn. FA: Bob Gaines and Mark Bowling, June 1988.
13. **Hey Vic, Over Here** 5.10a The short, thin crack on the block below the *Le Dent* Pillar. Pro: thin to 2 inches. FA: Kevin Powell and Mike Lechlinski, 1979.
14. **Le Dent** 5.6 R Climb the chimney formed by the right side of the *Le Dent Pillar.* The second pitch involves a 5.6 step-across to an unprotected slab. Pro: to 4 inches. FA: Ivan Couch, Jim Donini, and Mike Dent, 1970.

LE DENT PINNACLE AREA

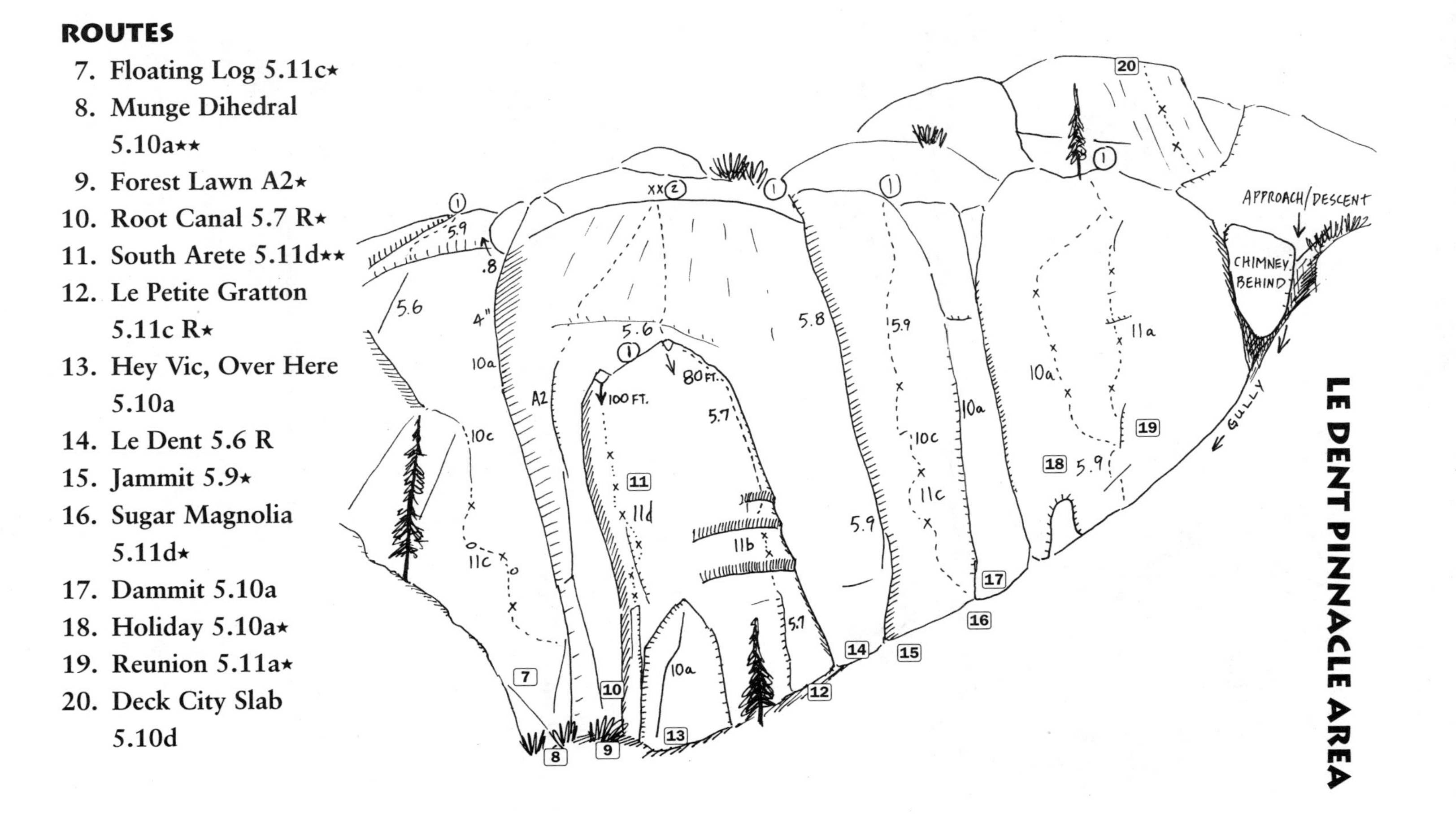

ROUTES

7. Floating Log 5.11c★
8. Munge Dihedral 5.10a★★
9. Forest Lawn A2★
10. Root Canal 5.7 R★
11. South Arete 5.11d★★
12. Le Petite Gratton 5.11c R★
13. Hey Vic, Over Here 5.10a
14. Le Dent 5.6 R
15. Jammit 5.9★
16. Sugar Magnolia 5.11d★
17. Dammit 5.10a
18. Holiday 5.10a★
19. Reunion 5.11a★
20. Deck City Slab 5.10d

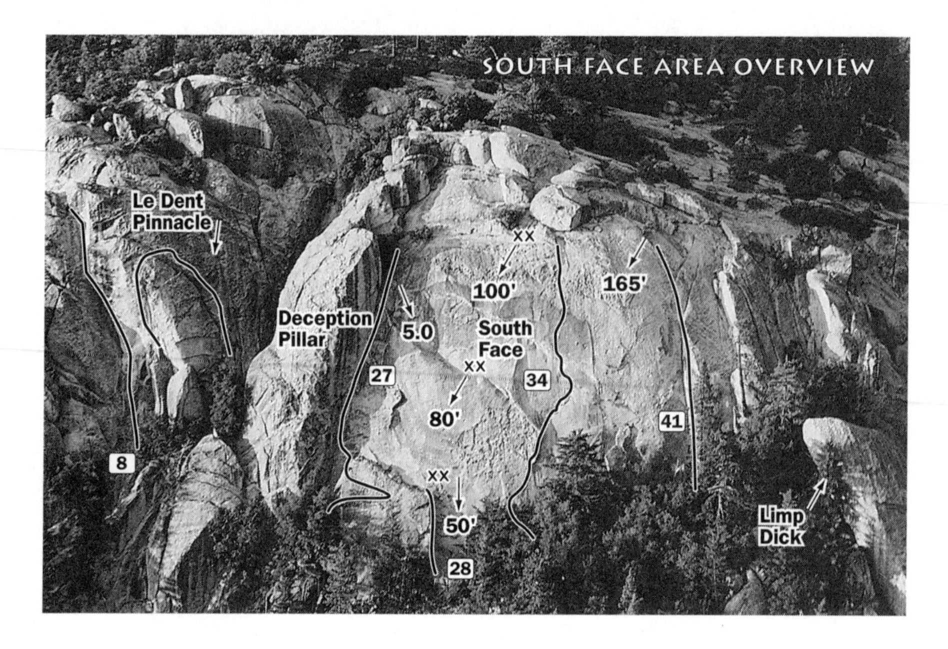

15. **Jammit** 5.9 ★ 20 feet right of *Le Dent* is this steep, left-facing corner starting with an overhanging alcove. Pro: to 3- inch. FA: Jim Donini, Ivan Couch, and Mike Dent, circa 1970.
16. **Sugar Magnolia** 5.11d ★ The face climb up the narrow pillar just right of *Jammit.* FA: Eric Erickson, 1978.
17. **Dammit** 5.10a This is a dirty, right-facing corner located just right of *Sugar Magnolia.* FA: Unknown.
18. **Holiday** 5.10a ★ This route and *Reunion* share the same start and are located on the face to the right of *Dammit.* This is the left-most route, passing 3 bolts. FA: Nick Conway, Stuart Critchlow, and Alan Bartlett, April 1992.
19. **Reunion** 5.11a ★ Start at the same point as *Holiday* and climb straight up past 3 bolts. Pro: to 2.5-inch. FA: Alan Bartlett and Dave Black, August 1991.
20. **Deck City Slab** 5.10d Short 2-bolt slab located just above the gully that leads down to the preceding routes. FA: Richard Tucker, 1986.
21. **Steal Your Face** 5.12b TR This steep face is located across the gully from (and facing) *Dammit.* It has 3 bolts but has not been led as of this writing. FA: (TR) Bill Leventhal and Mike Paul, 1988.
22. **Box of Rain** 5.10d (TR) 50 feet left of *Steal Your Face* is this dirty, left-leaning lieback flake that leads to a steep fist crack. FA: Bill Leventhal, 1988.

DECEPTION PILLAR

Deception Pillar is the prominent, 200-foot-high buttress that borders the left margin of the South Face. It is best reached from the vicinity of the South Face. The best way to approach the South Face is to head left along the base of the Buttress of Cracks and Sunshine Face, then up the gully (behind *Limp Dick*) until progress is obstructed by large blocks. Tunnel through (under) these blocks, then head down along the base of the rock to the South Face. It is also possible to reach the South Face from the Smooth Sole Walls by scrambling up and left. See Suicide Rock Overview Map.

DECEPTION PILLAR

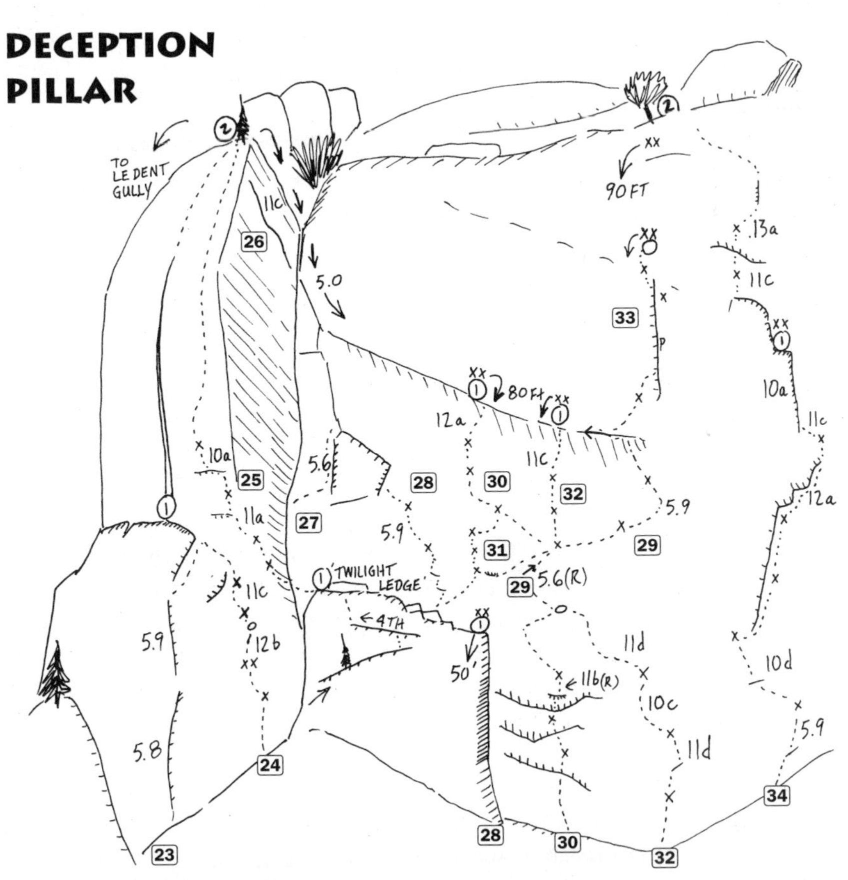

23. Deception Pillar 5.9★
24. The Great Pretender 5.12b★★
25. Brilliant Disguise 5.11a★★
26. Running a Rig 5.11c
27. Short Story 5.7
28. Twilight Delight 5.9
29. Boomerang 5.9
30. Hell's Angel 5.12a R★★
31. Midnight Sun Variation 5.12a★★
32. Archangel 5.11d★★
33. Bolts to Somewhere 5.11, A1
34. Hades 5.13a★★★

Descents: 1. Rappel off a small tree from the top of *Deception Pillar;* or 2. Downclimb the top of *Short Story* (5.0), then traverse out across the face on an exposed ledge to reach the bolt anchor atop *Hell's Angel;* two 80-foot rappels from here lead to the ground.

23. **Deception Pillar** 5.9 ★ Begin near a large oak at the base. 1. Up a deceptively difficult crack, then up easier but less protected face climbing to a ledge. 2. Enjoyable, knobby chimney; several horns can be tied off for pro. Pro: thin to 2 inches, long slings. FA: Pat Callis and Lee Harrell, July 1968.
24. **The Great Pretender** 5.12b ★★ Begin at the lower right margin of the Deception Pillar. Face climbing past several bolts leads to the first belay of the *Deception Pillar* route. FA: Jonny Woodward and Darrell Hensel, July 1986.
25. **Brilliant Disguise** 5.11a ★★ Begin by scrambling up to the broad ledge 40 feet up the *Short Story* corner. Climb up and left to a flake, followed by face and knob climbing past 4 bolts to a belay tree at the top of the pillar. 165-foot pitch. FA: Bob Gaines, Troy Mayr, Charles Cole, and Charlie Peterson, September 1987.
26. **Running a Rig** 5.11c (TR) Short, steep, thin crack at the top, right-hand side of the Deception Pillar Buttress, best approached by scrambling down the upper section of *Short Story.* FA: Troy Mayr, Charles Cole, Rick Ledesma, Curt Lyons, and Linda Abrahms, July 1988.

THE SOUTH FACE

The best way to approach the South Face is to head left along the base of the Buttress of Cracks and Sunshine Face, then up the gully (behind Limp Dick) until progress is obstructed by large blocks. Tunnel through (under) these blocks, then head down along the base of the rock to the South Face. It is also possible to reach the South Face from the Smooth Sole Walls by scrambling up and left. See Suicide Rock Overview Map.

Descents: Several descents are possible to get back to the base of the South Face, all require downclimbing and/or rappels. It is best to have two ropes. 1. Many climbers downclimb the top of *Short Story* (5.0), then traverse out on the face on an exposed ledge to reach the bolt anchor atop *Hell's Angel.* An 80-foot rappel from here leads to Twilight Ledge where another short (50-foot) rappel from 2 bolts leads to the deck. 2. It is also possible to make a 95-foot rappel from bolts at the top of the face directly to the bolted rappel anchor on *Archangel* (See topo). 3. A 165-foot rappel is possible from a tree at the top of *Miscalculation.* 4. A 120-foot rap is possible from a large block atop *Spring Cleaning.* 5. A 75-foot rap from a tree near the top of *Minor.*

SOUTH FACE ROUTES

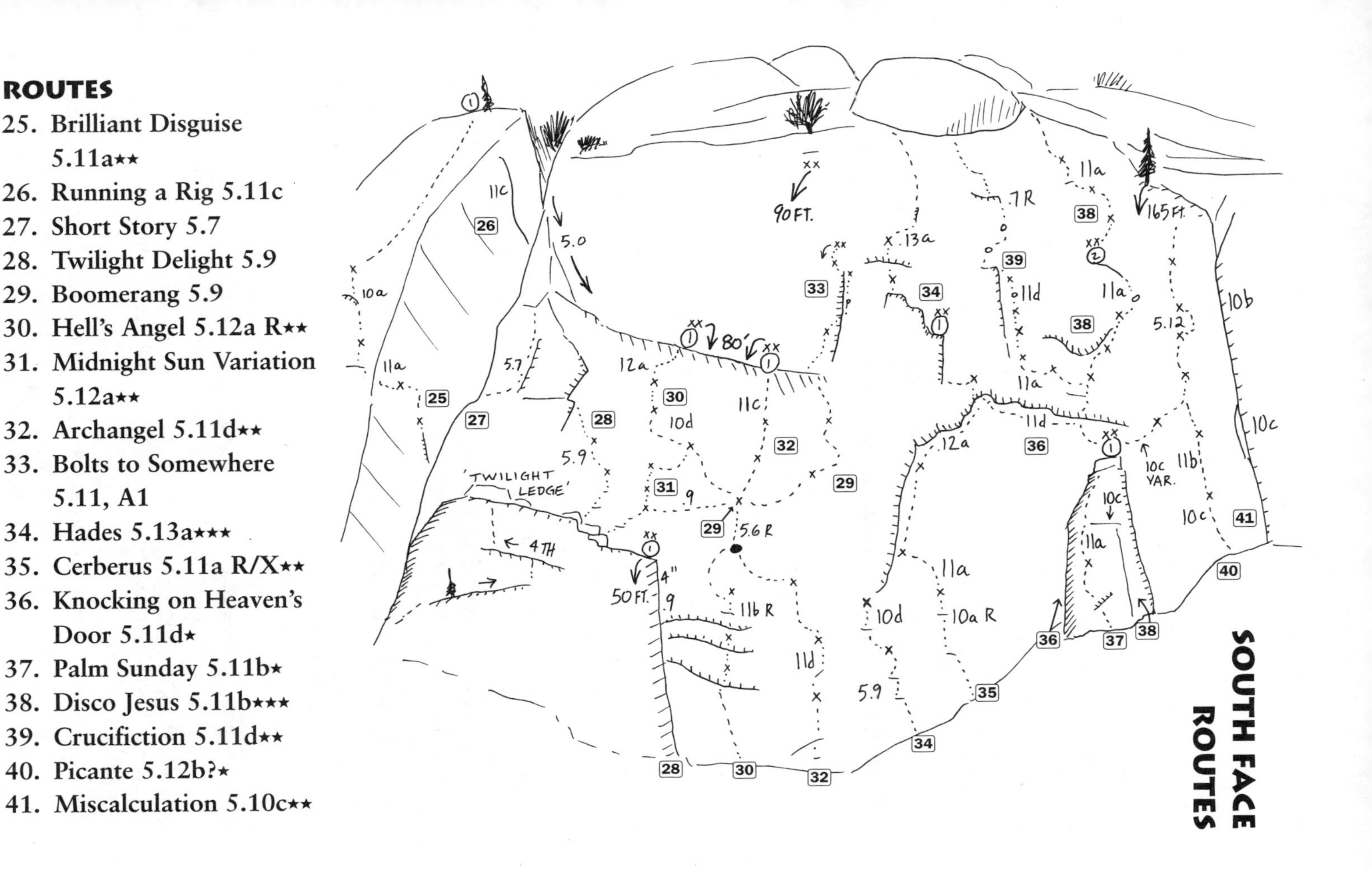

ROUTES

25. Brilliant Disguise 5.11a★★
26. Running a Rig 5.11c
27. Short Story 5.7
28. Twilight Delight 5.9
29. Boomerang 5.9
30. Hell's Angel 5.12a R★★
31. Midnight Sun Variation 5.12a★★
32. Archangel 5.11d★★
33. Bolts to Somewhere 5.11, A1
34. Hades 5.13a★★★
35. Cerberus 5.11a R/X★★
36. Knocking on Heaven's Door 5.11d★
37. Palm Sunday 5.11b★
38. Disco Jesus 5.11b★★★
39. Crucifiction 5.11d★★
40. Picante 5.12b?★
41. Miscalculation 5.10c★★

27. **Short Story** 5.7 Climb the prominent, right-facing corner formed by the right side of the Deception Pillar Buttress. FA: Unknown.
28. **Twilight Delight** 5.9 Begin about 60 feet right of *Short Story.* 1. A steep, 40-foot-high right-facing dihedral with a 4-inch crack to a broad ledge (this point can also be reached via a class 4 scramble just right of *Short Story*). 2. Up and left past 2 bolts to join *Short Story.* Pro: to 4 inches. FA: Clark Jacobs, Terry Martin, and Dave Black, September 1974.
29. **Boomerang** 5.9 From the ledge atop the first pitch of *Twilight Delight,* traverse right past three bolts, then loop back left and up past another bolt to a belay bolt. Rap 130 feet or continue left to reach the rap anchor on *Hell's Angel* (80 feet to Twilight Ledge) or farther left to finish on *Short Story* (5.0) to the top. FA: Alan Bartlett, et al., 1979.
30. **Hell's Angel** 5.12a R ★★ Start about 20 feet right of the *Twilight Delight* dihedral. The 5.11 mantle above the second bolt is the psychological crux. Easier climbing leads to some very thin slab moves up to the ledge system. FA: Bob Gaines, Paul Van Betten, and Jay Smith, June 1987.
31. **Midnight Sun Variation** 5.12a ★★ From Twilight Ledge climb straight up past bolts (moving right at the third bolt) to join the upper section of *Hell's Angel.* FA: Bob Gaines, October 1999.
32. **Archangel** 5.11d ★★ Start right of *Hell's Angel,* head up and left to meet *Boomerang,* then straight up to a 2-bolt belay on the big ledge. Rap 80 feet to Twilight Ledge. FA: Darrell Hensel and Jonny Woodward, July 1986.
33. **Bolts to Somewhere** 5.11, A1 A more appropriate name might be *Bolts to Nowhere,* as the pitch ends abruptly at 2 bolts in a blank wall. Start atop the first pitch of *Boomerang* (bolt belay). Climb into a tapering dihedral then up to the two-bolt anchor. FA: Troy Mayr and Charles Cole, August 1988.
34. **Hades** 5.13a ★★★ A classic test piece: outstanding quality, variety, and difficulty. 1. Begin 40 feet right of *Archangel* and climb past bolts (5.9 R to 1st bolt, then 10+ to the 2nd), step right into the arch, up past 2 more bolts; make crux moves where the arch curves right, then up to a bolt that protects a thin face move left (11b) to easier climbing and a 2-bolt belay stance. 2. The crux second pitch heads up a razor-like flake, then over a small overlap. Clipping the two bolts is difficult unless slings are in place. FA: (A3) Tobin Sorenson, et al., 1970s. FFA: 1st pitch: Kevin Powell and Darrell Hensel, 1980. 2nd Pitch, John Long and Bob Gaines, 1984.
35. **Cerberus** 5.11a R/X ★★ Begin 40 feet right of *Hades.* An unprotected 5.10a mantle about 40 feet up will keep most people away, although a large hook may be useful for protection. From here a bolt protects 5.11a

ROUTES

34. Hades 5.13a★★★
35. Cerberus 5.11a R/X★★
36. Knocking on Heaven's Door 5.11d★
37. Palm Sunday 5.11b★
38. Disco Jesus 5.11b★★★
39. Crucifiction 5.11d★★
40. Picante 5.12b?★
41. Miscalculation 5.10c★★
42. It's a Mayracole 5.11d★★
43. 10b or No 10b 5.10b★
44. Spring Cleaning 5.6★
45. Minuet 5.10c
46. Major 5.7
47. Minor 5.1
48. Orange Roughy 5.10b

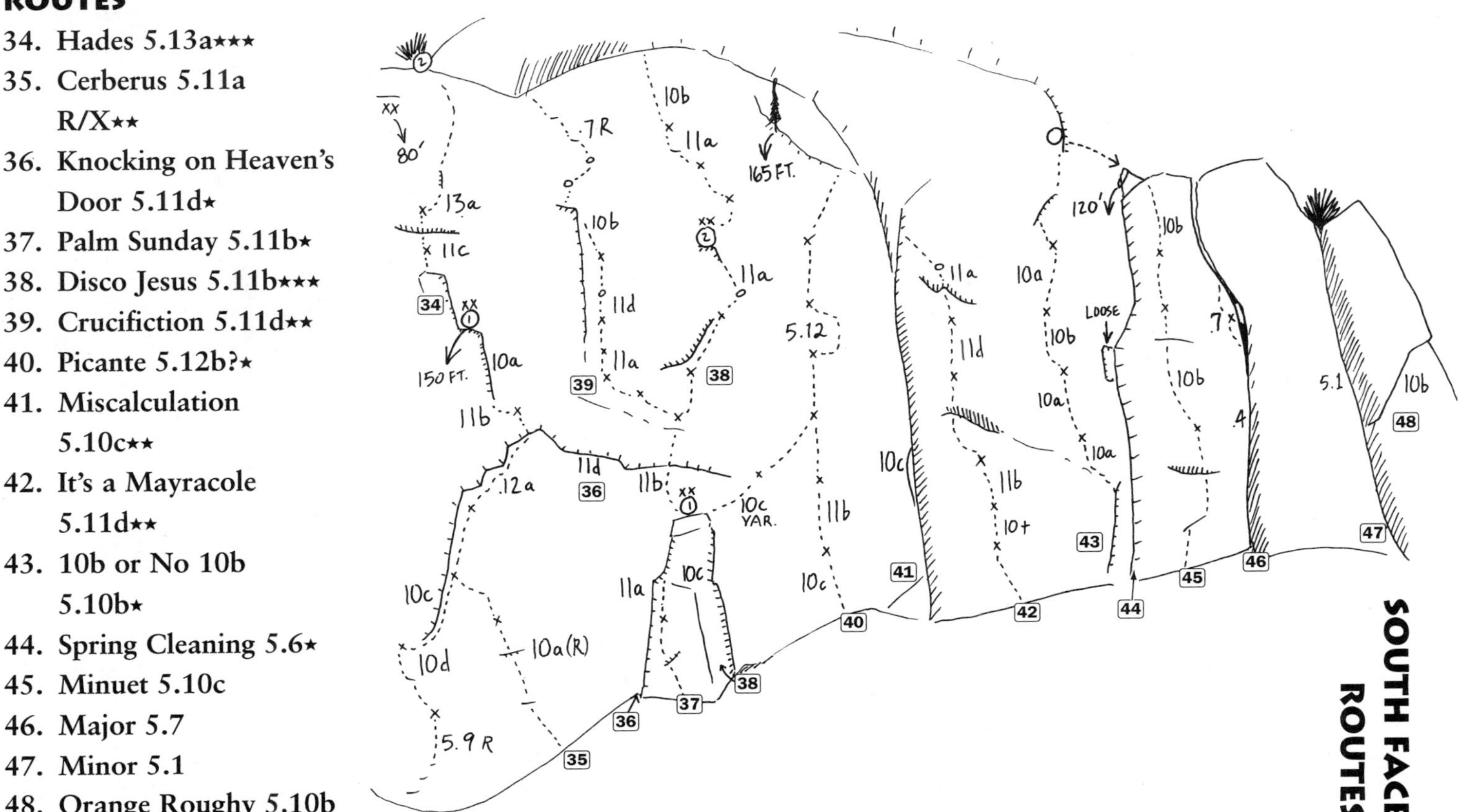

SOUTH FACE ROUTES

face move up and left to the third bolt on *Hades*. FA: Dave Tucker, Mike Paul, and Bob Gaines, August 1987.

36. **Knocking on Heaven's Door** 5.11d ★ Uphill from *Hades* a 50-foot-high exfoliation slab leans against the face. 1. Climb the left-facing dihedral to a 2-bolt belay atop the slab. 2. Left along the flake to join *Hades*. Pro: thin to 2 inches, pitons may be needed if none are in place. FA: (A2) Tobin Sorenson and Richard Harrison. FFA: Kevin Powell and Darrell Hensel, 1979.
37. **Palm Sunday** 5.11b ★ The short, sharp arete on the left side of the exfoliation slab. Pro: a TCU, 1 bolt. FA: Bob Gaines, Dwight Brooks, Paul Edwards, and John Long, June 1988.
38. **Disco Jesus** 5.11b ★★★ 1. Finger crack up the center of the exfoliation slab. 2. Straight up, then up and right to a 2-bolt belay. 3. Past 3 bolts to the top. Pitches 2 and 3 can be climbed in one 165-foot pitch. Pro: thin to 2 inches. FA: Eric Erickson and others, 1978.
39. **Crucifiction** 5.11d ★★ From the first bolt on the second pitch of *Disco Jesus,* tiptoe left across a quartz band past another bolt, then up the groove past 4 more bolts. FA: Bob Gaines, August 1987.
40. **Picante** 5.12b? ★ 6 bolt face 20 feet left of *Miscalculation*. Once rated 11+, small flakes have broken off the crux section. FA: John Long, Darrell Hensel, Kevin Powell, and Dave Wonderly, May 1987.
41. **Miscalculation** 5.10c ★★ The sustained, left-facing dihedral on the right margin of the South Face. At the top, go up and left to a belay tree. Rappel 165 feet. Pro: many thin to 3 inches. FA: Ivan Couch and Mike Dent, 1970.
42. **It's a Mayracole** 5.11d ★★ A sustained, 5-bolt slab located 30 feet right of *Miscalculation*. FA: Troy Mayr and Charles Cole, July 1987.
43. **10b or No 10b** 5.10b ★ Climb the first 40 feet of *Spring Cleaning,* then up and left past 4 bolts to the top. FA: Troy Mayr and Charles Cole, July 1987.
44. **Spring Cleaning** 5.6 ★ Lieback the large, left-facing corner, taking care to avoid a huge, loose flake about halfway up. Pro: to 3 inches. FA: Ivan Couch, Mike Dent and Larry Reynolds, 1970.
45. **Minuet** 5.10c 3-bolt climb up the narrow face between *Spring Cleaning* and *Major*. FA: Alan Bartlett, Steve Jennings, and Dave Black, December 1985.
46. **Major** 5.7 The low-angle chimney 30 feet right of *Spring Cleaning*. A bolt protects the crux near the top. Pro: to 3 inches. FA: Ivan Couch and Mike Dent, 1970.

47. **Minor** 5.1 The low-angle crack just right of *Major.* FA: Unknown.
48. **Orange Roughy** 5.10b The thin crack in an orange section of rock halfway up the right side of the 4th-class corner to the right of *Minor.* Pro: thin to 2 inches. FA: Troy Mayr and Steve Axthelm, October 1987.

THE LIMP DICK

This is the monolithic block that sits above the Smooth Sole Wall and below the right margin of the South Face. It can be reached by walking left, below the Sunshine Face, then up the gully. The huge boulder/pinnacle in the middle of the gully is The Limp Dick. South Side routes can be reached by heading left around the base. North Side routes are reached by heading right up the gully until progress is obstructed by large blocks. Tunnel through (under) these blocks. It is also possible to reach the South Side routes from directly above the Smooth Sole Wall, left side. See Suicide Rock Overview Map.

SOUTH SIDE ROUTES

49. **Limp Dick** 5.10a ★ Above the Left Side of the Smooth Sole Wall, left side, several large flakes sit at the base of the Limp Dick block. From the upper of these flakes, on the left margin of the block, two bolts protect a mantle

and undercling leading to unprotected class 4. Rap off the back side into the notch. FA: Mark Powell, Harry Daley, and Dave Rearick, May 1959. FFA: Tom Higgins, 1969.

50. **Fellatio** 5.10c Start 30 feet right of the *Limp Dick* route. An extended stem and strenuous mantle past one bolt to easier, unprotected climbing. FA: John Long, Rick Accomazzo, Tobin Sorenson, Royd Riggins, Richard Harrison, and Bruce Foster, 1973.

NORTH SIDE ROUTES

51. **Dick Tracy** 5.10c ★ The short, two-bolt route up the left margin of the North Side (facing *Tar and Feathers,* Route 78). There are two bolts just left of this, maybe an unfinished route? FA: Charles Cole and Gib Lewis, 1983.
52. **Dickhead** 5.11b R/X Solo (or toprope) the face about 30 feet right of *Dick Tracy.* There is a stray bolt near the bottom, added after the first ascent. FA: Jonny Woodward, July 1988.
53. **Five Tree** 5.3 Near the notch separating the South Face from the Limp Dick block a large pine tree will be found growing against the Limp Dick formation. Climb the tree as high as possible, then continue up the face to the top. FA: Charles Cole, et al.,1987.
54. **Pinhead** 5.12a/b ★★ Start in the tree, then climb the bulging face up and left past 4 bolts. Pro: 4 bolts. FA: Tom Gilje and Scott Erler, 1987.

SMOOTH SOLE WALLS

The Smooth Sole Walls are located to the left and below the large Sunshine Face of Suicide and face southeast. They are comprised of two slabs split by a chimney (*Chatsworth Chimney*); a large block/pillar sits atop the Smooth Sole Walls (Limp Dick). From the point where the trail up to Suicide meets the base of the rock (at the right side of The Buttress of Cracks), head left along the base of both The Buttress of Cracks and the larger Sunshine Face. Where the trail steepens and begins to head up a gully, traverse left along a ledge, then under a wedged boulder to reach the base of the Smooth Sole Walls. See Suicide Rock Overview Map.

SMOOTH SOLE WALLS

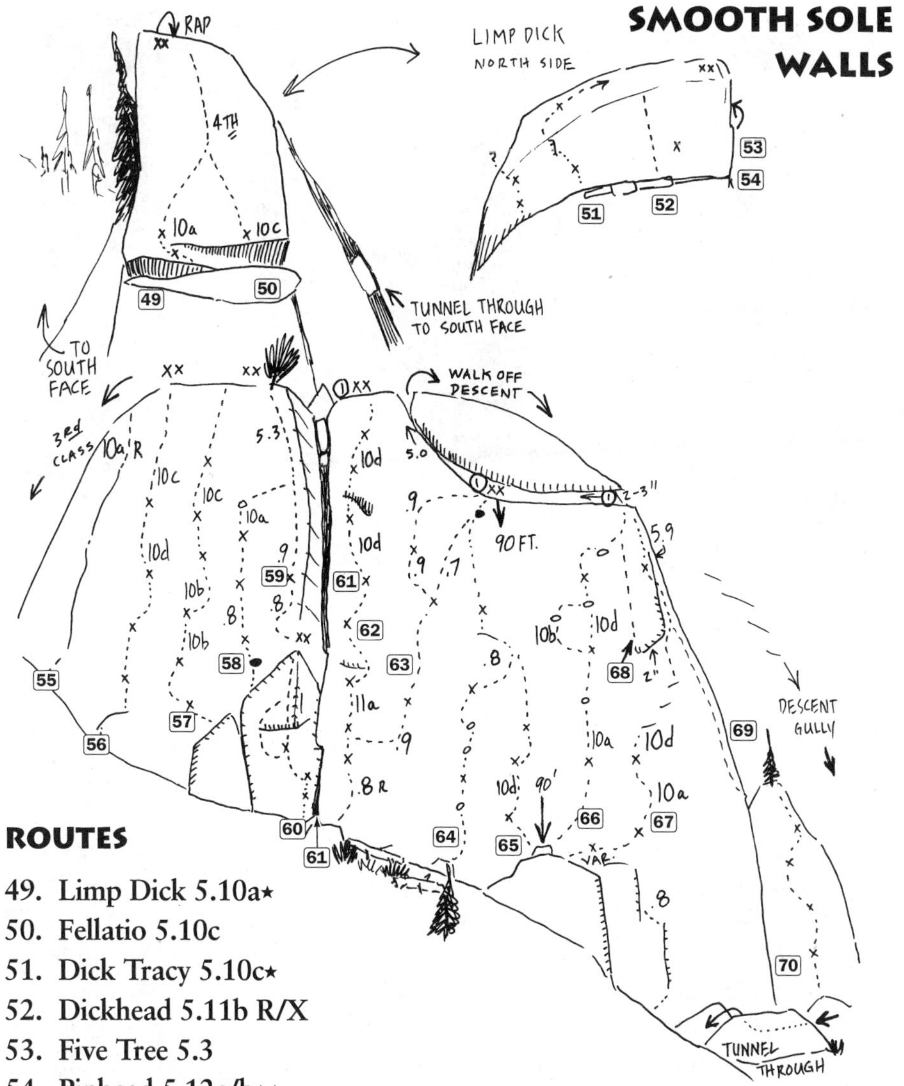

ROUTES

49. Limp Dick 5.10a★
50. Fellatio 5.10c
51. Dick Tracy 5.10c★
52. Dickhead 5.11b R/X
53. Five Tree 5.3
54. Pinhead 5.12a/b★★
55. Last Dance 5.10a R★
56. Blown Out 5.10d★
57. Down and Out 5.10c★★
58. Drowned Out 5.10a R★★
59. Over and Out 5.9 R★★
60. Steppin' Out 5.11d or 5.10d★★
61. Chatsworth Chimney 5.7 R★
62. Battle of the Bulge 5.11a R★★
63. The Fiend 5.9 R★★
64. Mickey Mantle 5.8 R★★★
65. Howard's Fifty-Footer 5.10d R★
66. Ultimatum 5.10b or 5.10d R★★
67. Pink Royd 5.10d R★★
68. Pink Royd Direct Finish 5.10c
69. Sensuous Corner 5.9★
70. Toxic Waltz 5.11c

LEFT SIDE

Descent: Walk/downclimb to the left.

55. **Last Dance** 5.10a R★ At the extreme left margin of the Smooth Sole Wall is this very thin crack. Pro: many very thin to 0.5-inch. There is a 2-bolt anchor on top. FA: Eric Erickson and Bill Squires, 1973.
56. **Blown Out** 5.10d ★ Approx. 25 feet down and right from *Last Dance,* climb straight up past 4 bolts. 2-bolt anchor. FA: Greg Bender and Phil Warrender, May 1972.
57. **Down and Out** 5.10c ★★ Near the right side of the left face, climb a crack to a ledge, then up and left past a bolt. Pro: 6 bolts, 2-bolt anchor. FA: Gib Lewis and Jim Wilson, March 1974.
58. **Drowned Out** 5.10a R ★★ Near the right side of the left face, climb a crack to a ledge, then go right up the ledge until a move up into a pocket leads to a bolt. Somewhat run-out. Pro: 3 bolts, slings, 2-bolt anchor. FA: J. Knutson and Phil Warrender, September 1972.
59. **Over and Out** 5.9 R ★★ Start as for *Drowned Out,* but head right to the top of the pedestal (2-bolt anchor here), climb the arete past 1 bolt. Pro: bolts. FA: Bob Gaines, Troy Mayr, and Mike Van Volkom, October 1987.
60. **Steppin' Out** 5.11d or 5.10d ★★ Start at the base of the pillar just left of *Chatsworth Chimney* and climb the arete past 3 bolts to a 2-bolt anchor. Continue up *Over and Out.* FA: Bob Gaines, October 1987.

SMOOTH SOLE WALLS—LEFT SIDE

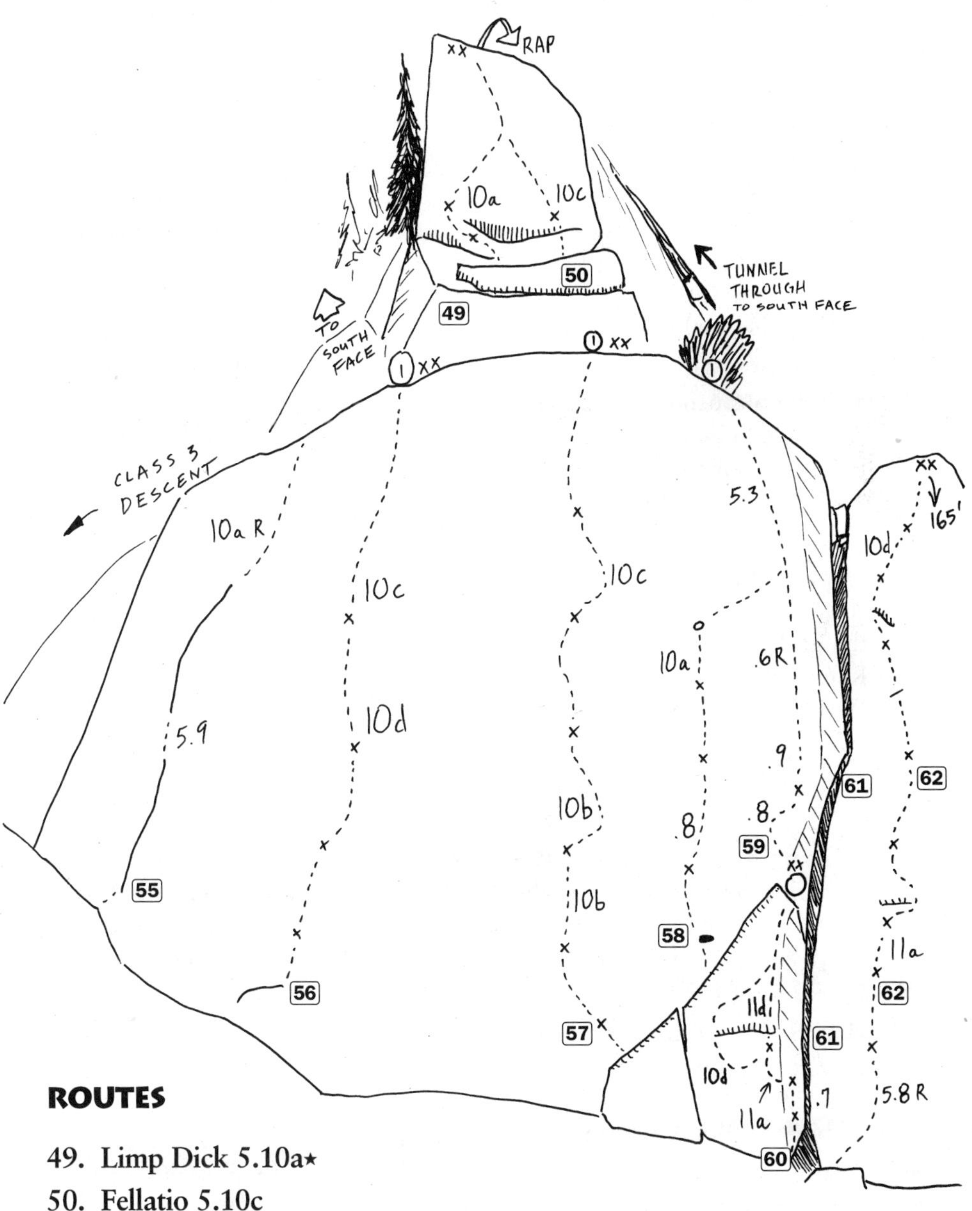

ROUTES

49. Limp Dick 5.10a★
50. Fellatio 5.10c
55. Last Dance 5.10a R★
56. Blown Out 5.10d★
57. Down and Out 5.10c★★
58. Drowned Out 5.10a R★★
59. Over and Out 5.9 R★★
60. Steppin' Out 5.11d or 5.10d★★
61. Chatsworth Chimney 5.7 R★
62. Battle of the Bulge 5.11a R★★

RIGHT SIDE

Descent: Rap off bolt/chain anchor above at the belay ledge (90 feet); rope barely reaches the highest rocks at the base. You can also climb a chimney/ramp about 40 feet higher to the top (5.0) and scramble down to the right or left back to the base.

61. **Chatsworth Chimney** 5.7 R ★ The long, deep chimney that splits the Smooth Sole Wall. FA: Unknown.
62. **Battle of the Bulge** 5.11a R ★★ Just right of *Chatsworth Chimney,* climb up to the first bolt of *The Fiend,* then straight up past 7 more bolts. 2-bolt anchor (140 feet). FA: Matt Cox, Randy Vogel, and Steve Emerson, 1976. (Chopped then rebolted later with additional bolts.)
63. **The Fiend** 5.9 R ★★ Start near the extreme left part of the right face, in a small hole, behind a boulder. A nasty 5.8 run-out leads to the first bolt; at the second bolt traverse straight right; then after the 3rd bolt, either go up and left to a 4th bolt (5.9), or up and right (5.7 R, a safer way for the second). Pro: 4 or 5 bolts. FA: Jim Wilson and Phil Warrender, June 1972.
64. **Mickey Mantle** 5.8 R ★★★ Start left of the middle of the face (40 feet right of *Chatsworth Chimney*). Several mantles lead up past 2 bolts. At the 2nd bolt move right, up, then left to the last bolt. Pro: 3 bolts. Rappel 90 feet or continue (5.0) up a short pitch to the top. FA: Jim Wilson and Phil Warrender, April 1972.
65. **Howard's Fifty-Footer** 5.10d R ★ Start about 20 feet up and right of *Mickey Mantle* and climb past 3 bolts to join *Mickey Mantle.* FA: Paul Morrell and Scott Erler, June 1992.
66. **Ultimatum** 5.10b or 5.10d R ★★ Start atop the pedestal about 30 feet right of *Mickey Mantle.* At the 2nd bolt climb out left, up, then back right to a large knob (5.10b) or straight up (5.10d). Pro: 3 bolts, slings for large knobs, 1.5- to 3-inch CDs for anchor. FA: John Long and Gib Lewis, April 1972.
67. **Pink Royd** 5.10d R ★★ Start about 40 feet down and right from *Ultimatum,* up loose flakes to a fixed pin. Continue up past two bolts to join *Sensuous Corner.* Pro: 2 Bolts, fixed pin, 1.5- to 3-inch CDs for anchor. FA: Eric Erickson and John Long, 1972.
68. **Pink Royd Direct Finish** 5.10c (TR) At the top, instead of moving right, climb straight up the arete to the top. FA: Bob Gaines, 1993.
69. **Sensuous Corner** 5.9 ★ Start about halfway up the right edge of the Smooth Sole Wall and climb a flared crack leading to a narrow prow with one bolt. Pro: to 3 inches. FA: Gib Lewis and G. Labadie, 1973.

SMOOTH SOLE WALLS—RIGHT SIDE

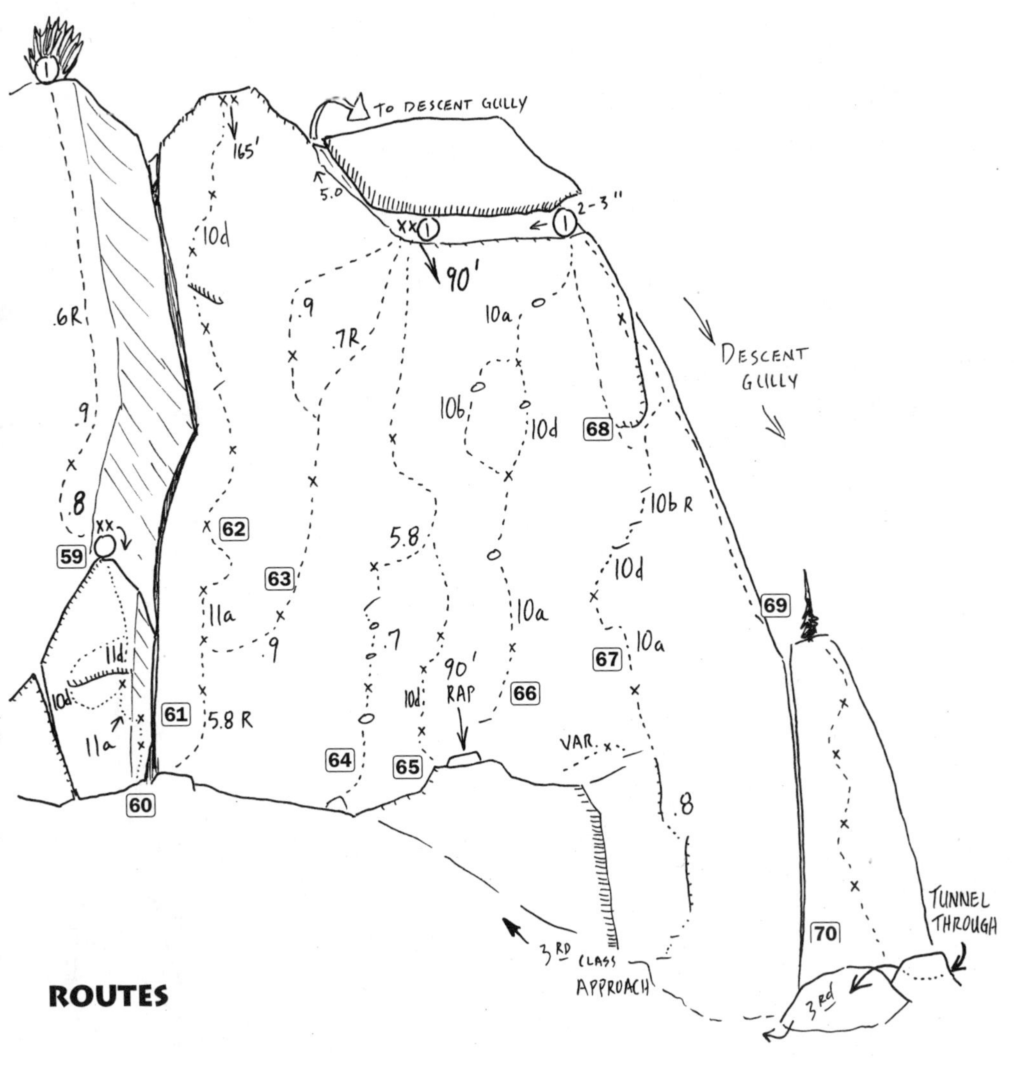

ROUTES

59. Over and Out 5.9 R★★
60. Steppin' Out 5.11d or 5.10d★★
61. Chatsworth Chimney 5.7 R★
62. Battle of the Bulge 5.11a R★★
63. The Fiend 5.9 R★★
64. Mickey Mantle 5.8 R★★★
65. Howard's Fifty-Footer 5.10d R★
66. Ultimatum 5.10b or 5.10d R★★
67. Pink Royd 5.10d R★★
68. Pink Royd Direct Finish 5.10c
69. Sensuous Corner 5.9★
70. Toxic Waltz 5.11c

70. **Toxic Waltz** 5.11c The four-bolt slab located at the extreme lower right edge of the Smooth Sole Wall. FA: Geoff Archer, Kay Buskirk, and Terry McCarthy, July 1989.

MY OBSESSION BOULDER

This boulder is located 40 yards below The Smooth Sole Walls. It can be approached either from the base of the Sunshine Face (traverse left and down along the base of the BSSW Face, some 25 feet below the ledge used to get to the base of the Smooth Sole Wall) then head downhill, or go down and somewhat right from the vicinity of *Chatsworth Chimney*. See Suicide Rock Overview Map.

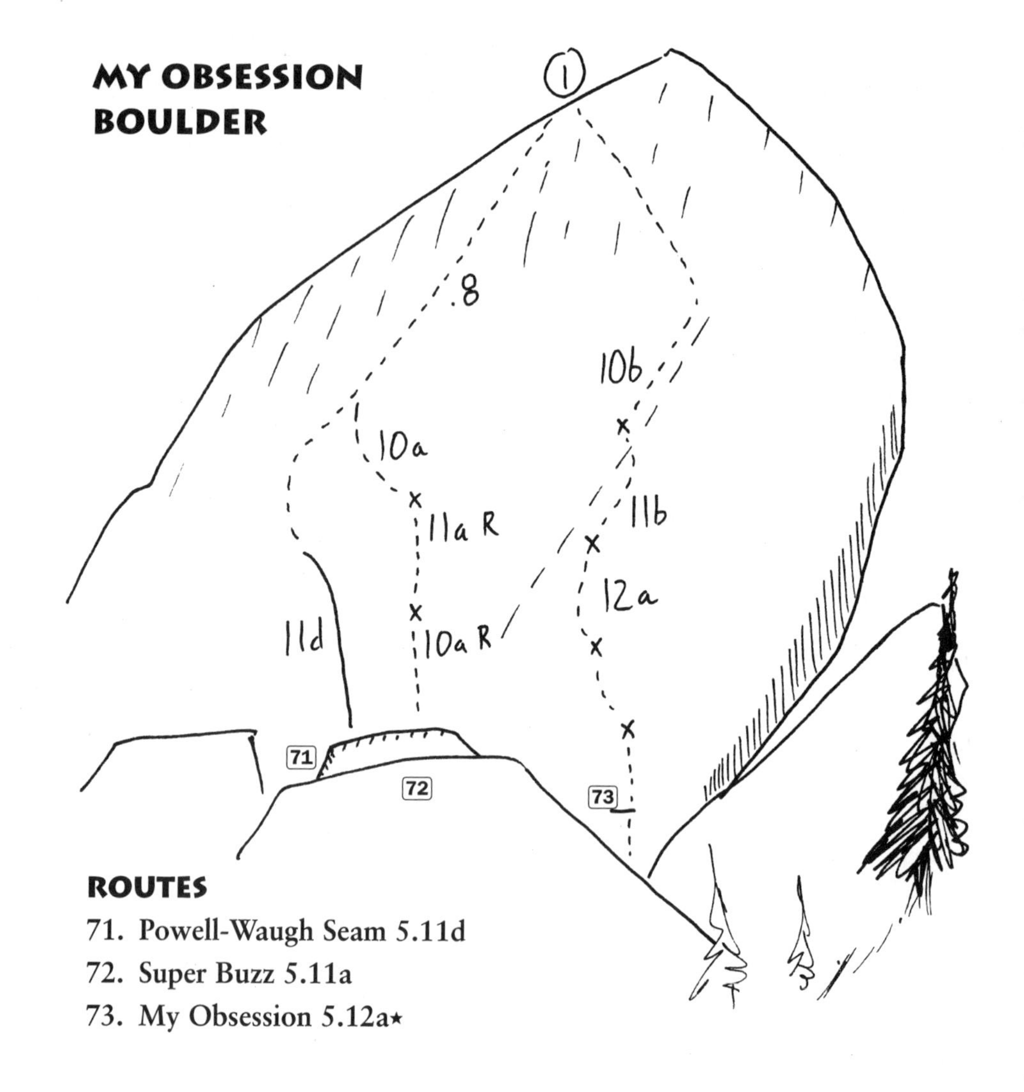

71. **Powell-Waugh Seam** 5.11d? (TR) The thin crack just left of *Super Buzz*. FA: Kevin Powell and Mike Waugh, 1979.
72. **Super Buzz** 5.11a R On the left side of the split boulder (facing Tahquitz) is this short, two-bolt face route. Clipping the bolts without breaking your ankles is a challenge in itself. FA: Eric Allen, Spring 1973.
73. **My Obsession** 5.12a ★ 20 feet right of *Super Buzz* is this short, 4-bolt test piece up a white crystal dike. FA: Darrell Hensel, 1979, (TR) First Lead: Hensel, 1987.

BELOW SMOOTH SOLE WALL (BSSW) FACE

The BSSW Face is located below the right-hand section of the Smooth Sole Wall. It can be approached either from the base of the Sunshine Face (traverse left and down along the base of the BSSW Face, some 25 feet below the ledge used to get to the base of the Smooth Sole Wall) or from the vicinity of *Chatsworth Chimney* (go down along the top of the BSSW Face). See Suicide Rock Overview Map.

74. **Endless Crack** 5.8 The left-curving crack that begins on the left side of the face. FA: Darrell Hensel and Kevin Powell, 1980.

BSSW FACE

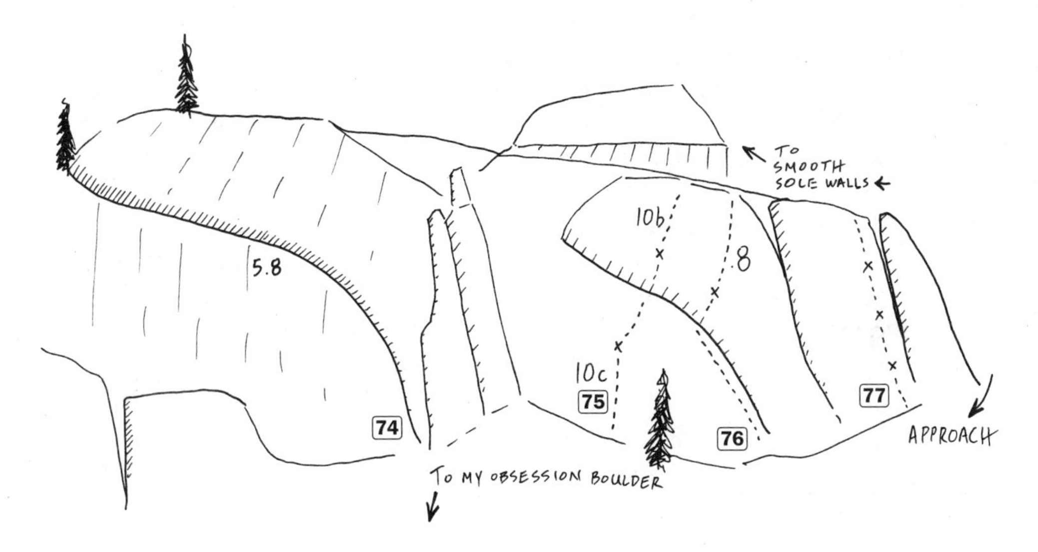

75. **Buffoonery** 5.10c This route starts left of a large pine tree located near the right side of the face. FA: Alan Bartlett, Steve Jennings, and Dave Black, December 1985.
76. **Shenanigans** 5.8 This route starts in a left-curving crack to the right of a large pine tree and left of a gully near the right side of the face. FA: Alan Bartlett, Steve Jennings, and Dave Black, December 1985.
77. **Mike and Larry's Excellent Adventure** 5.10c This 3-bolt route lies just left of a groove on the far right side of the face. FA: Mike Humphrey and Larry Kuechlin, June 1989.

THE SUNSHINE FACE

This is the largest face at Suicide; it faces southeast. In the summer, it is shaded in the late afternoon. The Sunshine Face has a large block sitting at its top (Paisano Pinnacle), and a large chimney system near its left side (*Paisano Chimney*). From the point where the trail up to Suicide meets the base of the rock (at the right side of The Buttress of Cracks), head left along the base of The Buttress of Cracks; a short uphill scramble leads to the Sunshine Face. See Suicide Rock Overview Map.

THE SUNSHINE FACE: UPPER LEFT SIDE

Walk along the base of the main Sunshine Face, then up the rock-filled gully. Go past the point where a deep chimney (*Paisano Chimney*) makes an obvious break in the Sunshine Face. The Left Side of the Sunshine Face lies below and left of Paisano Pinnacle.

Descent: Rappel (165 feet) from bolts near top of *Chisholm Trail* (easiest), or walk down and right to rappel anchors on a slab across from the top of Paisano Pinnacle. An 80-foot rappel gives access to a large ledge (the top of the main Sunshine Face); from here another 80-foot rappel, plus some downclimbing, leads to the base of the Weeping Wall.

78. **Tar and Feathers** (aka Woodpecker Crack) 5.11d ★ The arching, thin crack located across the notch from the top of the Limp Dick pillar. Sustained and difficult to protect. Pro: thin to 1.5-inch, including thin cams. FA: Spencer Lennard and Chris Robbins, 1977.
79. **Kill Them All** 5.10b/c On the right wall of the chimney leading up to the South Face is this nondescript, two-bolt face to a thin crack. FA: Don Bedford and Dan Haughelstine, July 1989.
80. **Miller Time** 5.10b 3-bolt slab to 2-bolt anchor left of Route 81. FA: Chris Miller and Cheryl Basye, August 2000.

SUNSHINE FACE—UPPER LEFT SIDE

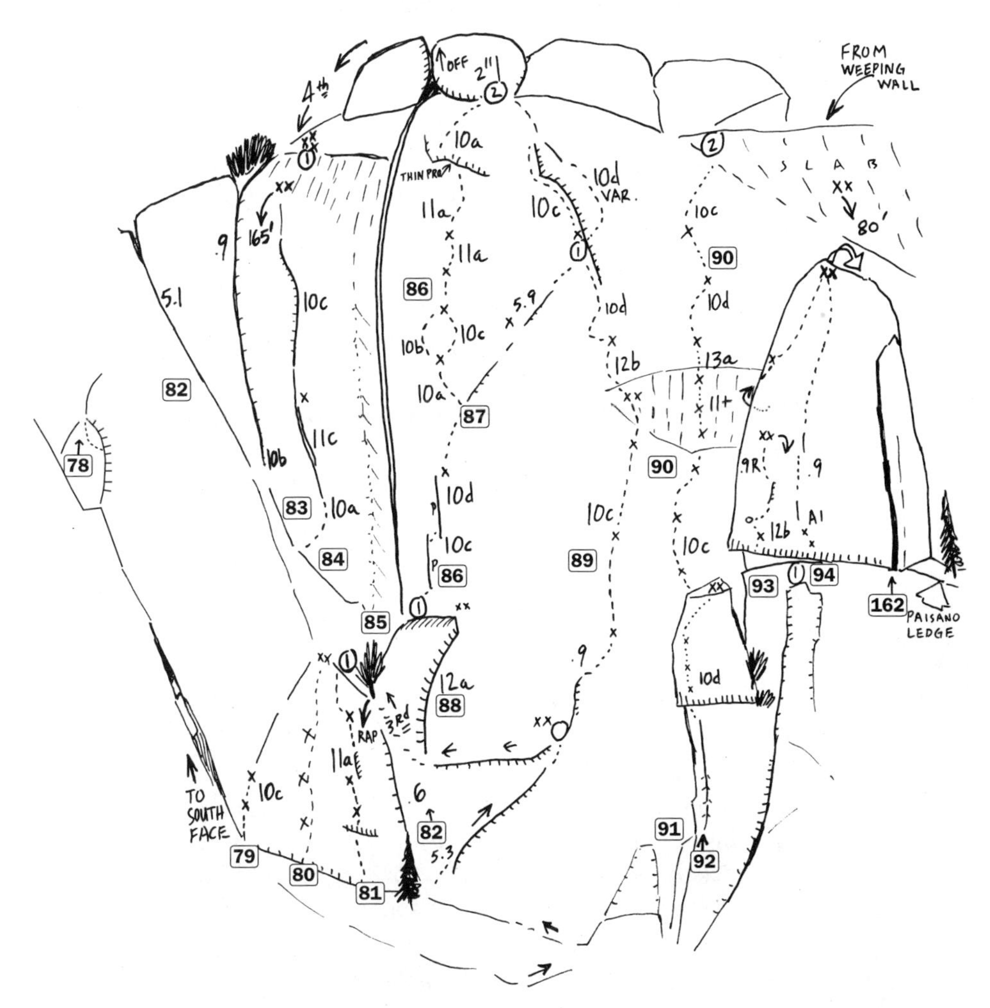

81. **Runout in Reverse** 5.11a/b At the start of the chimney, below a large tree, is this 3-bolt slab. FA: Troy Mayr and Charles Cole, July 1987.
82. **Garbage Gulch** 5.6 This is the loose gully left of *The Source*. FA: George Harr and others.
83. **The Source** 5.10b R This is mossy, flared chimney at the left edge of the face. So named as the first ascent party felt it was "the source of all evil." Pro: thin to 3 inches. FA: Ivan Couch and Mike Dent, early 1970s.
84. **Chisholm Trail** 5.11b/c ★★ This route lies in a right-facing flare between two long chimney systems (*The Source* and *B.C.'s Ouch Chimney*) on

the left side of the face. Watch out for bats living in the crack. Pro: several thin to 2-inch. FA: Fred Ziel, Eric Erickson and Tim Powell, 1977.

85. **B.C.'s Ouch Chimney** 5.9 The right-hand of the two chimneys. Pro: to 3.5 inches. FA: Ivan Couch, Mike Cohen, and Bob Kamps, early 1970s.
86. **The Man Who Fell to Earth** 5.11a ★★★ Scramble up a series of ledges (just right of *B.C.'s Ouch Chimney*) to the start of the route, a shallow discontinuous thin crack. Pro: 4 bolts, thin to 1.5-inch CDs. FA: Fred Ziel and Tim Powell, 1978.
87. **Starburst Variation** 5.9 R? From the first bolt, climb up and right on a ramp to a bolt; a short traverse right leads to the belay on *Caliente.*
88. **Yaniro's Arch** 5.12a/b (TR) The arching dihedral below and right of the start of *Man Who Fell to Earth*. FA: Tony Yaniro, 1978?
89. **Caliente** 5.12c ★★★ A Suicide Rock test piece. About 40 feet left of *Paisano Chimney,* scramble up and right to a ledge/ramp. Set up the belay here. Pro: 7 bolts, thin to 2 inches. FA: John Bachar, 1978.
90. **Someone You're Not** 5.13a ★★★ Start up *Paisano Chimney,* but belay on a pillar at a two-bolt belay. The second pitch involves steep face climbing past 9 bolts and one of the area's most baffling cruxes. Pro: 9 bolts, plus several to 2 inches for the anchor. FA: Darrell Hensel, November 1991.
91. **Paisano Chimney** 5.8 The large chimney that starts below, and then forms the left side of Paisano Pinnacle. Pro: to 4 inches. FA: Pat Callis and Lee Harrell, May 1968.
92. **Clockwork Orange** 5.10d ★ Begin from the alcove at the base of *Paisano Chimney.* This is directly below *Caliente* and *Someone You're Not.* Climb the crack to the 3-bolt arete on the orange block. 2-bolt, 100-foot rappel. Pro: to 1.5 inches. FA: Kelly Vaught, Bob Gaines, and Frank Bentwood, July 1998.
93. **Hit It, Ethel** 5.12b R ★ From the ledge under the outside face of Paisano Pinnacle, horrendous moves over the roof lead to a 5.8 or 5.9 run out and a 2-bolt anchor about 40 feet up. The crux is best protected by employing a double-rope belay, with one rope clipped to the bolt, and the other rope "tossed" over the obvious knob. FA: Tom Gilje, Terry Ayers, and Mike Lechlinski, 1991.
94. **Euphoria** 5.9 A1 ★ One of Suicide's last remaining aid routes. Just right of *Paisano Chimney,* scramble up third class and begin at a massive flake system. To surmount the overhang, two bolts and one piton can be used for aid. Above the roof, easy, but spectacular face climbing leads to the top. FA: Ivan Couch and Mike Dent, 1970.

Darrell Hensel on Someone You're Not *(5.13a), Suicide.* PHOTO BY KEVIN POWELL

MAIN SUNSHINE FACE

All the following routes lie on the main section of the Sunshine Face, to the right of *Paisano Chimney.* All routes end at or near a large ledge to the right of Paisano Pinnacle (Paisano Ledge).

Rappel Descents:

1. Rap (80 feet) and downclimb (see topo) *Bye Gully;* it leads down to the base of the Weeping Wall. Hike around the base of The Buttress of Cracks from here.

2. Look for bolts at the east brink of the large ledge atop the Sunshine Face (hidden from view by a boulder). Three 100-foot rappels (or two 165-foot rappels) from here reach the ground.

95. **Gates of Delirium** 5.11c ★ The first pitch is a somewhat popular 4-bolt slab and ends on a large ledge with a huge pine tree. From here, one can scramble off to the left (4th class), or rap 75 feet from the tree. The rarely-visited second pitch (5.10c R ?) begins with face climbing leading to a bolt and a steep flake system. Pro: many thin to 2.5 inches. FA: Tony Yaniro and Richard Leversee, January 1976.

96. **The Drain Pipe** 5.11b ★★ Start on the ledge atop the first pitch of *Gates of Delirium.* 1. Move right past a bolt to gain an S-shaped crack that leads to a small belay ledge. 2. A jamcrack that leads to a hand traverse right under Paisano Pinnacle. Pro: to 4.5 inches. FA: (5.7 A1) Lee Harrell and Charlie Raymond, March 1967. FFA: John Long, Richard Harrison, and Rick Accomazzo, 1973.

97. **Ishi** 5.12d R ★★★ Remarkable for its variety, although rarely done, due to one of the area's thinnest cruxes. About 50 feet right of *Gates of Delirium,* behind a large oak tree, climb past a 4-bolt ladder then up a narrow, 40-foot corner (protection difficult without pitons) to a small ledge and possible belay. Continue up another 7-bolt ladder to a 2-bolt belay. (This upper section can be accessed from the ledge atop *Gates of Delirium's* first pitch.) The last pitch is a classic 5.10 lieback up a thin flake. Pro: to 2.5 inches. FA: (A3) Tony Zeek, et al. FA: (upper section, 5.11c) Gib Lewis, Rick Accomazzo, and Jim Wilson, March 1976. FFA: Entire route, Darrell Hensel, 1985.

98. **Quiet Desperation** 5.11d ★★ From the belay at the top of *Iron Cross*'s first pitch, clip *Iron Cross*'s first bolt, then diagonal up and left on a razor-thin flake past a bolt to join *Ishi.* Pro: thin to 2 inches. FA: Rick Accomazzo, Gib Lewis, and Jim Wilson, March 1976.

SUNSHINE FACE/WEEPING WALL AREA OVERVIEW
rap xx
To
North Face
trail descent
Paisano
Pinnacle
185
Bye Gully
xx
xx
Weeping
Wall
Rebolting
Face
Main
Sunshine
Face
185
Escalator
103
East
Buttress

SUNSHINE FACE—LEFT

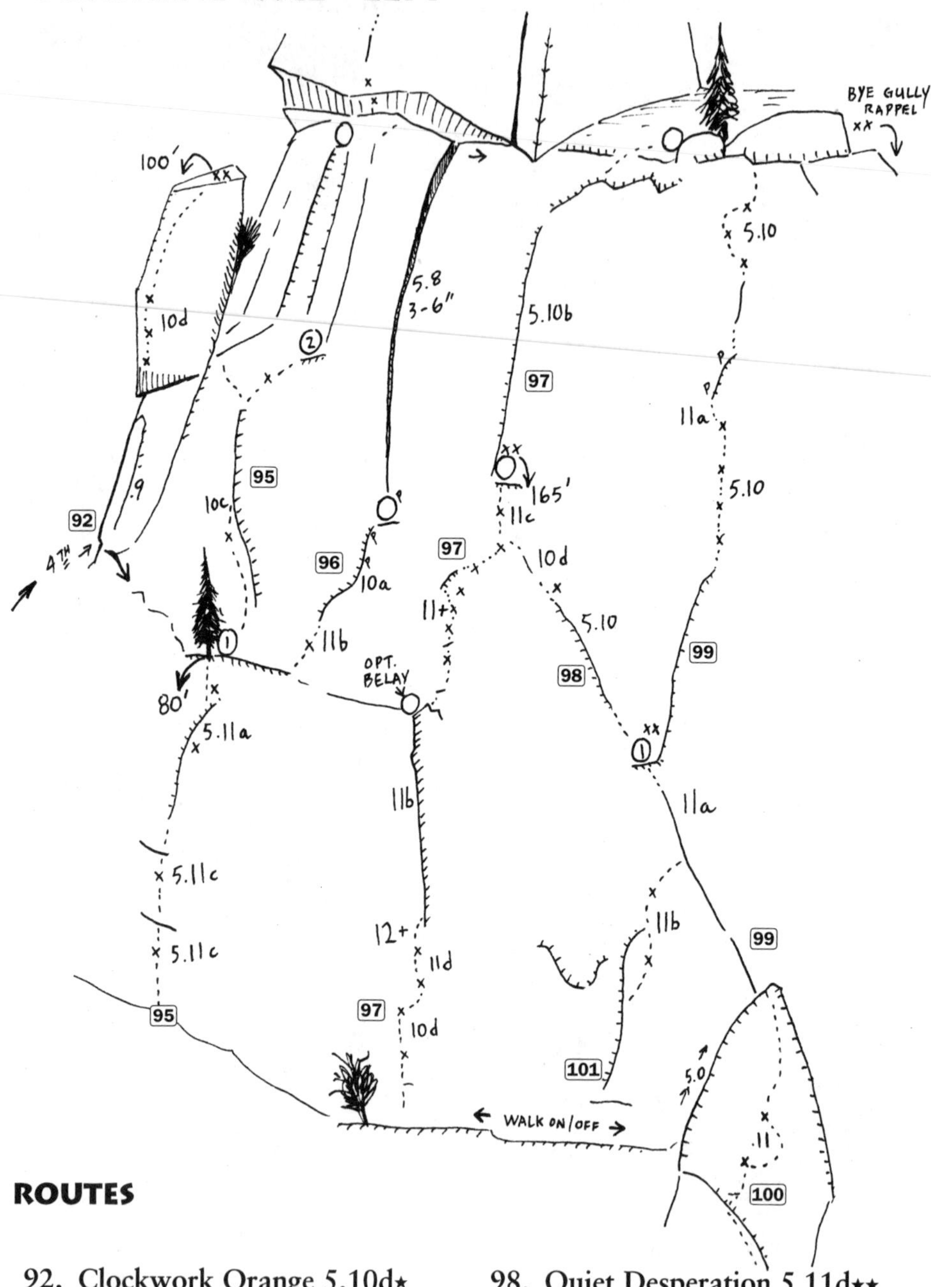

ROUTES

92. Clockwork Orange 5.10d★
95. Gates of Delirium 5.11c★
96. The Drain Pipe 5.11b★★
97. Ishi 5.12d R★★★
98. Quiet Desperation 5.11d★★
99. Iron Cross 5.11a★★★
100. Arrowhead 5.11a/b
101. Red Rain 5.11b★★

SUNSHINE FACE/WEEPING WALL RAPPEL DESCENT ROUTES

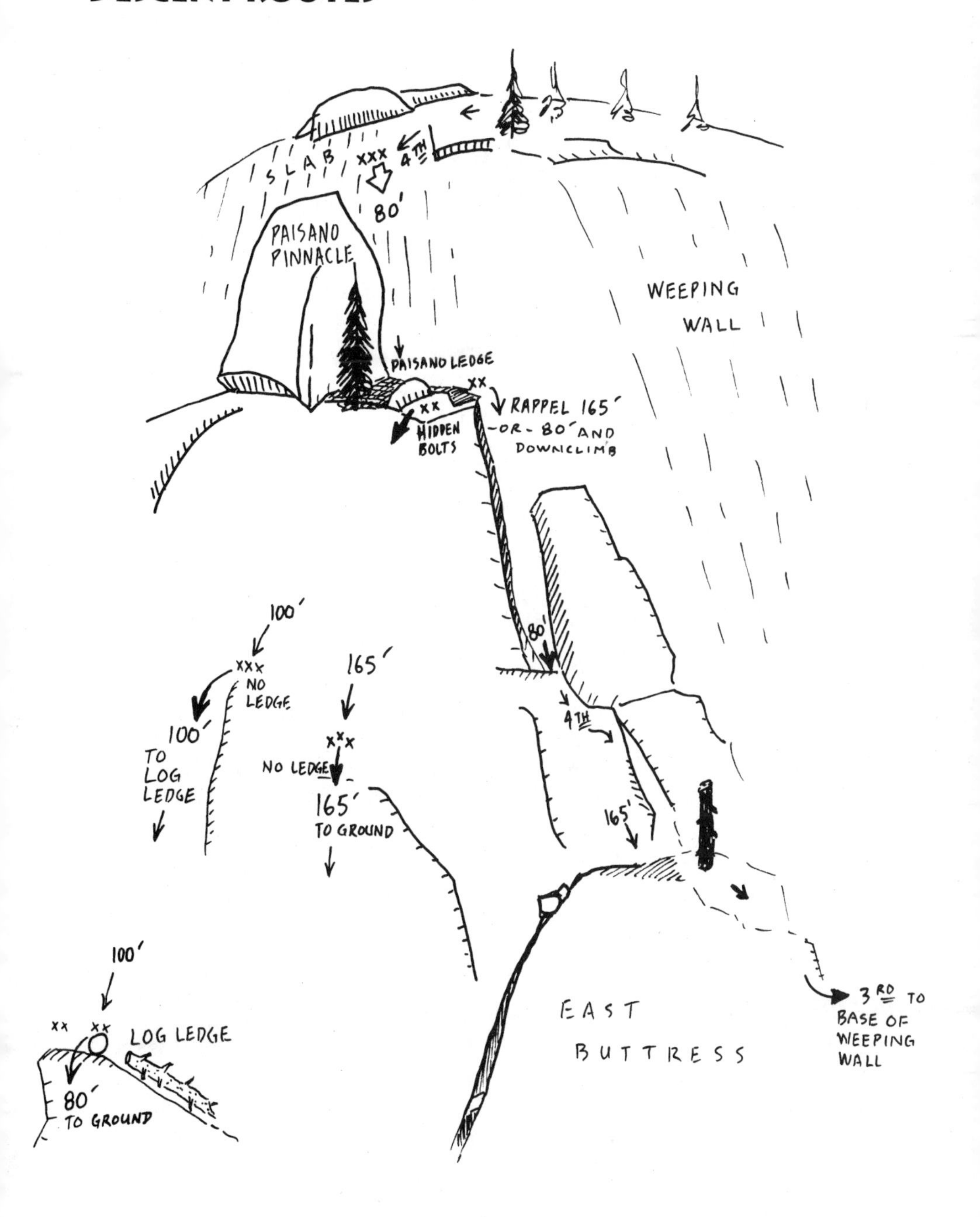

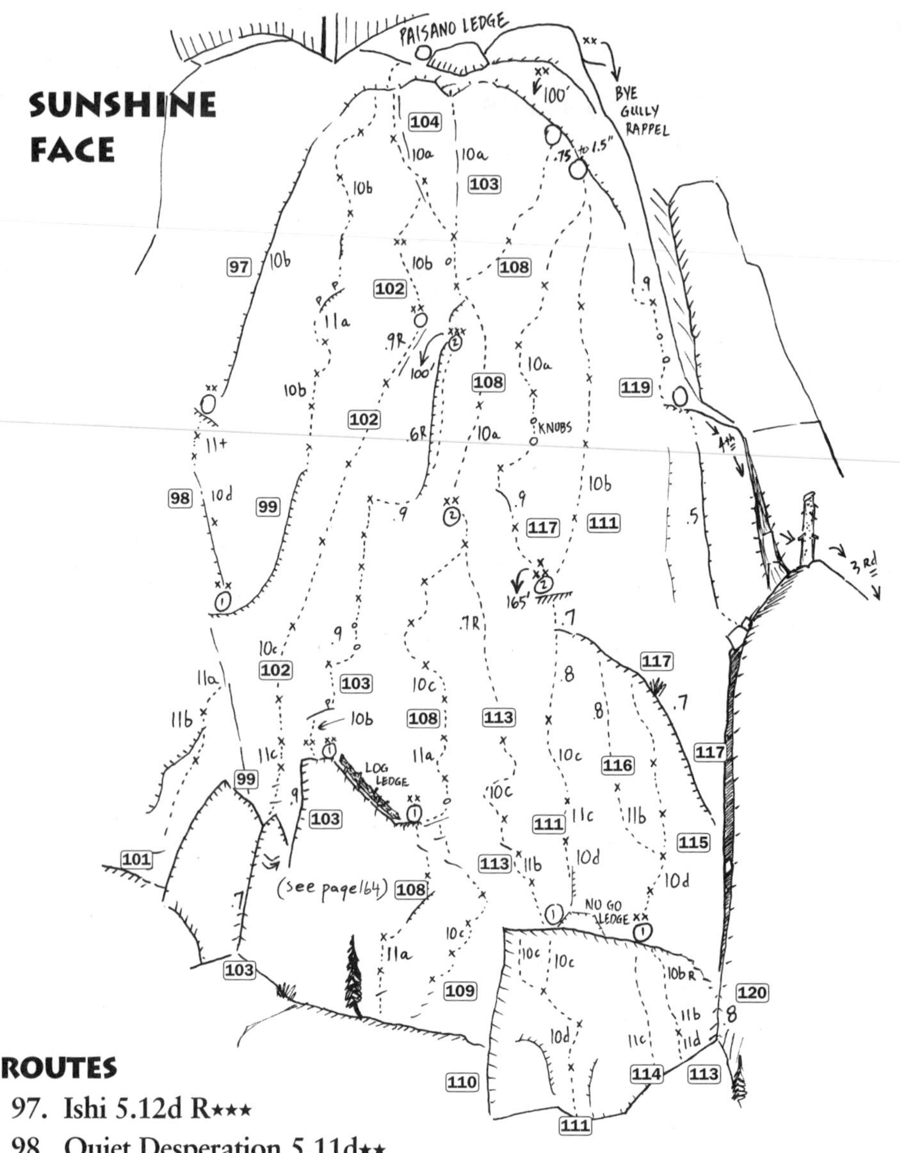

ROUTES

97. Ishi 5.12d R★★★
98. Quiet Desperation 5.11d★★
99. Iron Cross 5.11a★★★
100. Arrowhead 5.11a/b
101. Red Rain 5.11b★★
102. Moondance 5.11c★★★
103. Sundance 5.10b★★★
104. Sundike 5.10a★★★
108. Valhalla 5.11a★★★
109. Nirvana 5.11a★★★
110. First Pitch 5.8
111. New Generation 5.11c★★★
113. Race with the Devil 5.11d R★★
114. Speaking in Tongues 5.11d★
115. Hesitation Direct 5.10d★★
116. Voodoo Child (variation to Hesitation Direct) 5.11b R★★
117. Hesitation 5.10a★★
119. The Stretch 5.9★
120. Buttress Chimney 5.8

99. **Iron Cross** 5.11a ★★★ A magnificent route on superb rock. To start, either traverse right from *Ishi* on a long ledge to a massive flake, or (more rope drag) start on *Sundance,* but head up and slightly left to the right side of the flake. 1. Up the flake, then follow the left-leaning, thin crack (somewhat difficult to protect) to a ledge. 2. A long face pitch past 7 bolts and 2 fixed pins. Pro: many thin, up to 1.5-inch. FA: (5.10, A2) Charlie Raymond and Pat Callis, May 1968. FFA Pitch 1: Gib Lewis and Tobin Sorenson, 1973. FFA Complete Route: John Long and Richard Harrison, July 1973.

100. **Arrowhead** 5.11a/b Beginning at the base of *Sundance*, move left up a crack, then step right and climb the face of the immense flake past two bolts. A huge sling on the tip of the flake serves as an anchor. The last climber can remove it and downclimb the chimney to the ledge at the base of *Ishi.* Pro: to 3 inches. FA: Bob Gaines, September 1999.

101. **Red Rain** 5.11b ★★ Begin just left of the block; climb a thin corner to two bolts, then move up and right to join the crux of the first pitch of *Iron Cross*. Pro: thin. FA: Dave Evans and Darrell Hensel, August 1986.

102. **Moondance** 5.11c ★★★ Very sustained, on beautiful rock. 1. Start on *Sundance,* then climb the gold face left of Log Ledge. You can also traverse left to the third bolt from the Log Ledge belay for an easier (11a) variation. The 7th bolt is doubled for belaying (100 feet to Log Ledge). 2. Up and left past another set of double bolts to join the *Sundike* finish to the top. FA: (traversing left from Log Ledge) Dave Evans and Craig Fry, June 1986. FA Direct Start: Darrell Hensel and Dave Evans, September 1986.

103. **Sundance** 5.10b ★★★ A scenic cruise up the Sunshine Face. 1. Begin at a large ledge, up a corner, then move right to a short but strenuous lieback (5.9, 4-inch pro) to Log Ledge. 2. A steep, thin face move off Log Ledge leads to knobby face climbing; from the last bolt, traverse right to a corner, cross over it, then up (5.6 run-out) to a bolt belay. 3. Straight up past two bolts to a tricky thin crack (or up *Sundike*). Pro: thin to 4 inches. FA: Pat Callis, Charlie Raymond, and Larry Reynolds, January 1967.

104. **Sundike** 5.10a ★★★ From the 2nd bolt on the last pitch of *Sundance,* climb up and left up a white dike past 2 more bolts. FA: Clark Jacobs and Bob Harvey, March 1984.

105. **Sundance Arete** 5.12b R Start a few feet right of *Sundance* at a flake with a bolt, then up the arete past 2 more bolts, moving right above the last bolt, then up to Log Ledge. Pro: CDs to 0.75 inch. FA: Bob Gaines and Dave Mayville, September 1993.

106. **Sidewinder** 5.11d/12a Just right of *Sundance*, climb a short, thin crack past two very-difficult-to-clip bolts (12-); from the 3rd bolt, traverse

SUNSHINE FACE— CENTER BASE DETAIL

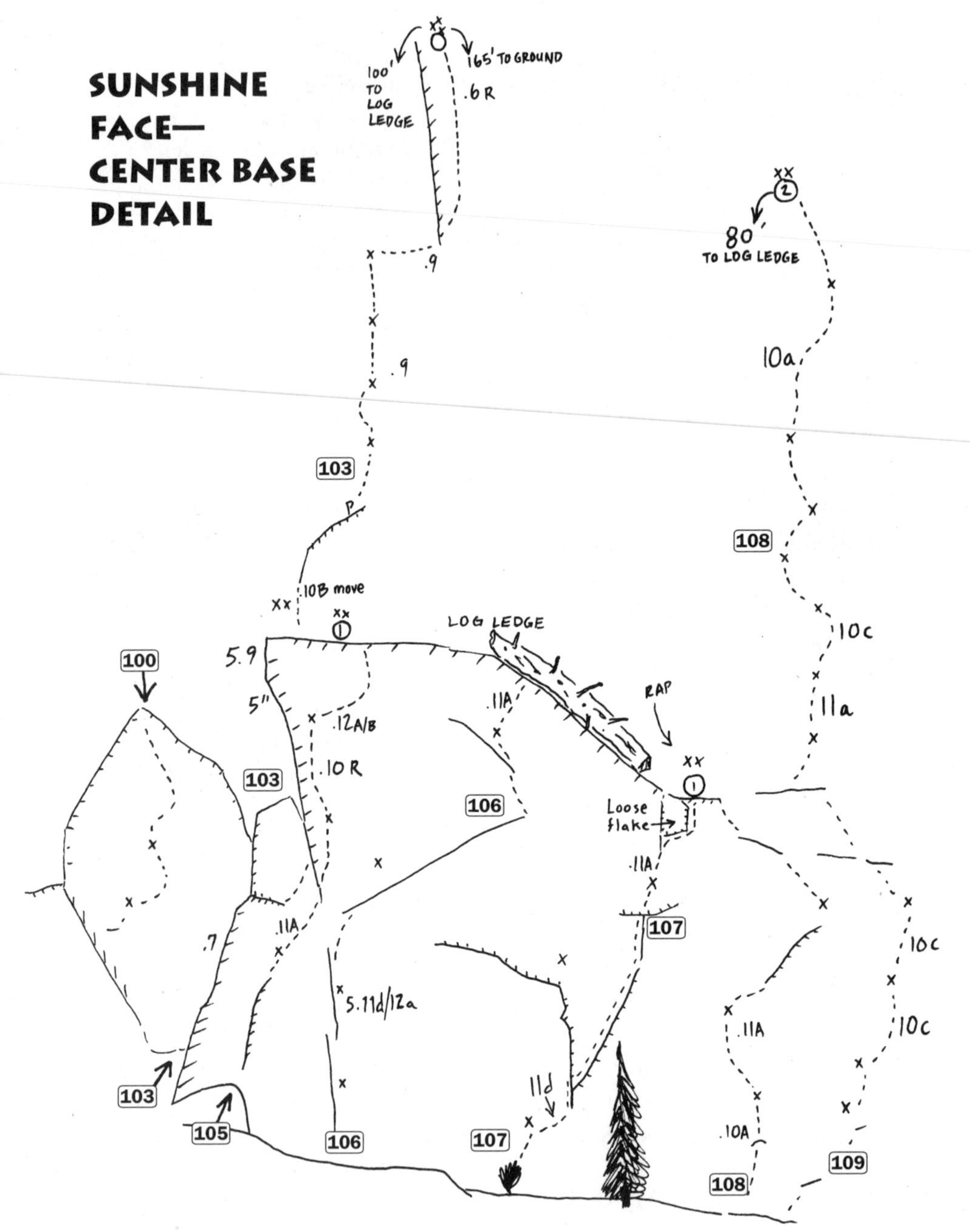

ROUTES

100. Arrowhead 5.11a/b
103. Sundance 5.10b★★★
105. Sundance Arete 5.12b R
106. Sidewinder 5.11d/12a
107. Bukatude 5.11d
108. Valhalla 5.11a★★★
109. Nirvana 5.11a★★★

Darrell Hensel on the second pitch of Valhalla *(5.11), Sunshine Face, Suicide.*
PHOTO BY KEVIN POWELL

right out a crack/ramp, then up past another bolt (11a) to Log Ledge. Pro: thin to 1.5 inches. FA: Don Bedford, Dan Haughelstine, and Greg Burroughs, February 1991.

107. **Bukatude** 5.11d Originally climbed by John Long via a direct start, a broken hold has rendered this line impossible. By traversing in from the left past a bolt, the line was resurrected at an easier grade. At the top, move right to avoid a very loose flake, then up to the two-bolt *Valhalla* belay. Pro: thin to 3 inches. FA Direct: John Long and Bob Gaines, 1985. FA: (traverse from left) Bob Gaines, September 1993.

108. **Valhalla** 5.11a ★★★ In the 1970s, the prerequisite to join the infamous Stonemasters was to climb this route. Start on a broad ledge near the center of the Sunshine Face, a short distance right of a small pine tree. 1. 3 bolts to Log Ledge. 2. Go right on a crack/ledge, then up past bolts to a hanging belay. 3. Past a bolt to the 1st bolt on the 3rd pitch of *Sundance,* then up and right past one more bolt to the top. Pro: 0.75 to 1.5 inches. FA: Ivan Couch, Larry Reynolds, and Mike Dent, November 1970.

109. **Nirvana** 5.11a ★★★ Start just right of *Valhalla* and climb a series of scoops past 4 bolts, then climb directly up to the crux of *Valhalla's* second pitch (7 more bolts, 11 bolts total). FA: Bob Gaines and John Long, August 1986.

110. **First Pitch** 5.8 This short, left-facing dihedral ends on No Go Ledge. Pro: to 3 inches. FA: Pat Callis, Charlie Raymond, and Trish Raymond, October 1966.

111. **New Generation** 5.11c ★★★ A new generation of climbers (Mike Graham and Tobin Sorenson; 17 and 18 years old) climbed this prized classic in July 1973. 1. Beginning just right of Route 110, 3 bolts to No Go Ledge. 2. Unprotected 5.10 leads to face climbing past 3 bolts to *Hesitation* belay. 3. Up and right past 4 bolts to the top. Pro: thin to 2 inches.

112. **My Generation variation** 5.11a (TR) ★ From the second bolt on the first pitch of *New Gen,* climb up and right to the *Race with the Devil* anchor. FA: Bob Gaines, July 1992.

113. **Race with the Devil** 5.11d R ★★ 1. 30 feet right of *New Gen,* a lone bolt marks the first pitch, which has a serious 5.10 run-out at the top. 2. Begin left of *New Gen,* face climbing up and left past 4 bolts to unprotected (5.7) face up a "finlike dike" to the join 2nd pitch of *Valhalla* at the last bolt. Above the fourth bolt you can also move up and right (5.8 R) to the *Hesitation* belay. Pro: thin to 2 inches. FA: Tony Yaniro, 1979.

Darrell Hensel and Tim Powell on Voodoo Child *(5.11), Suicide.*
PHOTO BY KEVIN POWELL

114. **Speaking in Tongues** 5.11d (TR) ★ Climb the clean, white face at an indistinct vertical dike between *Race with the Devil* and *New Generation.* FA: Bob Gaines, June 1984.

115. **Hesitation Direct** 5.10d ★★ From the two-bolt belay at the right end of No Go Ledge, climb past 4 bolts to the *Hesitation* belay. FA: John Long, Jim Wood, and Clark Jacobs, 1975.

116. **Voodoo Child** (Variation to Hesitation Direct) 5.11b R ★★ Near the second bolt on *Hesitation Direct,* traverse up and left to a bolt, then up (5.8 R) to the *Hesitation* belay. FA: John Long and Eric Erickson, 1978.

117. **Hesitation** 5.10a ★★ 1. From about 80 feet up *Buttress Chimney,* move left up a ramp/flake to a bolted belay. 2. Climb up and left, then back up and right, passing 5 bolts and a couple of tied-off chickenheads. Pro: small to 2 inches. FA: Pat Callis (rope solo!), July 1967.

118. **Deep Vertical Smiles** 5.10c R A girdle traverse of the upper Sunshine Face. Begin at the top of *Buttress Chimney* (base of *Bye Gully,* left of Weeping Wall) and traverse out left past the *Hesitation* belay to the *Valhalla* belay. Continue left, crossing *Sundance,* then exiting up *Iron Cross.* FA: Rob Muir and Tobin Sorenson, 1974.

119. **The Stretch** 5.9 ★ Begin at the top of *Buttress Chimney* (base of *Bye Gully* route), up and left from The Weeping Wall. Drop down a few feet, then climb an easy (5.5) crack system for about 80 feet to a ledge. The second pitch ascends the airy crest past a bolt, then up and left to a crack leading to Paisano Ledge. Most parties do just the second pitch. Pro: to 3 inches. FA: Pat Callis, Charlie and Trish Raymond, November 1966.

120. **Buttress Chimney** 5.8 Primarily used as an approach to No Go Ledge, *Hesitation,* and *Insomnia;* the crux is at the bottom. Pro: to 3 inches. FA: Pat Callsand and Lee Harrell, 1967.

THE BUTTRESS OF CRACKS

The Buttress of Cracks is the lowest point of Suicide Rock, and the approach trail ends near its right side. From the point where the trail up to Suicide meets the base of the rock, head left along the base of the Buttress of Cracks; a short uphill scramble leads to a small, flat spot near the left end of the Buttress (*The Pirate,* a very thin, straight crack, starts here). The Sunshine Face lies just around the corner to the left. See Suicide Rock Overview Map.

Descent from the top of The East Buttress: Scramble up and then right along the summit, then down a notch (the top of *East Buttress Gully*), then down class 3 to the base of The Weeping Wall.

Descent from East Buttress Ledge: Rappel 130 feet from bolts at the base of *Bocomaru* (100 feet if you swing left at the base), or rappel 80 feet from a

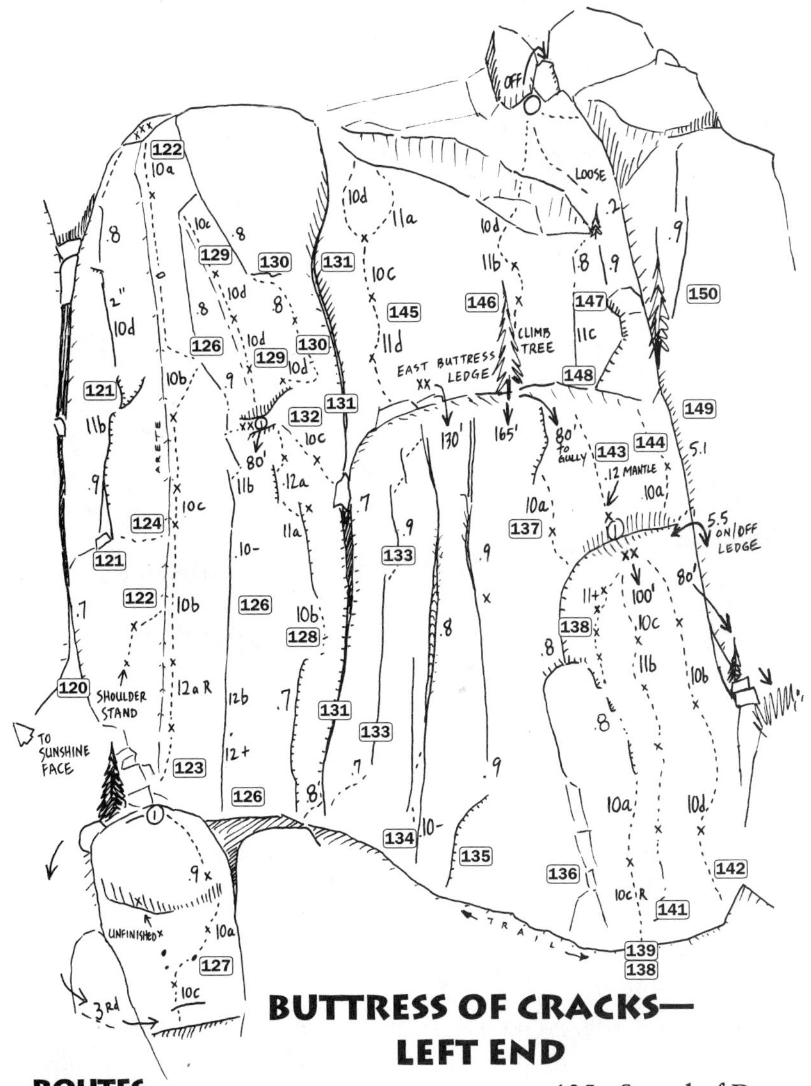

BUTTRESS OF CRACKS—LEFT END

ROUTES

120. Buttress Chimney 5.8
121. Insomnia 5.11b/c★★★
122. Double Exposure 5.10b, A1★★
123. Double Exposure Direct Start 5.12a R
124. Overexposed Variation 5.10c R
126. The Pirate 5.12c/d★★★
127. Bluebeard 5.10c
128. Walk the Plank 5.12a★
129. Pieces of Eight 5.10d R★
130. Swashbuckler 5.10d
131. Captain Hook 5.8★
132. Buccaneer 5.10c
133. Pass Time 5.9
134. Frustration 5.10a★
135. Sword of Damocles 5.9
136. The Hernia 5.8★
137. Hernia Direct Finish 5.10a
138. Bacon Bits 5.11b/c R★
139. Club Sandwich 5.10d R
141. Winter Solstice 5.11c★
142. Arcy Farcy 5.10d/11a★
143. Arcy Farcy Mantle 5.12a R
144. Arcy Farcy Direct Finish 5.7
145. Bocomaru 5.11d★
146. When You're Sap 5.11b
147. Aqualung 5.9★
148. Aqualung Direct 5.11c R
149. East Buttress Gully 5.2
150. Narcolepsy 5.9

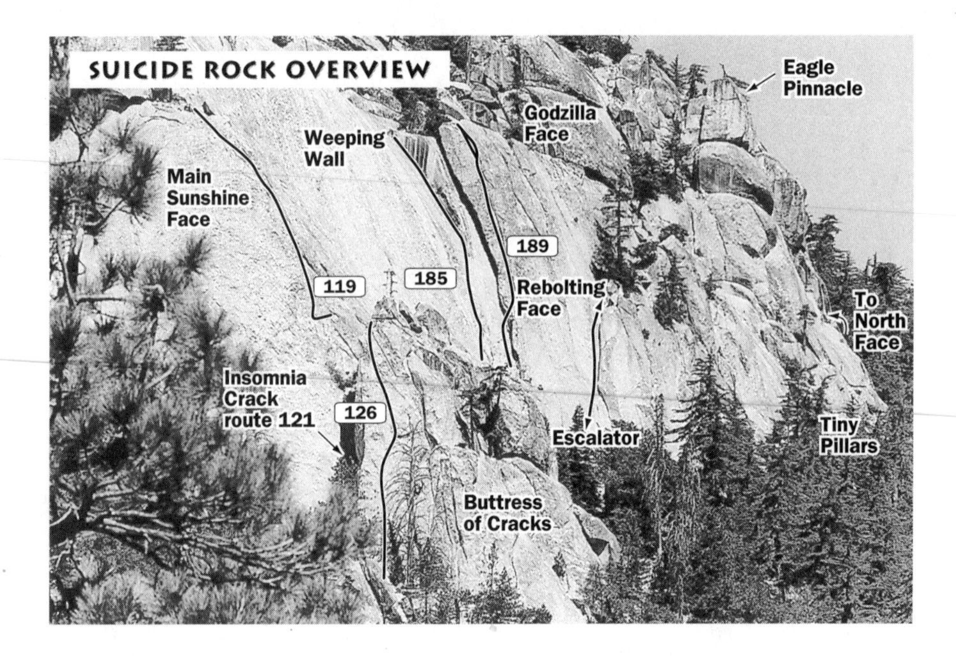

large pine tree (somewhat diagonally) to reach *East Buttress Gully* and the ledge at the base of *Spatula.*

121. **Insomnia** 5.11b/c ★★★ This is perhaps the finest crack climb in all of Idyllwild. It lies around the corner (left end) of The Buttress of Cracks and faces the Sunshine Face. Start on a small ledge about 25 feet up *Buttress Chimney.* Pro: several 1- to 3-inches. FA: (A3) Pat Callis and Larry Reynolds, June 1967. FFA: Jim Erickson and Scott Stewart, March 1972.

122. **Double Exposure** 5.10b, A1 ★★ This route ascends the spectacular arete formed by the left edge of The Buttress of Cracks The original route starts around the corner from *The Pirate,* using a shoulder stand and aid from two bolts to reach the arete. Pro: to 1 inch. FA: John Long, 1975.

123. **Double Exposure Direct Start** 5.12a R Climb the arete directly from the base, past two widely-spaced bolts. FA: (TR) Tony Yaniro, 1978. First lead, Terry Ayers, 1990.

124. **Overexposed variation** 5.10c R Traverse right from the flared chimney on *Insomnia* to the third bolt on *Double Exposure.* FA: Jonny Woodward, 1985.

125. **Sleepwalker variation** 5.10c (TR) After the crux of *Insomnia,* climb right to meet the upper section of *Double Exposure.* FA: Bob Gaines, August 1993.

126. **The Pirate** 5.12c/d ★★★ This is the very obvious, very thin crack that starts off the flat spot near the left end of The Buttress of Cracks. The first pitch can be aided clean (A2). The 2nd pitch moves up and left (5.9) to a 5.8 crack. Pro: many thin nuts and CDs to 2 inches. FA: (5.8,A2) Pat Callis and Larry Reynolds, June 1967. FFA: Tony Yaniro, 1978.
127. **Bluebeard** 5.10c This 3-bolt route lies on a small face below the flat area at the base of *The Pirate*. It is best approached by scrambling downhill from the base of *The Pirate*. The initial move requires creative belaying/spotting. FA: Bob Gaines and others, June 1989.
128. **Walk the Plank** 5.12a ★ Start up a lieback just right of *The Pirate*. Pro: thin to 3 inches, 2 bolts. FA: (5.10, A4) Bob and Yvonne Gaines, July 1987. FFA: Darrell Hensel, May 1989.
129. **Pieces of Eight** 5.10d R ★ From atop the first pitch of *The Pirate,* go straight up past 3 bolts, finish on *The Pirate*. Pro: to 3 inches. FA: Bob Gaines and Mike Van Volkom, June 1987.
130. **Swashbuckler** 5.10d From atop the first pitch of *The Pirate,* go right to an arete, left at a horizontal crack, then up a crack. Pro: to 3 inches. FA: Bob Gaines and Mike Confer, June 1987.
131. **Captain Hook** 5.8 ★ A few tricky face moves gain entry to the obvious deep chimney 25 feet right of *The Pirate*. Near the top of the first lead you encounter the infamous "Crocodile's Head." The second pitch is a slippery chimney dubbed "The Throat." Pro: to 3 inches. FA: Charlie Raymond and Larry Reynolds, October 1966.
132. **Buccaneer** 5.10c This route starts atop the first pitch of *Captain Hook*. One bolt protects moves to *The Pirate* belay. A good way of approaching *Pieces of Eight* and *Swashbuckler* or to toprope *The Pirate*. FA: Unknown.
133. **Pass Time** 5.9 Follow the discontinuous crack system just right of the *Captain Hook* chimney. Pro: thin to 2 inches. FA: Phil Gleason and Lee Harrell, March 1968.
134. **Frustration** 5.10a ★ Begin at the twin vertical cracks a short distance downhill from *Captain Hook* and climb up into an awkward groove. Pro: thin to 2.5 inches. FA: Pat Callis and Lee Harrell, March 1968.
135. **Sword of Damocles** 5.9 The faint crack system to the left of *Hernia*. Pro: thin to 2 inches. FA: J. Gosling and Lee Harrell, March 1968.
136. **The Hernia** 5.8 ★ Start just left of the lowest point of The Buttress of Cracks, climb a flake system up to a small overlap, then continue up a crack that curves up and right to a two-bolt anchor on a sloping ledge. (100-foot rappel) A 5.4 traverse right leads to *East Buttress Gully*. Pro: thin to 3 inches. FA: Lee Harrell and S. Wood, August 1967.

137. **Hernia Direct Finish** 5.10a Go straight up past a bolt where the regular route traverse right (165-foot pitch). FA: Ivan Couch and Mike Dent, 1969.

138. **Bacon Bits** 5.11b/c R★ aka Razor Games. Begin with a 5.10 run-out to reach a bolt just right of *The Hernia,* then climb a flake system to a face with 4 bolts leading up and right to a 2-bolt anchor. Pro: 0.5 to 1.5 inches. (100-foot rap.) FA: Russ Clune, October 1987, first lead Kelly Vaught, Clark Jacobs, and Rick Harlin, November 2000.

139. **Club Sandwich** 5.10d R Begin with a 5.10 run out to reach a bolt just right of *The Hernia,* then climb a flake system up and left to join *The Hernia* at its crux. Pro: 0.5 to 3 inches. FA: (without the bolt) Chongo Brothers, 1989.

140. **Ham Sandwich** 5.10b From 1st bolt on *Winter Solstice,* head left to a flake that joins *The Hernia*. Pro: to 3 inches. FA: Jim Hoagland and Dick Bird, early 1980s.

141. **Winter Solstice** 5.11c ★ This is the 4-bolt face just left of *Arcy Farcy.* (100-foot rappel) FA: Hamilton Collins and Greg Rzonka, December 21, 1985.

142. **Arcy Farcy** 5.10d/11a ★ The 3-bolt slab climb on the right-hand margin of the lowest section of Buttress of Cracks. Getting harder over the years as tiny flakes disappear (100-foot rappel). FA: Mike Kaiser, Greg Bender, Phil Warrender, and Jim Wilson, 1972.

143. **Arcy Farcy Mantle** 5.12a R This is the sloping mantle move over the bulge directly above the *Arcy Farcy* belay. One bolt provides rather inadequate protection. FA: John Long, 1974.

144. **Arcy Farcy Direct Finish** 5.7 From the right end of the ledge climb up past one bolt to the big pine tree. FA: Malcolm Best, mid-80s.

UPPER EAST BUTTRESS LEDGE ROUTES

Many of the routes on The Buttress of Cracks end on a large ledge (East Buttress Ledge). The following routes start on this ledge. The easiest approach is to climb *East Buttress Gully* to the right end of the ledge. Descent is off the back of formation where *East Buttress Gully* ends, then down and right to base of The Weeping Wall.

145. **Bocomaru** 5.11d ★ 3-bolt face beginning from the far left side of the ledge. FA: Clark Jacobs and Bob Bolton, 1983.

146. **When You're Sap** 5.11b Near the middle of the ledge, chimney and stem behind a large tree to reach face climbing. Pro: 2 bolts, several thin to 2 inches. FA: Bob and Yvonne Gaines, July 1988.

147. **Aqualung** 5.9 ★ This short but fun route follows a flake and thin crack up past a small tree to the top of the East Buttress. Beware of loose rock near the top. Pro: thin to 1.5 inches. FA: Steve Mackay and Alan Vick, January 1973.

148. **Aqualung Direct** 5.11c R The thin crack left of the original start, rurps were used for protection on the first free ascent! FA: Steve Mackay and Alan Vick, January 1973. FFA: John Yablonsky, early 1970s.

149. **East Buttress Gully** 5.2 Start up the right side of the gully left of *The Spatula* (Route 152) and climb the gully to a broad ledge with a huge pine tree (East Buttress Ledge). The second pitch goes up the big corner to the top of the East Buttress. Pro: to 2.5 inches. FA: Unknown.

150. **Narcolepsy** 5.9 From the right end of East Buttress Ledge this is the steep crack on the right wall, starting behind a large tree. Pro: to 2 inches. FA: Troy Mayr and Steve Axthelm, 1987.

BUTTRESS OF CRACKS—RIGHT END

The following climbs lie on the right end of The Buttress of Cracks, which lies above the lowest section of the rock, almost directly above where the trail up to Suicide first gains sight of (and meets) the rock. Routes 155 to 161 are most easily approched from the base of The Weeping Wall.

151. **Nawab** 5.8 Starting just right of the start of *East Buttress Gully,* climb a flared crack with a tough start to an undercling right. Pro: to 3.5 inches. FA: Unknown.

152. **Spatula** 5.10a R ★ This is the 2-bolt face left of *The Plague.* Pro: to 1 inch. FA: Clark Jacobs and Eric Erickson, 1974.

153. **Spatula Direct Start** 5.11R Past one bolt on the left side of the face to join *Spatula.* FA: Clark Jacobs and Lisa Fry, August 1992.

154. **The Plague** 5.8 1. The left-facing dihedral at the right margin of the face to a ledge with a pine tree (easy walk-off right here). 2. Lieback the flake on the left over a bulge. Pro: to 4 inches. FA: Fred Ziel and others, July 1971.

155. **Zorro Zucchinis from Alpha Centuri Four** 5.10b R A long name for a short route. Climb the steep, unprotected face and flake to a bolt that protects friction moves up and left. Pro: thin to 2 inches. FA: Jim Wilson, Peter Wilkening, and Dick Shockley, July 1975.

156. **Low Pressure** 5.10c ★ The prominent, right-facing corner and overhang. Pro: several 0.5- to 2-inch. FA: Tobin Sorenson and Gib Lewis, 1973.

157. **High Pressure Variation** 5.11b R Surmount the overhang where the normal route underclings right. FA: (TR) John Long. First Lead: Kelly Vaught, 1999.

BUTTRESS OF CRACKS—RIGHT END

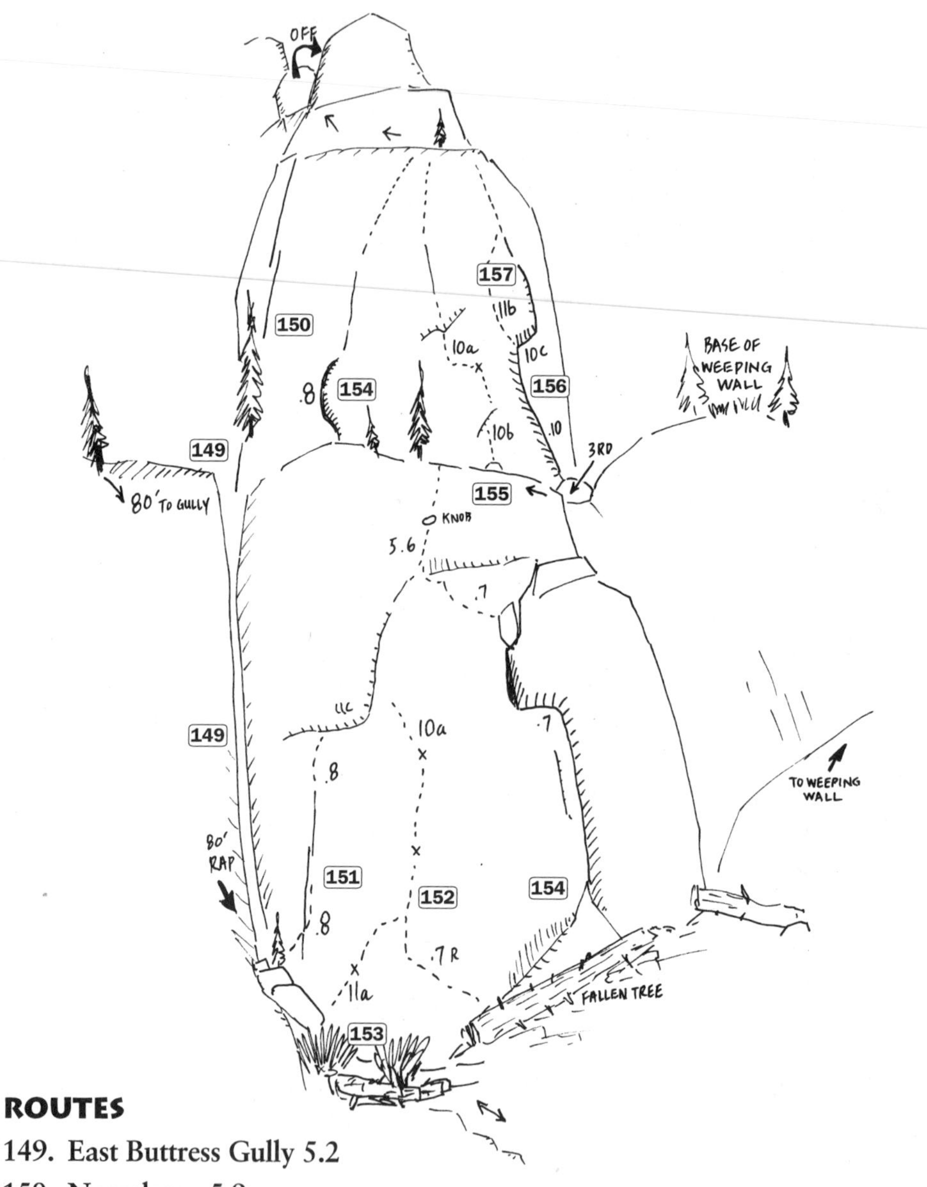

ROUTES

149. East Buttress Gully 5.2
150. Narcolepsy 5.9
151. Nawab 5.8
152. Spatula 5.10a R★
153. Spatula Direct Start 5.11R
154. The Plague 5.8
155. Zorro Zucchinis from Alpha Centuri Four 5.10b R
156. Low Pressure 5.10c★
157. High Pressure Variation 5.11b R

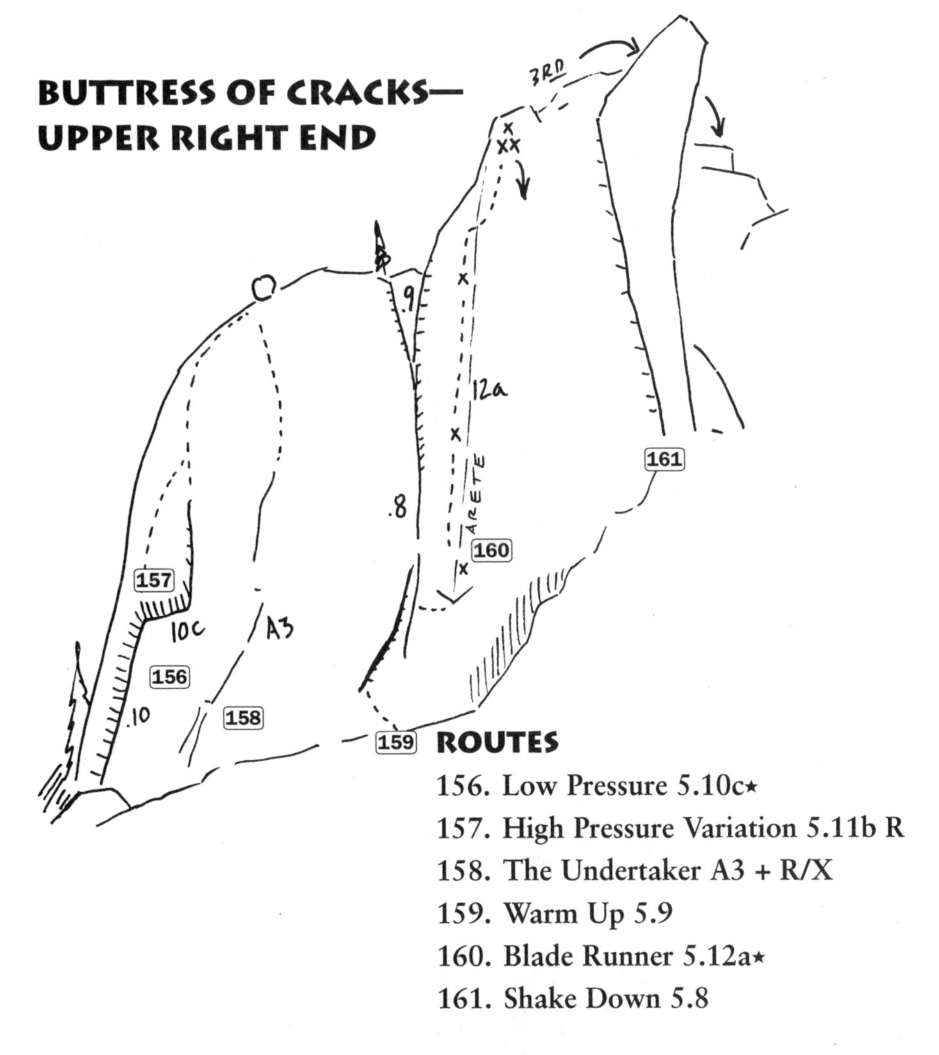

158. **The Undertaker** A3+ R/X This is a short, overhanging aid crack on the wall just right of *Low Pressure*. FA: Jay Smith, 1971.

159. **Warm Up** 5.9 From the base of The Weeping Wall, the obvious crack in a flared chimney on the left. Pro: to 2 inches. FA: R. Lindgen, E. Evans and R. DeRusha, August 1970.

160. **Blade Runner** 5.12a ★ After the first few moves of *Warm Up*, reach out right and climb the sharp arete past 3 bolts. FA: (TR) Bob Gaines, September 1986. First Lead: Steve Sutton and Clark Jacobs, December 1991.

161. **Shake Down** 5.8 A short distance right and uphill from *Warm Up* is this uninspiring little crack. Pro: to 2 inches. FA: Unknown.

PAISANO PINNACLE

Paisano Pinnacle is the 50 foot-high block that sits on a large ledge (Paisano Ledge) atop the Sunshine Face. Part of its base overhangs the face below, forming the spectacular *Paisano Overhang,* one of the country's first 5.12s. The easiest approach is via *Bye Gully.* It is also passed when descending from The Weeping Wall via a rappel. Routes 93 and 94 also lie on the pinnacle, but are best approached from the left side of the Sunshine Face. See Suicide Rock Overview Map.

162. **Paisano Overhang** 5.12c ★★ One of the first routes in America to receive the 5.12 grade. Climbs the horizontal 4- to 5-inch roof crack overhanging the Sunshine Face. Pro: several to 5 inches. FA: (5.7, A3) Pat Callis and Charlie Raymond, January 1968. FFA: John Long, 1973.

163. **The Easement** 5.11b ★ This is the 2-bolt face climb just left of *Paisano Jam Crack.* FA: David Katz, June 1987.

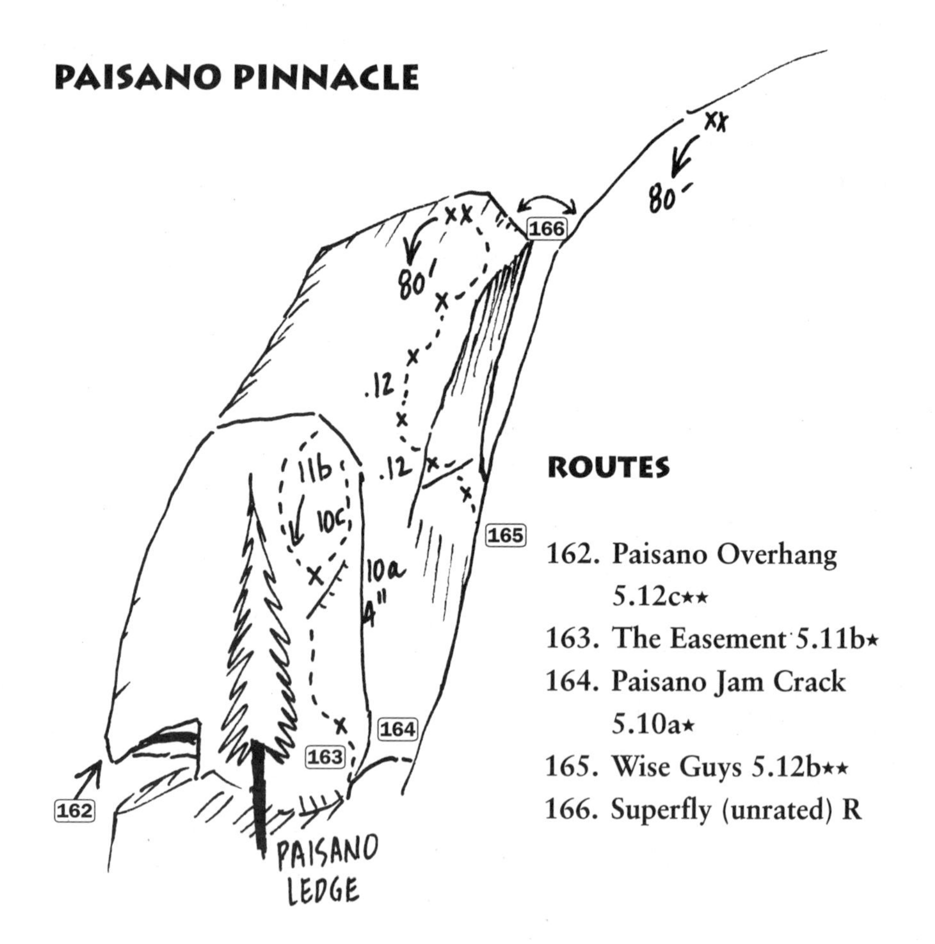

PAISANO PINNACLE ROUTES

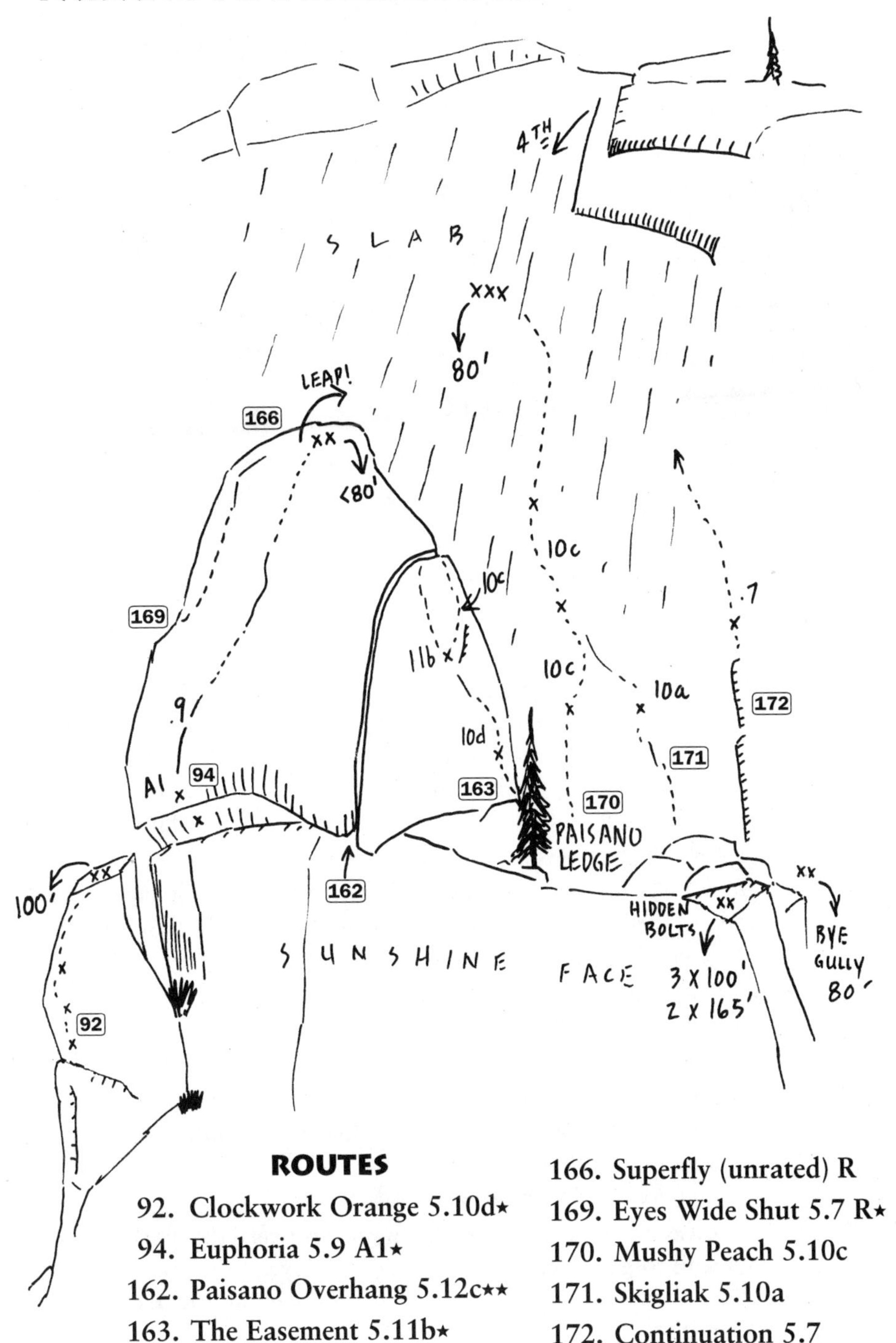

ROUTES

92. Clockwork Orange 5.10d★
94. Euphoria 5.9 A1★
162. Paisano Overhang 5.12c★★
163. The Easement 5.11b★
166. Superfly (unrated) R
169. Eyes Wide Shut 5.7 R★
170. Mushy Peach 5.10c
171. Skigliak 5.10a
172. Continuation 5.7

Darrell Hensel making the leap on Superfly. PHOTO BY KEVIN POWELL

164. **Paisano Jam Crack** 5.10a ★ This is the 4-inch-wide crack on the inside face of the block. The first ascent party rated the climb 5.8, although they had distinct advantages; a snowbank to shorten the route and cushion their falls, lug-soled boots, which fit well into the crack, and a jug of wine for courage. Sober climbers in rock shoes have found the crack to be considerably more difficult. Pro: to 4 inches. FA: Mark Powell, Don Wilson, and Frank Hoover, February 1955.
165. **Wise Guys** 5.12b ★★ Stem the wide chimney behind the pinnacle, then traverse left (12-) around the overhanging arete to a delicate (12) face. FA: Bob Gaines, Kelly Vaught, and Frank Bentwood, August 1999.
166. **Superfly** (Unrated) R Not really a route, this is a leap from the pinnacle onto the slab. FA: Bill Antel, Mike Graham, Tobin Sorenson, and Rick Accomazzo, 1973.
167. **Mantle of No Return** 5.8/9 R The rating depends a lot upon your reach. From the rappel bolts on the slab above, downclimb until an extended move is required to grab the lip of the block and mantle. FA: Jim Wilson, Gib Lewis, and Kyle Cooper, October 1973.
168. **The Step Away** 5.8 R Climb the wide chimney between the pinnacle and the main wall to gain a crack high on the southwest corner of the pinnacle. Pro: thin to 1.5 inches. FA: Charlie Raymond and Pat Callis, November 1966.

169. **Eyes Wide Shut** 5.7 R ★ The easiest way to the top of the pinnacle—ironically, the last route to be found. Best approached from the rappel anchor on the slab above the pinnacle; rap down 90 feet into the chimney. Stem up to a shelf, then climb the outside face of the block. Pro: 2 bolts. FA: Bob Gaines, Kelly Vaught, and Frank Bentwood, September 1999.
170. **Mushy Peach** 5.10c This is the 3-bolt face route up the wall just right of Paisano Pinnacle. FA: Randy Leavitt and Paul Neal, 1978.
171. **Skigliak** 5.10a The face just left of *Continuation.* Originally had 2 bolts, but the second one was sheared off by rockfall. You can traverse left to *Mushy Peach*'s 2nd bolt. FA: Dave Hanbury and Dave Black, July 1971.
172. **Continuation** 5.7 This one-pitch climb leads from Paisano Ledge to the top of Suicide Rock. Pro: to 2 inches, one bolt. FA: Unknown.

THE WEEPING WALL

The 300-foot Weeping Wall faces east and receives morning sun and afternoon shade. From the point where the trail up to Suicide meets the base of the rock (at the right side of The Buttress of Cracks), head up and right about 50 yards to reach the base of The Weeping Wall. The deep break/chimney on the left side of the face (*Bye Gully*) is lower part of the standard descent route. See Suicide Rock Overview Map.

Descents

Bye Gully Descent: Head left along the top of the wall, then downclimb (class 4) a smooth slab to rap anchors across from and overlooking the top of Paisano Pinnacle. A single-rope (80-foot) rappel gives access to Paisano Ledge (the top of the Sunshine Face); below, make a 165-foot rappel (or 80 feet plus some 4th class downclimbing) to the base.

Godzilla's Descent: Another descent begins by scrambling right and down (some 5th class) to near the *Godzilla's Return* block to an 80-foot rappel. From here either downclimb *The Escalator* (5.6) or make another 80-foot rappel from a tree at the top of *The Escalator.*

North Face Descent: To avoid any rappelling or technical downclimbing, walk up and right along the summit of the rock until you reach a trail. Near the north end of the rock, cut down off the main trail to the base of the North Face.

173. **Bye Gully** 5.5 From the base of the Weeping Wall, scramble up and left to this long, low-angle chimney leading up to Paisano Ledge. Caution: This route is the standard descent route, and as a result, is NOT recommended as a climb. FA: Unknown.

WEEPING WALL

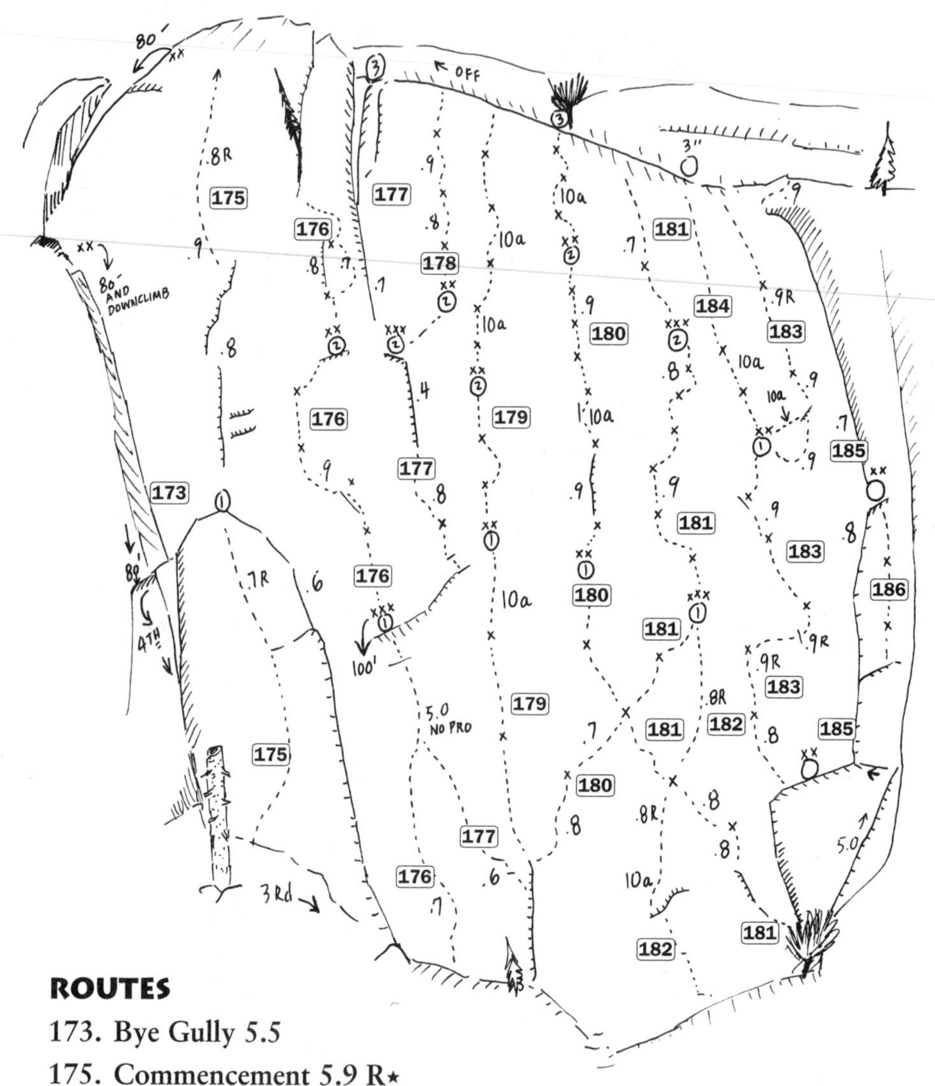

ROUTES

173. Bye Gully 5.5
175. Commencement 5.9 R★
176. Clam Chowder 5.9 R★★
177. Surprise 5.8 R★★
178. Surprise Direct 5.9★★
179. Duck Soup 5.10c R★★
180. Revelation 5.10a★★
181. Serpentine 5.9★★★
182. Dire Straits 5.10a R/X★
183. Ten Karat Gold 5.10a R★★★
184. White Line Fever 5.10a★★
185. Sampson 5.9 R
186. Change in the Weather 5.10b

Climbers on the Weeping Wall. PHOTO BY BOB GAINES

174. **Green Monster** 5.10a This short route begins about halfway up *Bye Gully,* ascending the short, left wall past 3 bolts. FA: Dave and Rich Tucker (The Chongo Brothers), May 1989.

175. **Commencement** 5.9 R ★ 1. Climb the 100-foot-high slab at the extreme left side of the Weeping Wall to a belay stance atop the flake. 2. Up to a small right-facing flake, then move up and left on low-angle friction to the top. Pro: small to 3 inches. FA: Bob Kamps and Ivan Couch, May 1970.

176. **Clam Chowder** 5.9 R ★★ 1. Start about 20 feet left of *Surprise,* then climb straight up to the 3-bolt belay ledge. 2. Straight up to a bolt, then up and left past 3 bolts to a small belay ledge with a two-bolt anchor. 3. Up past 2 bolts to a pine tree. FA: Jay Smith, Bruce Foster, Jim Wood, and Clark Jacobs, May 1973.

177. **Surprise** 5.8 R ★★ 1. Start at a very small crack/corner left of the center of the base, then head up and left to a 3-bolt belay. 2. Head right on a tapering ledge, then up past a bolt to a small corner, then up to a belay stance at 3 bolts. 3. The long, flared crack/chimney to the top. Take care not to kick off loose rocks from the top. Pro: small to 2 inches. FA: Pat Callis and Larry Reynolds, April 1966.

178. **Surprise Direct** 5.9 ★★ Instead of taking the 3-bolt belay atop the second pitch, traverse out right on a pronounced rib and belay at a pair of bolts. A sustained 5.9 lead past several bolts leads to the top. FA: Pat Callis and Mike Dent, August 1966.

179. **Duck Soup** 5.10c R ★★ 1. Climb the initial corner of *Surprise,* then proceed directly up the face past 2 bolts. 2. Past 2 bolts up a faint, orange-tinted waterstreak. 3. Up past 5 bolts to the top. Pro: to 2 inches for the start. FA: Marty Woerner, 1971.

180. **Revelation** 5.10a ★★ 1. Start on *Surprise,* but head up and right, using the 3rd bolt of *Serpentine,* then go straight up. Pro: to 2 inches. FA: Ivan Couch and Mike Dent, August 1970.

181. **Serpentine** 5.9 ★★★ Start next to the large oak tree near the right side of the base. A short crack leads to face climbing up and left. At the 3rd bolt go right. Pro: a medium nut protects the start. FA: Pat Callis and Lee Harrell, 1967.

182. **Dire Straits** 5.10a R/X ★ Begin midway between *Revelation* and *Serpentine,* and climb over a small overlap (small pro here) past the 2nd bolt on *Serpentine,* then directly up to the *Serpentine* belay. FA: Bob Gaines, July 1987.

183. **Ten Karat Gold** 5.10a R ★★★ From the large oak near the right side of the face, class 4 climbing up a groove leads to a ledge with a two-bolt

anchor. Start off the left edge of this ledge. Pro: several 1- to 3-inch for the top anchor. FA: John Long, Richard Harrison, and Rick Accomazzo, June 1973.

184. **White Line Fever** 5.10a ★★ This popular finish climbs directly up past 2 bolts above the belay stance. FA: Clark Jacobs and Jack Roberts, 1982.

185. **Sampson** 5.9R Follows the long left-facing dihedral the forms the right border of The Weeping Wall. 1. A short corner just right of *Serpentine* to the broad ledge. 2. Up the flake (5.8R) to a 2-bolt belay at a small ledge. 3. Continue up the corner; a 5.9 mantle is required to exit. Pro: to 2.5 inches. FA: Pat Callis and Lee Harrell, August 1967.

186. **Change in the Weather** 5.10b This is a one-pitch climb past two bolts up the narrow face between *Sampson* and *Goliath* to the *Sampson* belay. FA: John Allen and Kenji Hirotunian, September 1988.

REBOLTING FACE

Immediately to the right of The Weeping Wall is a large slab (The Rebolting Face). A large, flaring chimney (*Goliath,* Route 187) separates The Weeping Wall from The Rebolting Face. A long right-angling chimney/gully system (*The Escalator,* Route 197) marks the right margin of The Rebolting Face. See Suicide Rock Overview Map.

Rappel Descents:

1. Scramble right and down to near the *Godzilla's Return* block to an 80-foot rappel. From here, either downclimb *The Escalator* (5.6) or make another 80-foot rappel from a tree at the top of *The Escalator.*

2. Third class leads down to two bolts at the top of *Rebolting Development.* Three 100-foot (30-meter) rappels lead to the ground.

North Face Descent:

To avoid any rappelling or technical downclimbing, scramble up and right to the summit of the rock until you reach a trail. Near the north end of the rock, cut down off the main trail to the base of the North Face.

187. **Goliath** 5.7 *Goliath* scales the giant flaring chimney just beyond the right margin of The Weeping Wall. Start at the oak tree and climb 4th-class groove to reach a good belay ledge. Pro: to 3 inches. FA: Charlie Raymond and Pat Callis, June 1966.

188. **Goliath Direct Finish** 5.8 ★ Exit right up the hand crack that splits the right wall near the top of the chimney. A great way to finish. FA: Unknown.

189. **David** 5.7 R ★ From the large ledge at the start of *Goliath,* go right over the overhanging lip of the *Goliath* dihedral to airy face climbing up the

REBOLTING FACE

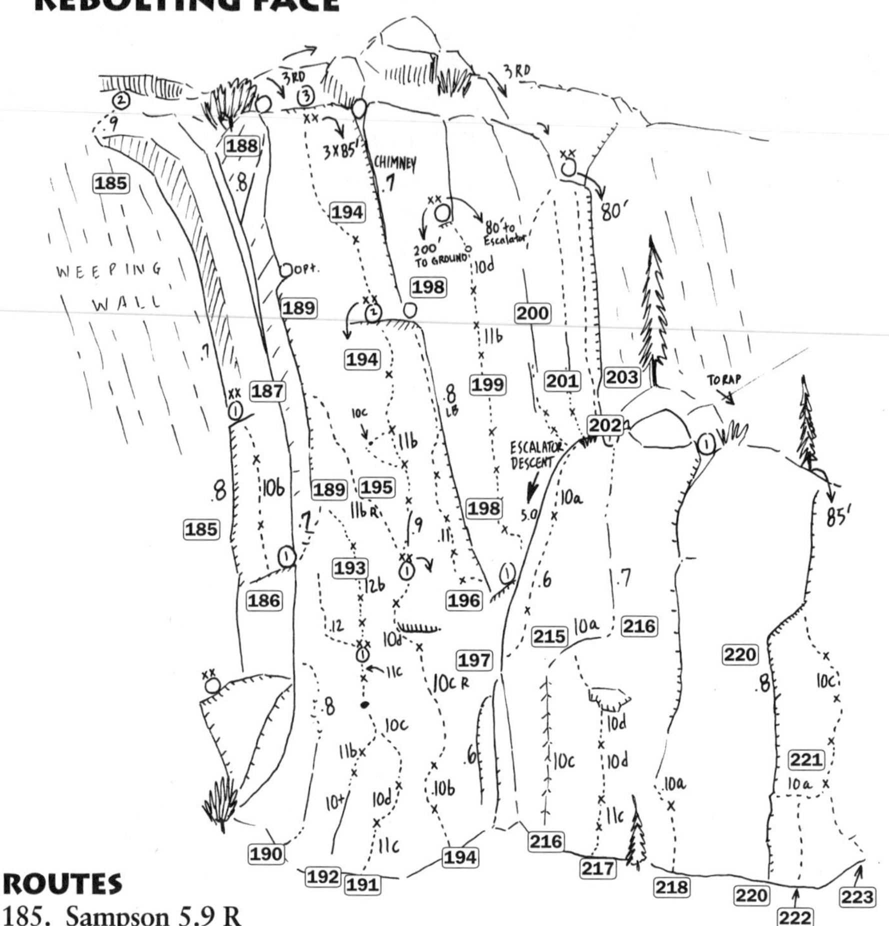

ROUTES

185. Sampson 5.9 R
186. Change in the Weather 5.10b
187. Goliath 5.7
188. Goliath Direct Finish 5.8★
189. David 5.7 R★
190. Mogen David 5.8 R★
191. Playing on the Freeway 5.11d/12a★★
192. Diamond Lane 5.11c★
193. Reckless Driving 5.12a/b★★
194. Rebolting Development 5.11b R★★★
195. Midnight Lumber Variation 5.11b R/X
196. Urban Development 5.11a R★
197. The Escalator 5.6
198. Delila 5.9
199. Season's End 5.11c★★
200. The Dilemma 5.11c
201. Tucker's Crack 5.10c
202. Pickpocket 5.8
203. Rap Flake 5.8
215. Mad Dogs and Edgingmen 5.10a
216. The Jackal 5.10b/c R★
217. Graceland 5.11c R★
218. The Breeze 5.10a
220. The Shadow 5.8 R★
221. Free Lance 5.10c R★
222. Freebase Variation 5.11+
223. Javelin Variation 5.10d

knobby arete. Pro: to 3 inches. FA: Charlie Raymond and Pat Callis, June 1966.

190. **Mogen David** 5.8 R ⋆ This thin crack is a direct start to *David*. Pro: very thin to 3-inch. FA: Ken Cook, et al., 1977.

191. **Playing on the Freeway** 5.11d/12a ⋆⋆ The first pitch is popular and hard. The original second pitch traverses left on minuscule edges. Pro (for second pitch): to 3 inches. FA: Troy Mayr and Charles Cole, July 1987.

192. **Diamond Lane** 5.11c ⋆ This variation starts just left of the *Playing on the Freeway* and climbs a thin crack, then up and right past 2 bolts to join *Playing on the Freeway* at the third bolt. Pro: thin nuts. FA: Dave Tucker, Mike Paul, and Paul Wilson, August 1987.

193. **Reckless Driving** 5.12a/b ⋆⋆ A direct finish to the 2nd pitch. Pro: to 3 inches. FA: Troy Mayr and Charles Cole, November 1987.

194. **Rebolting Development** 5.11b R ⋆⋆⋆ This route lies on the narrow face just right of The Weeping Wall. Start near the right side of the face. A 10c runout above the 2nd bolt on 1st pitch keeps most people away. On the second pitch, it is possible to avoid the scary crux by moving left above the second bolt to a knob tie-off, then moving back right (10c) to clip the third bolt. You can rap the route with three 100-foot (30-meter) rappels. Pro: bolts. FA: D. Wert, Mike Kaeser, and Greg Bender, October 1971.

195. **Midnight Lumber Variation** 5.11b R/X From the first belay on *Rebolting* climb up and left via difficult (5.11) and unprotected climbing to easier, but still unprotected ground. FA: John Long, rope solo, 1986.

196. **Urban Development** 5.11a R ⋆ From a point about 40 feet up *The Escalator* place pro, then traverse left and climb the face past 4 bolts to easier climbing with no protection. FA: Unknown.

197. **The Escalator** 5.6 The first 20 feet present a pair of rounded lieback flakes, above which the climbing is 4th class, up the slanting ramp/chimney, leading to tree-covered ledges. This route is used primarily as an approach and descent route, and is not recommended as a climb. FA: Unknown.

198. **Delila** 5.9 Begin up *The Escalator*. 1. Lieback the slick, right-facing open book that widens into a chimney to a good belay ledge. 2. Continue up the chimney to the top. Pro: to 3.5 inches. FA: Pat Callis, Charlie Raymond, and Trish Raymond, January 1968.

199. **Season's End** 5.11c ★★ A sustained face pitch beginning a short distance up *The Escalator,* just right of *Delila.* Some pro is useful before reaching the first bolt. Rap 165 feet and downclimb *The Escalator* (5.6), or rap 200 feet to the deck. Pro: 0.5 to 2.5 inches. FA: (5.10) Tobin Sorenson and Mike Graham (to the fifth bolt, then traversed left), early 1970s. FA complete route: Eric Erickson, 1978.
200. **The Dilemma** 5.11c Begin near the top of *The Escalator* and climb up and left past two closely spaced bolts to reach a thin crack. Pro: very thin nuts. FA: (A3) John Long and Jim Wilson, 1973. FFA: Dave and Rich Tucker (the Chongo Brothers), August 1987.
201. **Tucker's Crack** 5.10c 2 bolts leading to a thin crack a short distance right of *The Dilemma.* FA: Dave and Rich Tucker, August 1987.
202. **Pickpocket** 5.8 Climb the small overhang just right of *Tucker's Crack,* then up the easier face above. FA: Paul Wilson, 1987.
203. **Rap Flake** 5.8 This is the lieback flake directly below the *Godzilla's* rappel, near the top of *The Escalator.* FA: Unknown.

THE GODZILLA FACE

The Godzilla Face is a huge, blocklike formation split by two horizontal ledges, located at the top of *The Escalator* (Route 196).

The Godzilla Face and The Sunkist Face are easily reached by following *The Escalator* to its end, or climbing one of the routes to the right of *The*

GODZILLA FACE

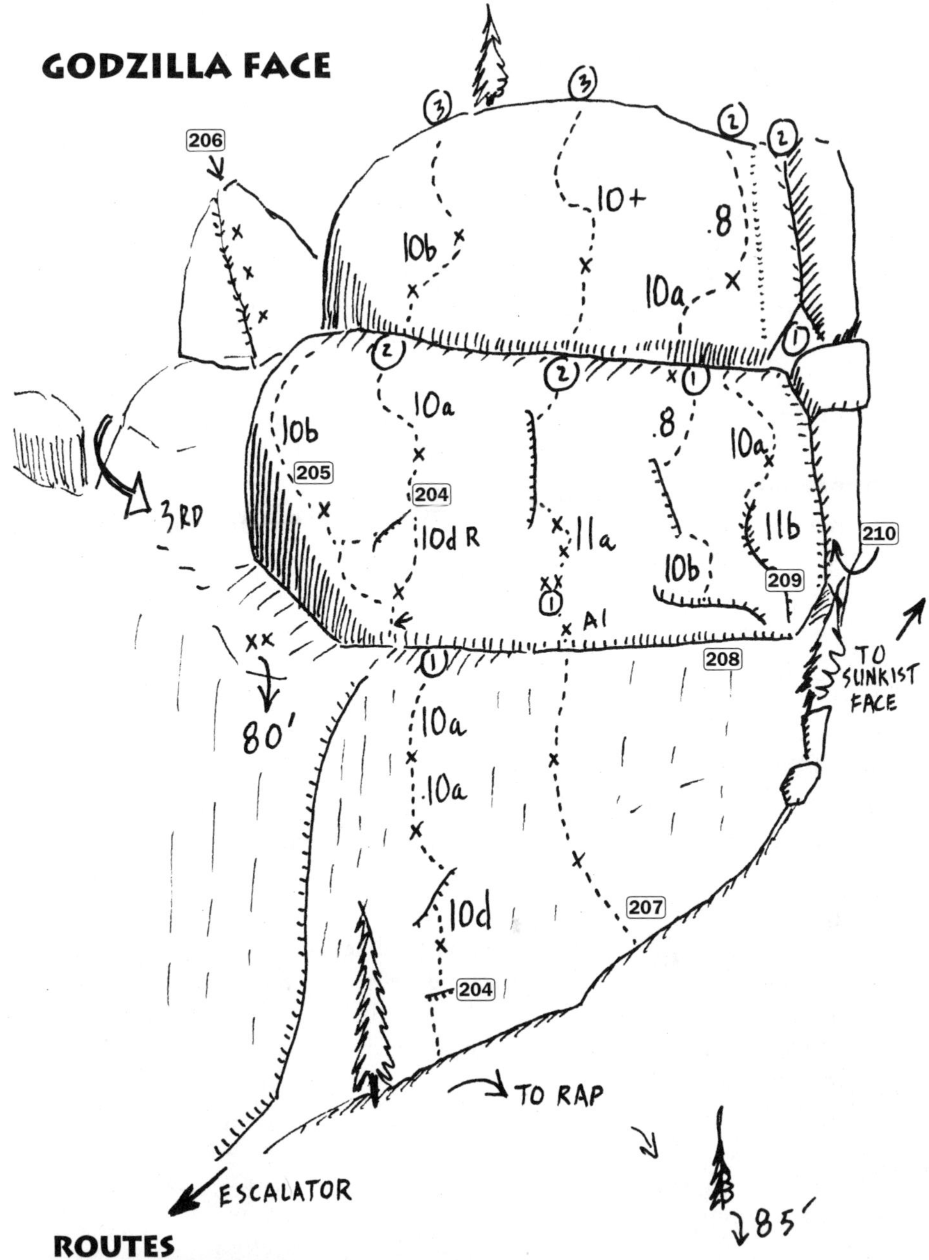

ROUTES

204. Godzilla's Return 5.10d R★★★
205. Godzilla's Arete Variation 5.10b R★
206. Rodan's Arete 5.11a
207. Mecca Godzilla 5.11a, A1★★
208. Montezuma's Revenge 5.10b R★★
209. Baby Cobra 5.11b★
210. Komodo Corner 5.7

Escalator (Routes 215 to 234) to ledges below these faces. See Suicide Rock Overview Map.

Descent: Scramble down and left (easy 5th) to an 80-foot rappel located to the left of the Godzilla's Face.

204. **Godzilla's Return** 5.10d R ★★★ 1. Up the initial slab past 3 bolts and belay on the ledge. 2. Begins with the infamous "Toad's Lip" mantle, which is most easily accomplished farther left. After the first bolt, either move out left (5.9) or go straight up (5.10d R) past another bolt to a belay ledge. 3. Up past 2 bolts to the top. FA: John Long and Hooman Aprin, April 1972.
205. **Godzilla's Arete Variation** 5.10b R ★ Climb the left arete to the left on the 2nd pitch of *Godzilla's* past one bolt (placed after the first ascent). FA: Dave Evans and Margy Floyd, July 1989.
206. **Rodan's Arete** 5.11a The 3-bolt arete on a small formation left of the 3rd pitch of *Godzilla's*. FA: Unknown.
207. **Mecca Godzilla** 5.11a, A1 ★★ Begin near the center of the face. 1. Climb the slab past two bolts to the overhang, where one bolt is used for aid, to a two-bolt stance. 2. Face climb past two bolts into a small corner that leads to a belay on a flat ledge. 3. Climb the block past one bolt to the top. Pro: thin cams to 2 inches. FA: Scott Erler and Paul Wilson, 1988.
208. **Montezuma's Revenge** 5.10b R ★★ Start at the right margin of the Godzilla Face. 1. Up and left over a tricky overhang to knobby face climbing. 2. Mantle the overhang to a bolt, easier climbing to the top. Pro: to 3 inches. FA: Tobin Sorenson, Gib Lewis, and Jim Wilson, 1973.
209. **Baby Cobra** 5.11b ★ This is the small dihedral/arch just right of the *Montezuma's Revenge*. There should be a couple of fixed pins in the arch and one bolt on the face above. Pro: thin. FA: (5.10, A1) Alan Nelson and Karl Mueller, 1978. FFA: Darrell Hensel, Dave Evans, and Todd Gordon, July 1986.
210. **Komodo Corner** 5.7 This route follows a corner system on the extreme right border of the face. The second pitch ascends the prominent, short dihedral. Pro: to 3 inches. FA: Clark Jacobs and Jeff Best, 1974.

SUNKIST FACE

This short, yet nearly featureless, steep slab is located just right of The Godzilla Face. Both The Godzilla Face and The Sunkist Face are easily reached by following either *The Escalator* to its end or by climbing *North Gully East* (5.1, Route 240). One can also climb one of the routes between *The Escalator* and *North Gully East* directly to ledges below these faces. See Suicide Rock Overview Map.

SUNKIST FACE

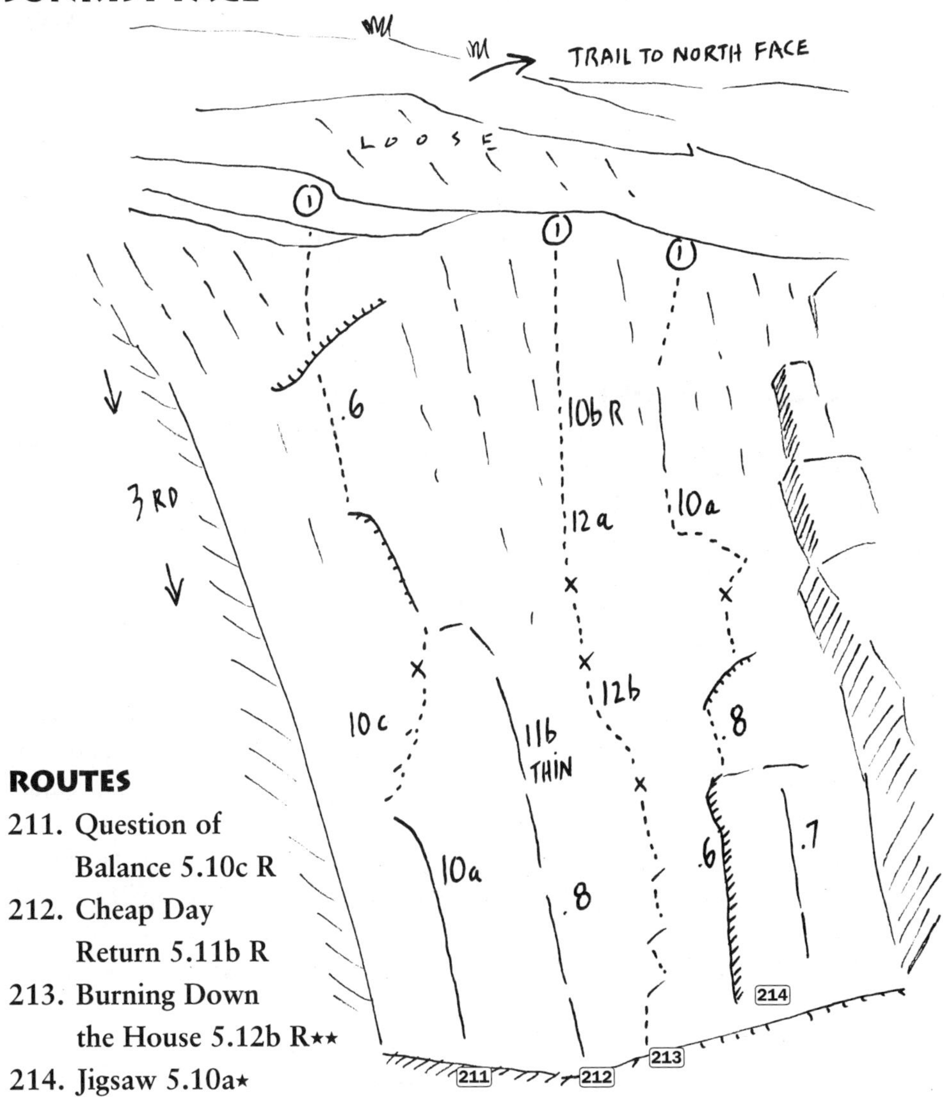

Descent: Go left along the top of The Godzilla Face, then scramble down (easy 5th) to an 80-foot rappel located to the left of the Godzilla's Face.

211. **Question of Balance** 5.10c R Begin at the hairline crack at the far left side of the face. Exit right as soon as possible, then climb up past a bolt. This route is often toproped, as the initial crack is difficult to protect without pitons. Pro: several thin to 2 inches. FA: Tobin Sorenson and Bill Antel, July 1973.

212. **Cheap Day Return** 5.11b R This is the thin crack just right of *Question of Balance*. Pro: several very thin to 1.5 inches. FA: (TR) Kevin Powell; First Lead: Dave Evans and John Frericks, August 1983.

213. **Burning Down the House** 5.12b R ★★ This test piece climbs the center of the clean, white slab past three bolts. FA: Darrell Hensel, October 1987.

214. **Jigsaw** 5.10a ★ Begin at the right side of the face; a lieback or finger crack leads to face climbing past a bolt. Pro: to 2.5 inches. FA: Tobin Sorenson, Bill Antel, John Long, Rob Muir, Richard Harrison, and Bruce Foster, July 1973.

ROUTES RIGHT OF THE ESCALATOR

The following climbs are found on the faces and cracks that lie to the right (and below the upper part) of *The Escalator* (Route 197). From the Weeping Wall, just walk right. The routes all start along the base of the rock.

Descent: Either downclimb *The Escalator,* or rappel 80 feet from a tree above *The Shadow.*

215. **Mad Dogs and Edgingmen** 5.10a After the initial section of *The Escalator,* climb the blunt arete on the right past 2 bolts. Pro: to 2.5 inches. FA: John Long and Jim Wilson, early 1970s.

216. **The Jackal** 5.10b/c R ★ Climb a deceptive groove, then traverse right to the vertical crack system leading to the top. Pro: thin to 2 inches. FA: Marty Kaeser, Phil Warrender, Jon Lonnie, and T. Emerson, November 1971.

217. **Graceland** 5.11c R ★ Begin at the pine tree midway between *The Jackal* and *The Breeze*. Climb past 3 bolts to gain a flake; finish up *The Jackal.* Pro: thin to 2 inches. FA: Bob Gaines, July 1987.

218. **The Breeze** 5.10a Start about 50 feet right of *The Escalator,* face climb past a bolt to reach a crack system. Pro: to 3 inches. FA: Charlie Raymond, Trish Raymond, and Janie Taylor, February 1968.

219. **The Ghost** 5.12b (TR) This is the blank face between *The Breeze* and *The Shadow.* FA: Bob Gaines, 1991.

220. **The Shadow** 5.8 R ★ 30 feet right of *The Breeze* is this classic lieback flake. Pro: several thin to 2.5 inches. FA: Charlie Raymond, February 1968.

221. **Free Lance** 5.10c R ★ Lieback the first few feet of *The Shadow,* then traverse right and climb up past 4 bolts. Pro: small to 2 inches. FA: John Long and Brian Pottorff, November 1971.

222. **Freebase Variation** 5.11+ (TR) A direct start. FA: Bob Gaines, August 1992.

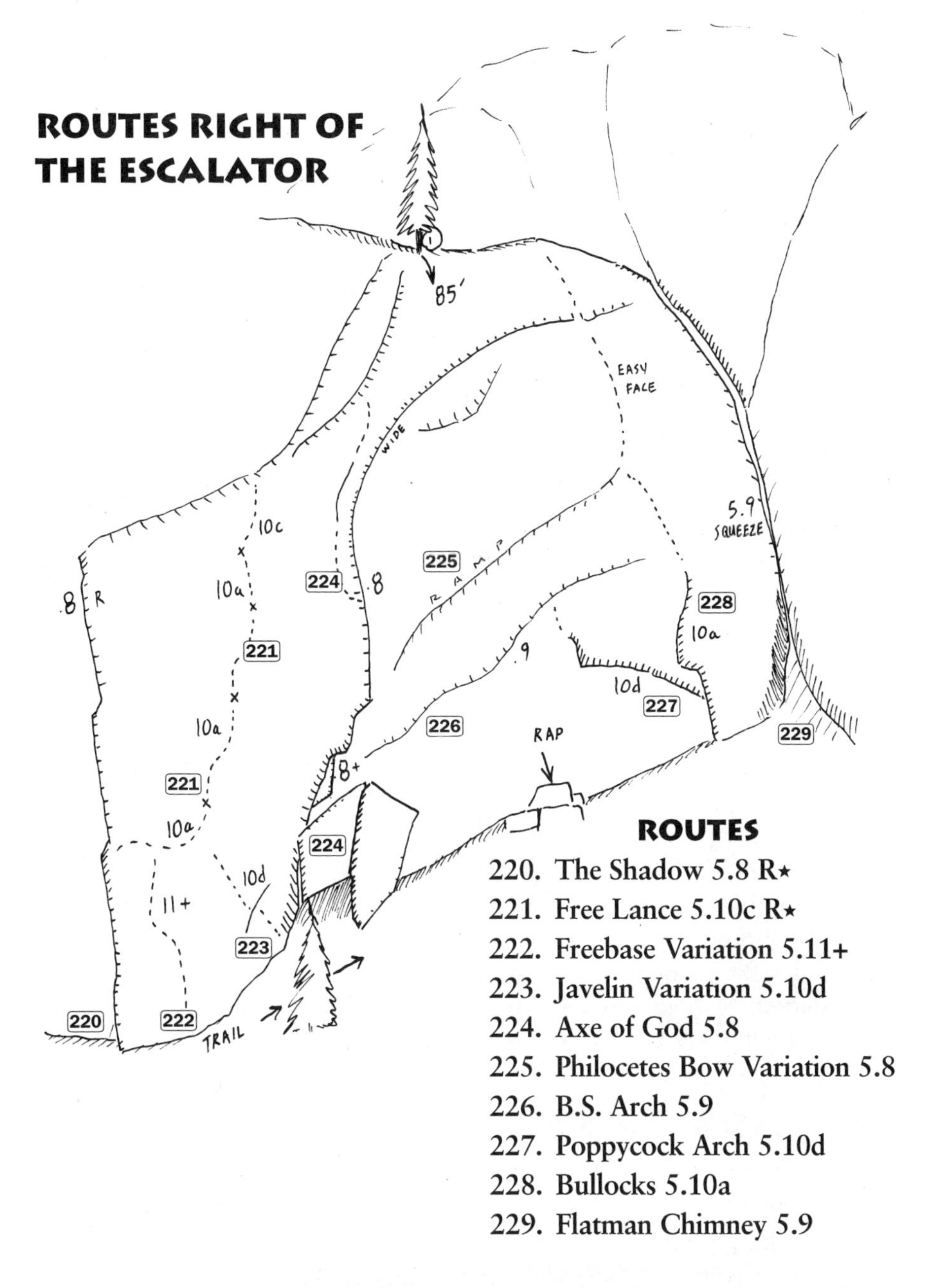

223. **Javelin Variation** 5.10d Traverses in from the right to gain the first bolt. FA: Kevin Powell and Darrell Hensel, 1990.

224. **Axe of God** 5.8 Directly above an ominous, wedged flake, follow the right-facing, right-curving crack. Pro: to 2.5 inches. FA: Lee Harrell and Pat Callis, May 1968.

225. **Philocetes Bow Variation** 5.8 After about 20 feet, traverse up and right along a ramp to join *B.S. Arch* near the top. FA: Unknown.

226. **B.S. Arch** 5.9 From the start of *Axe of God,* move out right on a thin undercling, then climb easy face to the top. Pro: thin to 2.5 inches. FA: Jay Smith and Tom Burns, August 1973.

227. **Poppycock Arch** 5.10d (TR) Begin about 40 feet to the right of *B.S. Arch* and move left under a small overhang. FA: Unknown.

228. **Bullocks** 5.10a Begin at the same point as Route 227 and lieback straight up a flake. FA: Unknown.

229. **Flatman Chimney** 5.9 The narrow slot just right of *B.S. Arch*. FA: Pat Callis and Lee Harrell, May 1968.

230. **Herkimer** 5.10c R The face just right of *Flatman Chimney.* Pro: 2 bolts, fixed pin, to 2 inches. FA: Craig Fry, Dave Evans, and Jim Angione, June 1988.

231. **Hair Pie** 5.10a Start on *Hair Lip* but continue straight up. Pro: thin to 2 inches. FA: Tom Burns and Larry Swearingen, August 1973.

232. **Hair Lip** 5.10a ★★ This route is located approximately 60 yards right of the Weeping Wall. Look for a right-arching, very flared chimney (*Hot Buttered Rump*) located on the left margin of a smooth slab. This route starts 15 feet left of the chimney. Climb up a thin flake, then traverse right to the very exposed "lip" past 3 bolts. Two 80-foot rappels (or one 165-foot rappel) to the ground. Pro: thin-to-medium nuts/CDs. FA: Ivan Couch and Larry Reynolds, October 1970.

233. **Hair Face Variation** 5.8+ Go to first bolt on *Hair Lip,* then head back left to finish on *Hair Pie.*

234. **Hot Buttered Rump** 5.10a About 60 yards right of the Weeping Wall is this right-arching, very flared chimney located on the left margin of a smooth slab (Sideshow Slab). Pro: many to 2 inches. FA: Charlie Raymond and Lee Harrell, April 1968.

SIDESHOW SLAB

This smaller version of the Weeping Wall is located just right of *Hot Buttered Rump,* about 60 yards right of the Weeping Wall.

235. **Sideshow** 5.9 R A two-bolt face climb with a ramp in the middle section, and unprotected (5.7) slab above, located a few feet right of *Hot Buttered Rump*. FA: Ivan Couch and Mike Dent, November 1970.

236. **Step Right Up** 5.10a 4 bolts to a two-bolt anchor just right of *Sideshow.* FA: Chris Miller, Pete Parades, and Cheryl Basye, July 1999.

237. **It's Showtime** 5.9 (TR) 10 feet right of *Step Right Up,* to the 2-bolt anchor. FA: Chris Miller, July 1999.

SIDESHOW SLAB

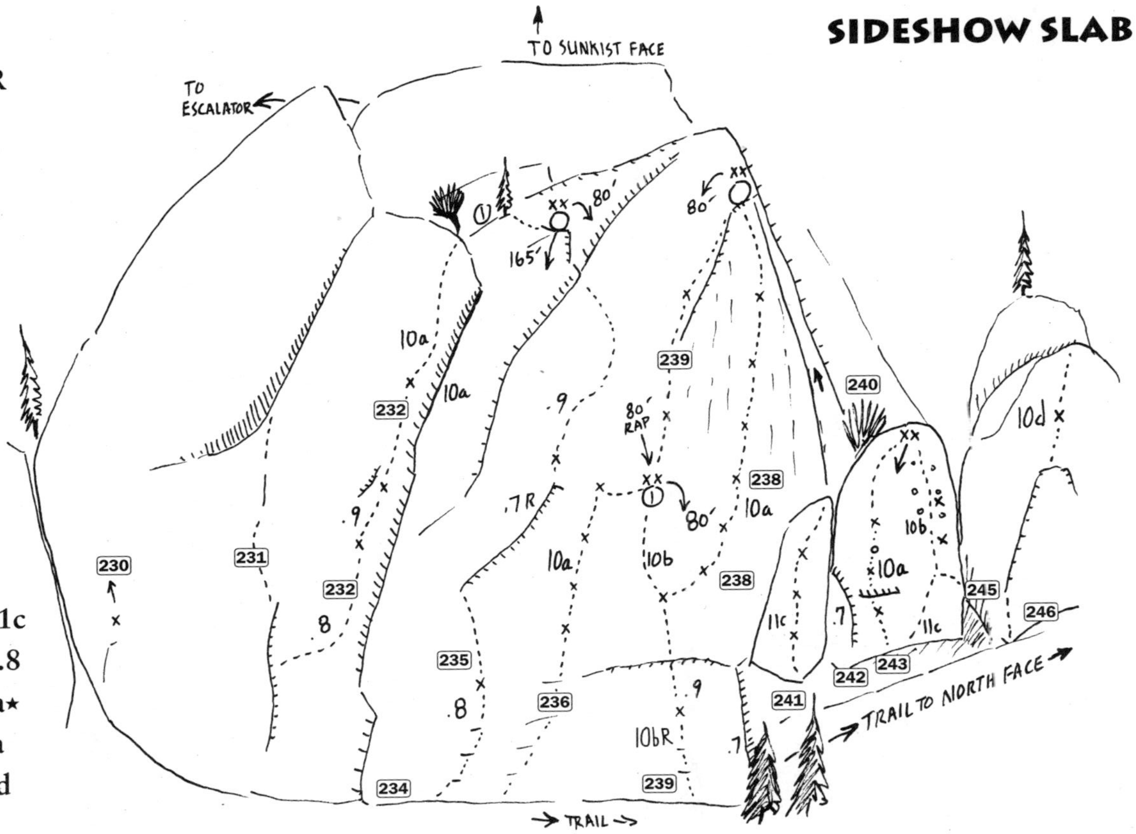

ROUTES

230. Herkimer 5.10c R
231. Hair Pie 5.10a
232. Hair Lip 5.10a★★
234. Hot Buttered Rump 5.10a
235. Sideshow 5.9 R
236. Step Right Up 5.10a
238. Show Stopper 5.10a R★
239. Ours 5.10b R★
240. North Gully East 5.1
241. Tiny Bubbles 5.11c
242. Crack of Noon 5.8
243. Noondance 5.10a★
245. Funny Face 5.10a
246. Coyote Girl 5.10d

238. **Show Stopper** 5.10a R ★ Begin with the first two bolts of *Ours,* then move up and right past 6 more bolts to a two-bolt anchor. A less runout variation can be done starting up the crack on the right. Two 80-foot rappels (or 165 feet) to the ground. FA: Chris Miller, Pete Parades, and Cheryl Basye, July 1999.

239. **Ours** 5.10b R ★ Follow four bolts up slippery, runout, low-angle slab about 40 feet right of *Sideshow.* FA: Mike Graham, Steve West, and Alan Vick, October 1972.

240. **North Gully East** 5.1 This low-angle gully is located on the right side of the Sideshow Face and offers an easy approach to the Sunkist Face and the Godzilla Face. FA: Unknown.

TINY PILLARS

These next routes are located on a series of small pillars just right of the Sideshow Slab and below and left of The Eagle Pinnacle area. The Pillars are located just above the trail along the base of the rock, about 80 yards right of The Weeping Wall. See Suicide Rock Overview Map.

241. **Tiny Bubbles** 5.11c 3 bolts on a short, pocketed left-hand "pillar." FA: Dave Evans, Jim Angione, and Dave Tucker, July 1989.

242. **Crack of Noon** 5.8 The short, left-arching flake left of *Noondance.* Pro: to 3.5 inches. FA: unknown.

243. **Noondance** 5.10a ★ 3 bolts protect the face just right of the 5.7 crack. 2-bolt anchor (50 feet). FA: Chongo Brothers, July 1989.

244. **Crater Face** 5.11c (TR) A direct start to *Funny Face* from the bottom of the right-hand pillar. FA: Chongo Brothers, July 1989.

245. **Funny Face** 5.10a Avoid the difficult lower section of *Crater Face* by traversing in from the right. 2 bolts to a 2-bolt anchor. FA: Troy Mayr and Amy Sharpless, 1987.

246. **Coyote Girl** 5.10d Look for a bolt above a slab/flake a short distance right of the Tiny Pillars. FA: Dave Evans and Margy Floyd, 1989.

EAGLE PINNACLE

This interesting and complex formation lies between the *North Gully East* (Route 240) and the *North Gully West* (Route 270), culminating in a blocklike pinnacle. The face above the trail is characterized by a large sloping "bowl" near its middle, several routes begin out of this "bowl." See Suicide Rock Overview Map.

EAGLE PINNACLE

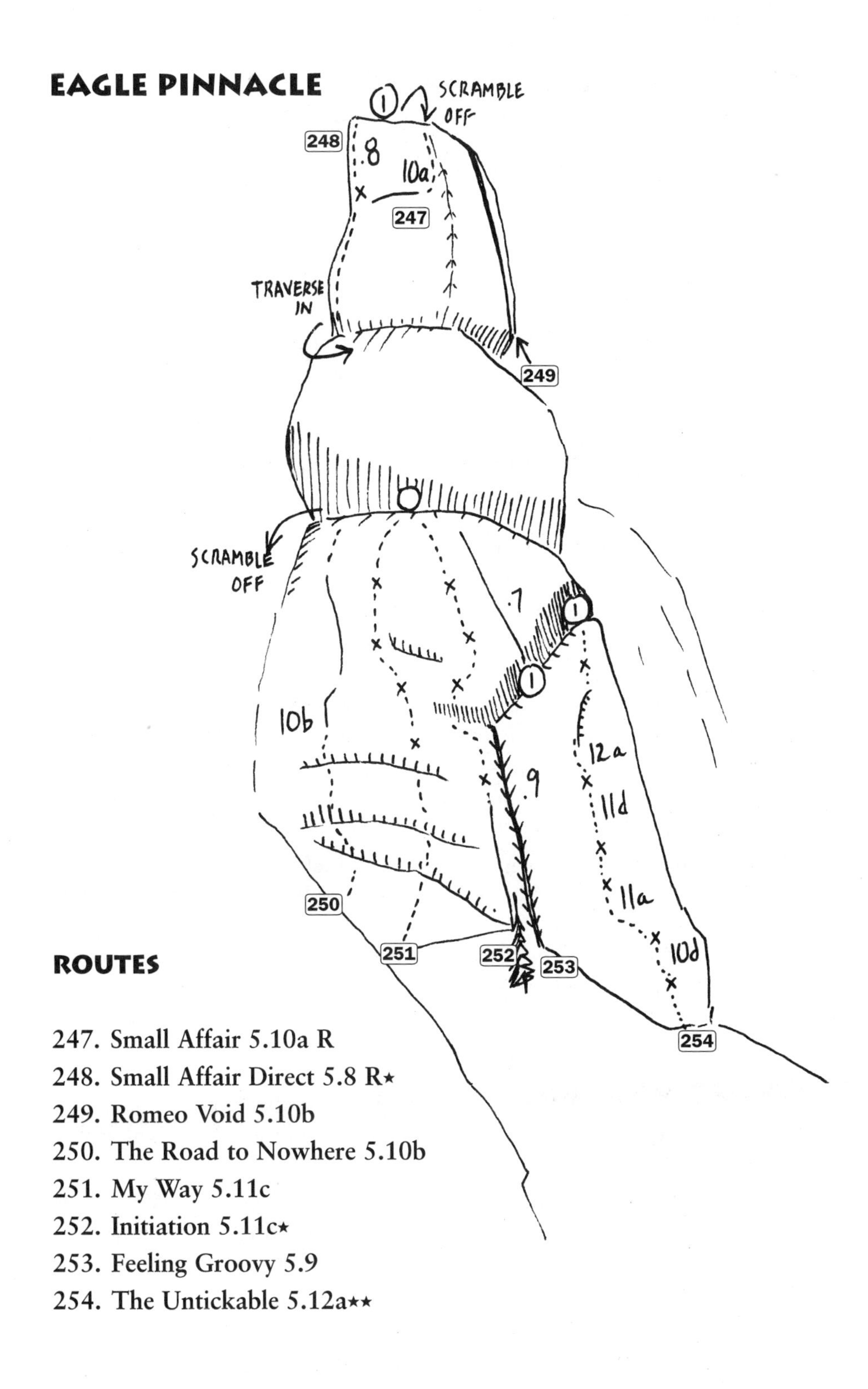

ROUTES

247. Small Affair 5.10a R
248. Small Affair Direct 5.8 R★
249. Romeo Void 5.10b
250. The Road to Nowhere 5.10b
251. My Way 5.11c
252. Initiation 5.11c★
253. Feeling Groovy 5.9
254. The Untickable 5.12a★★

SOUTH PINNACLE ROUTES

Routes 247 to 249 are located on the orange "block" forming the south and east sides of the summit of the Eagle Pinnacle formation, and are best approached from near the right end of the Sunkist Face and/or up *North Gully East* (Route 240).

247. **Small Affair** 5.10a R From the bolt, traverse right along a horizontal crack to an edge, then up to the summit. Pro: to 3 inches. FA: John Long and Bill Antel, 1977.

248. **Small Affair Direct** 5.8 R ★ This is a short, classic pitch up the left-hand arete, protected by a medium nut and one bolt. Pro: to 3 inches. FA: John Long and Rick Accomazzo, 1978.

249. **Romeo Void** 5.10b (TR) From *Small Affair,* walk 30 feet right, start in a chimney, then move left up the arete. FA: Bob Gaines, 1982.

SOUTH SIDE ROUTES

Routes 250 to 253 are located on the southern side of the Eagle Pinnacle Formation, below the summit block. They are located to the right of, and are best approached from, partway up *North Gully East* (Route 240).

250. **The Road to Nowhere** 5.10b This route is located on the rounded buttress on the far left side of the formation and involves face and thin-crack climbing. FA: Dave Evans and Craig Fry, July 1985.

251. **My Way** 5.11c The four-bolt face between *Road to Nowhere* and *Initiation.* First lead (Bolts placed by unknown party): Darrell Hensel and Kevin Powell, 1990.

252. **Initiation** 5.11c ★ Start at a thin crack just left of the flared chimney on *Feeling Groovy*. The face above is protected by four bolts. Pro: include thin wires, TCUs. FA: Dave Evans and Craig Fry, August 1988.

253. **Feeling Groovy** 5.9 Best done in two short pitches. 1. The prominent flared chimney, exiting right onto a broad ledge. 2. A brief crack over a bulge. Pro: thin to 3 inches FA: Bob and Yvonne Gaines, August 1987.

LOWER EAST FACE ROUTES

Routes 254 to 259 can be accessed by scrambling up from the trail along the base of the rock.

254. **The Untickable** 5.12a ★★ This is the prominent buttress with 6 bolts between *Feeling Groovy* and *Sloppy Seconds.* FA: Darrell Hensel, July 1986.

EAGLE PINNACLE

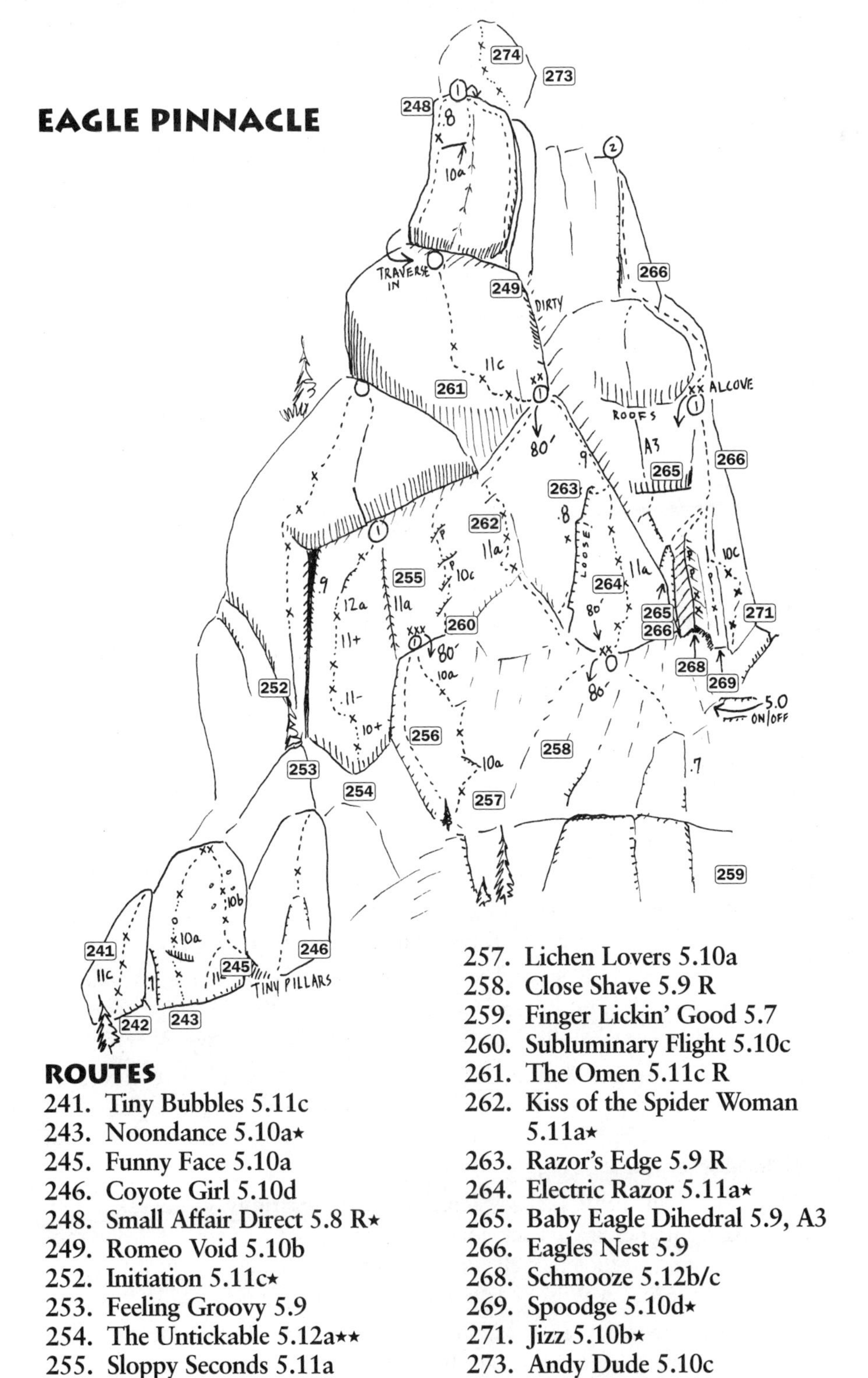

ROUTES

241. Tiny Bubbles 5.11c
243. Noondance 5.10a★
245. Funny Face 5.10a
246. Coyote Girl 5.10d
248. Small Affair Direct 5.8 R★
249. Romeo Void 5.10b
252. Initiation 5.11c★
253. Feeling Groovy 5.9
254. The Untickable 5.12a★★
255. Sloppy Seconds 5.11a
256. Razor Burn 5.11a
257. Lichen Lovers 5.10a
258. Close Shave 5.9 R
259. Finger Lickin' Good 5.7
260. Subluminary Flight 5.10c
261. The Omen 5.11c R
262. Kiss of the Spider Woman 5.11a★
263. Razor's Edge 5.9 R
264. Electric Razor 5.11a★
265. Baby Eagle Dihedral 5.9, A3
266. Eagles Nest 5.9
268. Schmooze 5.12b/c
269. Spoodge 5.10d★
271. Jizz 5.10b★
273. Andy Dude 5.10c
274. Compound Eyes 5.11

255. **Sloppy Seconds** 5.11a A deceptive groove on the left border of the face above the base of the rock. Pro: to 3 inches. FA: Fred Ziel and Eric Erickson, late 70s.

256. **Razor Burn** 5.11a (TR) From the two-bolt anchor atop *Lichen Lovers* you can toprope the rounded arete just right of the gully. FA: Bob Gaines, August 1989.

257. **Lichen Lovers** 5.10a Begin near the left margin of the slab below *Razor's Edge* (below and right of *Sloppy Seconds*). Friction past 3 bolts to a two-bolt anchor. FA: Dan and Debbie Haughelstine, August 1989.

258. **Close Shave** 5.9 R Insignificant route up the thin crack and slab a short distance right of *Lichen Lovers*. FA: Bob Gaines, 1987.

259. **Finger Lickin' Good** 5.7 The corner to finger crack a short distance right of *Close Shave*. Pro: to 3 inches. FA: Owen Gunther and Mark Minor, 1970.

UPPER EAST FACE ROUTES

Routes 260 to 269 are most easily reached from the bottom of *North Gully West* (route 270). Walk past Eagle Pinnacle, up and right on talus, to near the base of the North Face. Walk back left on a rocky ledge. This ledge ends at the base of *North Gully West;* traverse left around the arete of *Spoodge* (5.2) to access the sloping "bowl." Alternatively, you can climb Routes 257 to 259 to reach the sloping "bowl." There is a two-bolt belay/rappel anchor in the center of the bowl (80-foot rappel).

260. **Subluminary Flight** 5.10c This route ascends the dark, lichen-covered face between *Sloppy Seconds* and *Kiss of the Spider Woman*. Pro: 2 fixed pins, thin to 2 inches. FA: Dave Evans and Todd Gordon, June 1988.

261. **The Omen** 5.11c R Second pitch to either *Kiss of the Spider Woman* or *Subluminary Flight;* can be reached from atop *Razor's Edge*. Traverse left and up past 3 bolts. FA: Dave Evans and Todd Battey, May 1989.

262. **Kiss of the Spider Woman** 5.11a ★ The obtuse "corner" left of *Razor's Edge* with 3 bolts. Ends at the *Razor's Edge* belay. Pro: thin nuts, CDs to 2.5 inches. FA: (TR) Dave Evans and Jim Ivanko, October 1983. First Lead: Bob Gaines, August 1987.

263. **Razor's Edge** 5.9 R Lieback (gingerly) the precarious, loose flake, then move right and jam/lieback a left-slanting crack to a two-bolt belay/rappel station (80-foot rappel). Pro: 2 bolts, CDs including several 2.5- to 3.5-inch. FA: Jim Wilson, Tobin Sorenson, and John Long, 1974.

264. **Electric Razor** 5.11a ★ Sustained, thin face just right of *Razor's Edge* with 5 bolts; join *Razor's Edge* for its final crack section. Pro: a few 2.5- to 3.5-inch CDs. FA: Scott and Robin Erler, Paul Morrel, August 1991.

265. **Baby Eagle Dihedral** 5.9, A3 From the big sloping ledge, climb a crack just left of *Eagles Nest,* then climb up to and nail the huge roof. Pro: rurps, KBs, thin pitons, etc. FA: Craig Fry and Kelly Carignan, July 1986.

266. **Eagles Nest** 5.9 1. A short, awkward, 5.9 flake leads off the right side of the ledge to easier face and a 2-bolt belay in an alcove. 2. Step right, then 4th-class climbing leads to the top. FA: (5.5, A2) Chuck and Ellen Wilts, 1970. FFA: Mike Graham, Tobin Sorenson, and Bill Antel, 1972.

267. **Raker's Escape** 5.11a From the belay alcove, climb a crack out the left side of the overhang. FA: Rob Raker, Dave Evans, and Doug Munoz, October 1983.

268. **Schmooze** 5.12b/c ★ Wild stemming up the slightly overhanging dihedral with 2 bolts and 2 fixed pins, located just right of the start of *Eagles Nest* and just left of the prow of *Spoodge.* Pro: thin to 2.5 inches. FA: Bill Leventhal and Bob Gaines, July 1989.

269. **Spoodge** 5.10d ★ The thin crack/groove up the prow of the buttress leading to the alcove belay on *Eagles Nest.* One bolt and one fixed pin. FA: Eric Erickson and John Long, 1978.

NORTH SIDE ROUTES

These routes are located on the northern side of Eagle Pinnacle and/or above the top of *North Gully West* (Route 270). See description of North Gully West for best approach. Other approaches are possible.

270. **North Gully West** 5.2 This is the low-angle gully forming the right boundary of the Eagle Pinnacle formation. Walk past Eagle Pinnacle, up and right on talus, to near the base of the North Face. Walk back left on ledges to a broad sloping ledge which ends at the base of *North Gully West,* where *Spoodge* (Route 269) begins. Primarily an approach route, it also makes a good descent/rappel. FA: Unknown.

271. **Jizz** 5.10b ★ On the right side of the Eagle Pinnacle, near the base of *North Gully West,* on the left wall, interesting face moves past 3 bolts. Belay at the *Eagles Nest* alcove. FA: Dave Evans and Todd Battey, 1989.

272. **Flower of Low Rank** 5.10b This is the dirty, uninviting crack system to the right of *Jizz.* FA: Randy Grandstaff, 1978.

273. **Andy Dude** 5.10c This route is located at the top of *North Gully West,* on the blocklike formation which is above and behind Eagle Pinnacle, separated by a notch/gully. *Andy Dude* is the 40- foot, flared, arching crack. Pro: to 4 inches. FA: Randy Grandstaff, 1980.

274. **Compound Eyes** 5.11 This is a short, height-dependent pitch with a couple of bolts, located around the corner left of *Andy Dude,* directly above

the notch behind Eagle Pinnacle. FA: Dave Evans and Todd Gordon, August 1980.

NORTHEAST BUTTRESS AND NORTH FACE ROUTES

The Northeast Buttress and North Face of Suicide Rock lie at the extreme right side of the rock. The Northeast Buttress lies right of Eagle Pinnacle and is separated from that formation by *North Gully West* (Route 270). The North Face is the broad, slabby section of rock farther right, separated from the Northeast Buttress by a chimney system (*Cat's Cave Inn,* Route 292). Hike up to the base of The Weeping Wall, then head right along the base of the crag for about 200 yards. See Suicide Rock Overview Map.

NORTHEAST BUTTRESS

This section of the rock is somewhat steeper than most of the faces at Suicide; most of the routes follow crack systems. Walk past Eagle Pinnacle, up and right on talus, to near the base of the slabby North Face. Routes 275 to 283 are reached by walking back left along a rocky ledge. This ledge ends at the base of *North Gully West.* Many of the Eagle Pinnacle routes are also approached from this point.

275. **Gone in 30 Seconds** 5.10a Scramble (5.2) 100 feet up *North Gully West.* This is the right-diagonaling crack that passes a roof that starts out of *North Gully West,* up and left of *Johnny Quest.* Pro: thin to 2 inches, fixed pin. FA: Charles Cole, Troy Mayr, and Gib Lewis, August 1987.
276. **Johnny Quest** 5.10b ★★ Climb (5.2) up the bottom of *North Gully West,* then traverse right to a ledge with an oak tree and a pine tree. A 5.8 direct start is also possible up the crack just right of *Race Bannon.* Stem and lieback a short, vertical corner to a classic, straight-in finger crack. Rap 100 feet from bolts or continue on *Flakes of Wrath* (5.9 R) or *Flake Out* (5.6) to the top. Pro: thin to 2 inches. FA: Craig Fry and Spencer Lennard, 1979.
277. **Race Bannon** 5.11a (TR) ★ This is the short face with a thin crack directly below the start of *Johnny Quest.* FA: Bob Gaines and Mike Moretti, July 2000.
278. **Flakes of Wrath** 5.10c R ★★ Start just down and right of *Johnny Quest.* 1. A thin lieback that turns into a flake that curves left. 2. Loose flakes lead to a bolt and run-out 5.9 face climbing. Pro: to 3.5 inches. FA: John Bachar, Gib Lewis, Jim Wilson, John Long, Eric Erickson, and Tobin Sorenson, 1978.

NORTHEAST BUTTRESS

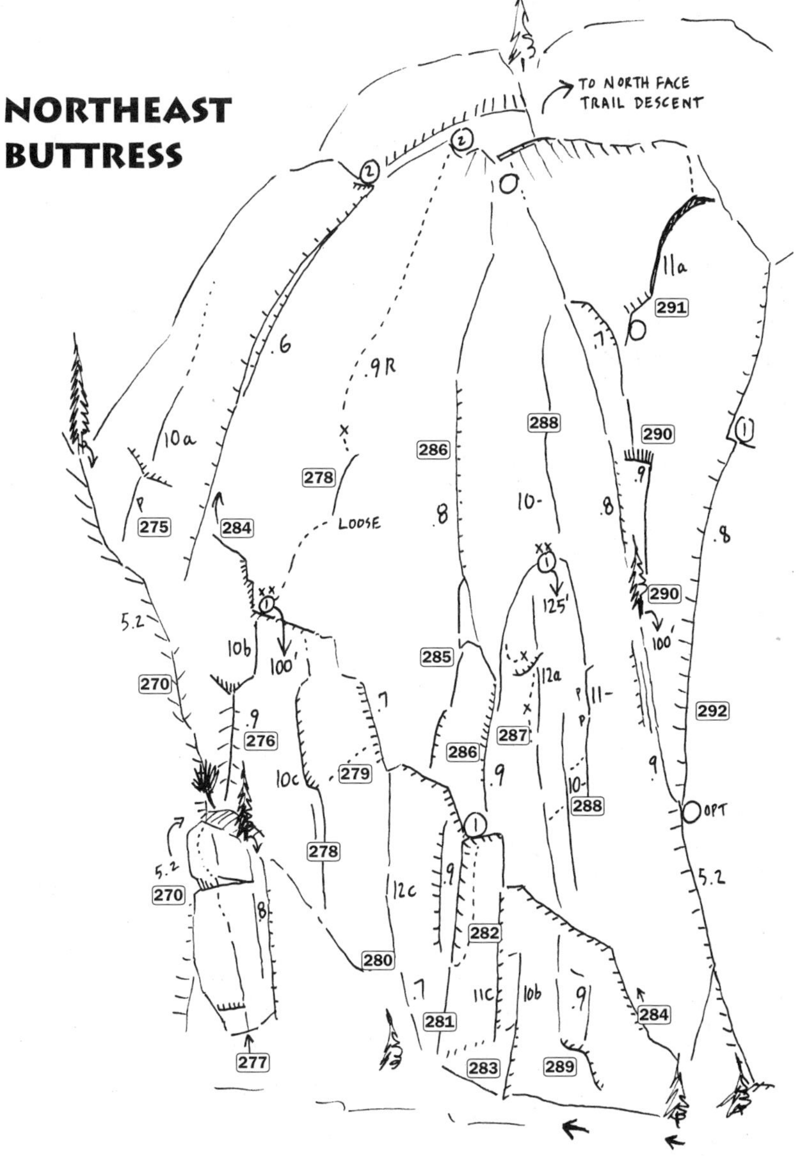

ROUTES

270. North Gully West 5.2
275. Gone in 30 Seconds 5.10a
276. Johnny Quest 5.10b★★
277. Race Bannon 5.11a★
278. Flakes of Wrath 5.10c R★★
279. Flakes of Rad 5.10d R?
280. Rock Hudson 5.12c★
281. Spooky Spike Direct 5.9 R★
282. My Brothers 5.11d
283. Vicious Rumors 5.11c★
284. Flake Out 5.7
285. Hidden Crack 5.8
286. Spooky Spike 5.9★
287. Hey Dude 5.12a★
288. Etude 5.11a★★★
289. Etude Direct Start 5.9
290. Flower of High Rank 5.9★★★
291. Wet Dreams 5.11a★
292. Cat's Cave Inn 5.8

279. **Flakes of Rad** 5.10d R? After the initial lieback, move right and up the face. FA: Dave Wonderly, et al., 1991.

280. **Rock Hudson** 5.12c ★ The fingertip crack on the slightly overhanging wall right of *Flakes of Wrath*. The climbing is restless and relentless; a difficult lead. Pro: many thin to 1.5-inch. FA: (A3, clean) Dave Evans and Margy Floyd, June 1985. FFA: Bob Gaines (TR), June 1987. First lead: Andy Puhvel, 1989.

281. **Spooky Spike Direct** 5.9 R ★ Interesting bridging between the shallow corners right of *Rock Hudson*. Usually toproped, this one might need a piton or two to adequately protect. Pro: thin to 2 inches. FA: Randy Leavitt and Brett Maurer, June 1981.

282. **My Brothers** 5.11d (TR) Climb a short way up *Spooky Spike Direct,* then step right and climb the arete. FA: Scott Cosgrove and Bob Gaines, October 1993.

283. **Vicious Rumors** 5.11c ★ Climb the left-facing dihedral with a hairline crack on the wall below *Flake Out,* to the right of *Spooky Spike Direct.* Pro: many thin to 1.5 inches. FA: Mike Lechlinski, Randy Leavitt and Mari Gingery, 1982.

284. **Flake Out** 5.7 Begin at the right-hand toe of the Northeast Buttress; scramble up and left (3rd and 4th class) to a ledge system that leads left (interspersed with several short vertical corners). Belay atop a squeeze chimney at the ledge shared with *Johnny Quest.* The second pitch ascends the long, low-angle, right-facing dihedral on the left to the top. Pro: to 3 inches. FA: Pat Callis, Charlie Raymond, and Trish Raymond, September 1967.

285. **Hidden Crack** 5.8 Begin as for *Flake Out.* Climb past the first vertical corner and belay as for *Spooky Spike. Hidden Crack* is found by traversing up and left about 30 feet to just before *Flake Out*'s wide crack section. Lieback a thin flake system over a bulge. Continue up *Spooky Spike.* Pro: to 3 inches. FA: Bob Gaines and Dayle Mazzarella, August 1996.

286. **Spooky Spike** 5.9 ★ Climb past the first vertical corner on *Flake Out* and belay. Follow the right-facing corner above, taking care not to dislodge the infamous "spooky spike." Pro: very thin to 2.5 inches. FA: Charlie Raymond, Bill Burke, and Trish Raymond, December 1968.

287. **Hey Dude** 5.12a ★ Start up *Etude,* but continue up the left branch of the crack to a fingertip lieback past two bolts to the *Etude* belay stance. Pro: very thin to 2.5 inches. FA: Bob Gaines, Clark Jacobs, and Lisa Fry, July 1991.

288. **Etude** 5.11a ★★★ 1. On the right side of the Northeast Buttress (left of *Flower of High Rank*) climb thin cracks on the left until it becomes feasible to traverse right over to the two right cracks (where fixed pins protect the crux), then a finger crack leads up to a two-bolt stance (125-foot rappel). 2. A steep finger crack leads to easier climbing. FA: (5.8 A2) Larry Reynolds, R. Wendell, September 1969. FFA: John Long, Rick Accomazzo, Richard Harrison, Tobin Sorenson, 1974.

289. **Etude Direct Start** 5.9 Lies on the wall below. FA: Jay Smith, Bob Gaines, and Yvonne Gaines, 1987.

290. **Flower of High Rank** 5.9 ★★★ The area's most popular 5.9 crack climb. This route lies on the right margin of the Northeast Buttress, just left of a giant right-facing dihedral (*Cat's Cave Inn*) that separates the main north face from a buttress to the left. This route lies just left of *Cat's Cave Inn,* following a thin crack on the left wall to a pine tree growing out of the crack some 100 feet off the ground. Pro: many 0.5 to 3 inches. FA: Rob Muir and Mike Graham, October 1972.

291. **Wet Dreams** 5.11a ★ More like a nightmare. Above the roof on *Flower* move right around the corner and jam an interesting, slanting crack that widens into a horizontal slot. Pro: to 3.5 inches. FA: Tobin Sorenson and John Bachar, 1974.

THE NORTH FACE

The North Face of Suicide lies at the extreme right-hand end of the crag and is characterized by a gradually diminishing and slabby face with numerous flakes and small corner systems. The left side of the North Face is marked by a large right-facing dihedral system (*Cat's Cave Inn,* Route 292). From The Weeping Wall, walk right along the base for about 200 yards. See Suicide Rock Overview Map.

Descent: Walk right across exfoliation slabs to a trail that curves back around to the base.

292. **Cat's Cave Inn** 5.8 Climb the gigantic, right-facing dihedral in 2 somewhat grungy pitches. Pro: to 4 inches. FA: Charlie Raymond and Pat Callis, September 1968.

293. **Yours** 5.8 Between *Cat's Cave Inn* and *Graham Crackers* the face is broken by a series of cracks with interconnecting ledges. Several combinations of 2- or 3-pitch 5.7 or 5.8 routes can be done here. Refer to the topo. Pro: to 2 inches. FA: Pete White, Larry Reynolds, D. Gilbert, March 1972.

NORTH FACE

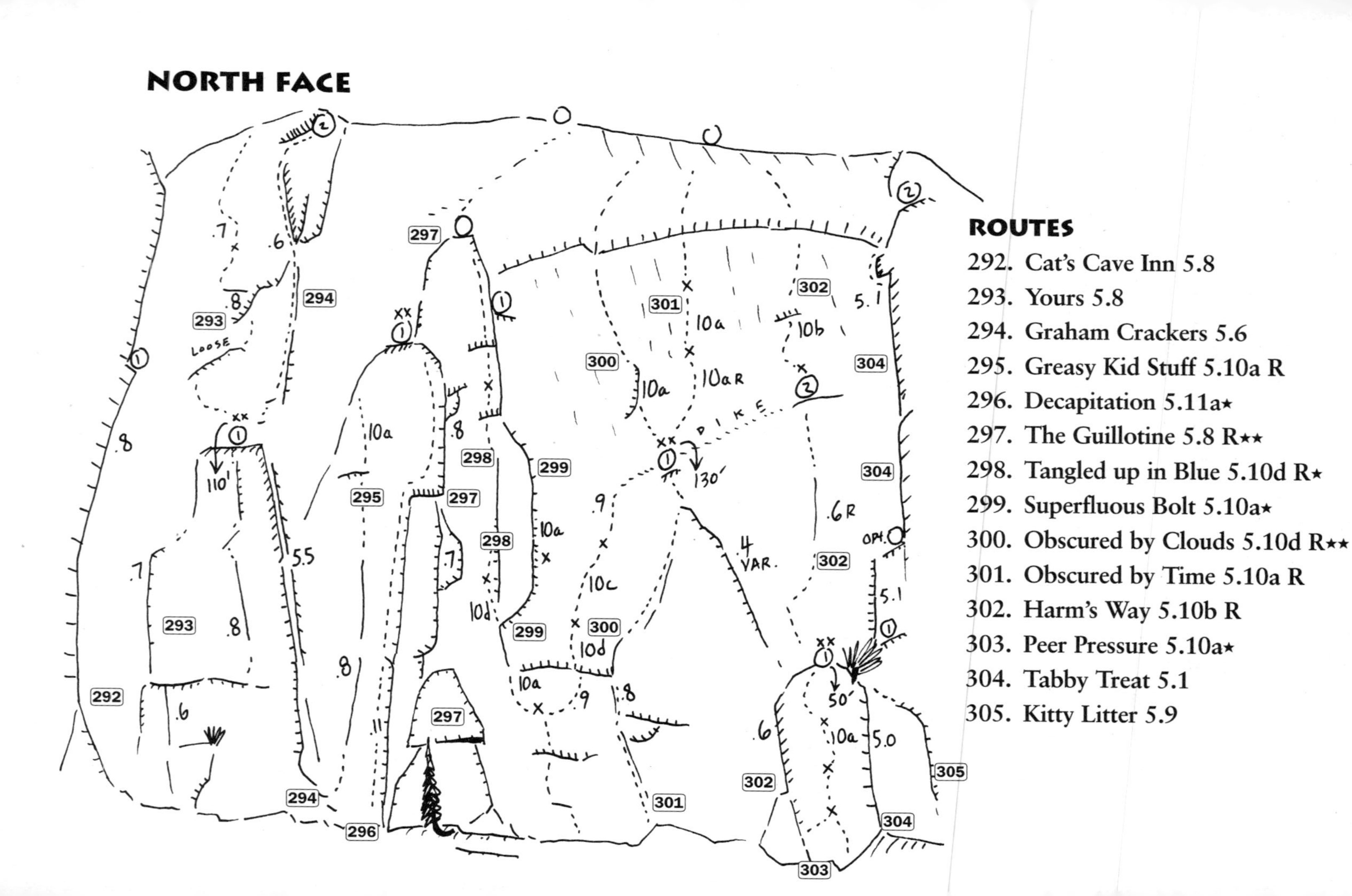

ROUTES

292. Cat's Cave Inn 5.8
293. Yours 5.8
294. Graham Crackers 5.6
295. Greasy Kid Stuff 5.10a R
296. Decapitation 5.11a★
297. The Guillotine 5.8 R★★
298. Tangled up in Blue 5.10d R★
299. Superfluous Bolt 5.10a★
300. Obscured by Clouds 5.10d R★★
301. Obscured by Time 5.10a R
302. Harm's Way 5.10b R
303. Peer Pressure 5.10a★
304. Tabby Treat 5.1
305. Kitty Litter 5.9

294. **Graham Crackers** 5.6 Begin 30 feet right of *Cat's Cave Inn,* immediately above a small sugar pine. 1. Up the obvious break on somewhat loose holds to a nice belay ledge on the left with two bolts (110-foot rappel). 2. Continue up a smooth trough to the crux: surmounting the left side of a down-pointing horn just below the top. Pro: to 3 inches. FA: Don Lashier and Trish Raymond, April 1968.

295. **Greasy Kid Stuff** 5.10a R The thin crack and face climb up the narrow slab between *Graham Crackers* and *Guillotine.* Pro: very thin to 2 inches. FA: Alan Bartlett, 1970.

296. **Decapitation** 5.11a (TR) ⋆ Follow the outer edge or arete formed by *Guillotine*'s corner, to the belay atop *Guillotine*'s first pitch. FA: Bob Gaines, John Long, Yvonne Gaines, Paul Edwards, and James Watts, June 1988.

297. **The Guillotine** 5.8 R ⋆⋆ Start directly behind a large fir tree with a curved trunk, where two huge granite flakes are ominously stacked against the wall. 1. A series of liebacks lead to a point where the flake widens to form a committing lieback. (The scene of several disastrous leader falls.) The run-out can be avoided by squeezing inside the chimney for pro (very awkward). Move left to a nice ledge with two bolts (130-foot rappel). 2. Begin with an easy crack to a 5.7 friction slab finish. Pro: to 3 inches. FA: Allen Steck and Chuck Wilts, October 1969.

298. **Tangled up in Blue** 5.10d R ⋆ Climb the initial section of *Superfluous Bolt,* then instead of moving right, climb straight up past a bolt to a slim, right-facing corner with a widening thin crack, then surmount an overlap to face climbing past another bolt. Pro: thin to 3 inches. FA: Bob Gaines and Yvonne Gaines, 1987.

299. **Superfluous Bolt** 5.10a ⋆ Start about 20 feet right of *The Guillotine.* 1. Climb up and left past a bolt, then up to a shallow, low-angle dihedral, past a bolt and up to a belay stance in the dihedral. 2. Continue up the corner to the top. Pro: to 2.5 inches. FA: Ivan Couch, Mike Cohen, and Mike Dent, early 1970.

300. **Obscured by Clouds** 5.10d R ⋆⋆ 1. Start up *Superfluous Bolt.* At the first bolt move up and right to an overlap (thin nuts and cams here) then up run-out face climbing past two bolts to a two-bolt belay at a diagonal quartz dike. 2. Unprotected face leads to a small flake (thin pro here), then easier friction leads to the top. Pro: thin to 2.5 inches. FA: Mike Graham, Tobin Sorenson, and Gib Lewis, 1974.

301. **Obscured by Time** 5.10a R 1. Ascend any number of variations up a series of cracks and flakes between *Obscured by Clouds* and *Harm's Way* to the belay on *Obscured by Clouds.* 2. Friction up and right past 2 bolts to the final overhang. Pro: to 3 inches. FA Pitch 1: Bob Gaines,

1984. FA Pitch 2: Eddie Bedout, Dave Mayville, and Bruce Gill, July 1988.

302. **Harm's Way** 5.10b R 1. Follow the left-facing corner that forms the left side of the *Peer Pressure* slab, then up run-out 5.8 slab to a belay at a small ledge with one bolt a short distance left of the *Tabby Treat* corner. 2. Smear straight up the slab with the only pro being the belay. Pro: to 3 inches. FA: Ivan Couch, Mike Dent, and Larry Reynolds, October 1970.

303. **Peer Pressure** 5.10a ★ A popular, 3-bolt friction romp up the small exfoliation slab between *Harm's Way* and *Tabby Treat.* Pro: 3 bolts, 2-bolt anchor (50-foot rappel). FA: Troy Mayr, Charles Cole, and Gib Lewis, 1987.

304. **Tabby Treat** 5.1 1.Climb the short, right-facing corner forming the right side of the *Peer Pressure* slab to a ledge above a bush. 2. Climb the long, left-facing corner that leads to the top. Pro: to 3 inches. FA: Charlie Raymond and Trish Raymond, May 1968.

305. **Kitty Litter** 5.9 This nondescript variation begins just right of *Tabby Treat*'s first pitch and climbs the small, left-facing corner that joins *Tabby* just above the bush. FA: Gib Lewis, Charles Cole, and Troy Mayr, 1987.

306. **Cat's Meow** 5.8 R Look for a small left-facing corner/flake system about 40 feet right of *Tabby Treat.* This leads to a short lieback flake. Stay left and lieback/undercling the slanting roof to a belay ledge. Continue up *Breakout* to the top. Pro: thin to 2.5 inches. FA: Unknown.

307. **Thin Man** 5.9 R Start with the short thin crack between *Cat's Meow* and *Breakout.* The crux is just off the ground and can be protected with thin nuts. Traverse up and left to a finger crack that leads to the lieback on *Cat's Meow.* Pro: to 2.5 inches. FA: Richard Copeland, et al., mid-1970s.

308. **Bunny Slope** 5.10c/5.11b Contrived, but interesting face pitch up the narrow slab between *Thin Man* and *Break Out,* past 3 bolts and a dubious fixed pin. After the third bolt the moves are easier if you move left. Pro: to 2.5 inches. FA: Bob Gaines and Mike Van Volkom, August 1987.

309. **Break Out** 5.6 Begin at a huge pine tree. 1. Climb up and left to a short, straight-in crack that leads to a small, right-facing dihedral to a nice belay ledge. 2. Enjoyable face climbing on knobs. Pro: to 2.5 inches. FA: Larry Reynolds and Hooman Aprin, October 1970.

310. **Hillside Strangler** 5.10c ★ Interesting balance and friction past 3 bolts on the arete forming the outer edge of the *Little Murders* dihedral. Pro: to 3 inches. FA: Bob Gaines and Bill Leventhal, July 1989.

NORTH FACE

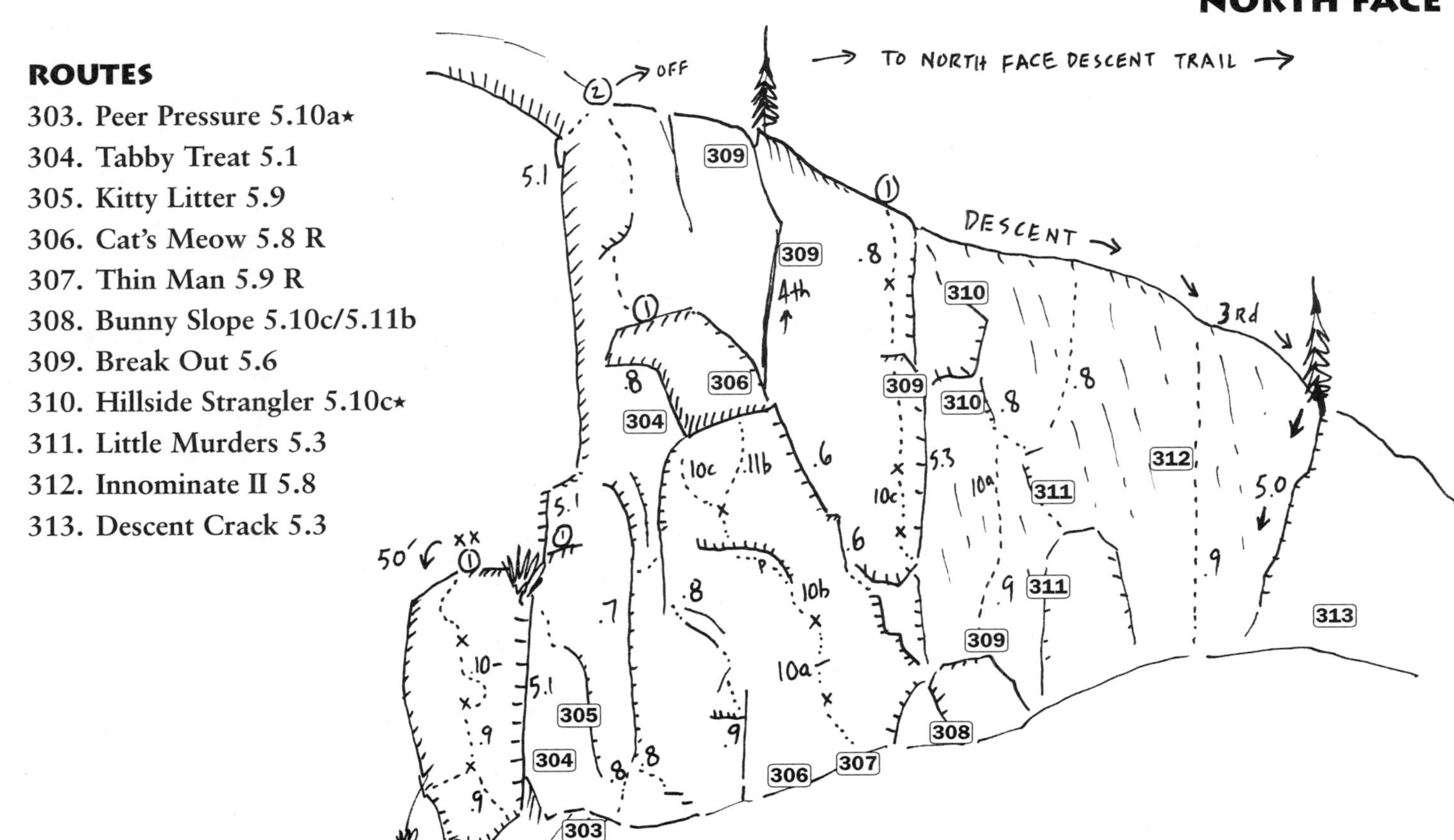

ROUTES

303. Peer Pressure 5.10a★
304. Tabby Treat 5.1
305. Kitty Litter 5.9
306. Cat's Meow 5.8 R
307. Thin Man 5.9 R
308. Bunny Slope 5.10c/5.11b
309. Break Out 5.6
310. Hillside Strangler 5.10c★
311. Little Murders 5.3
312. Innominate II 5.8
313. Descent Crack 5.3

311. **Little Murders** 5.3 This is the big, low-angle, right-facing dihedral near the far-right margin of the North Face. A 5.5 variation underclings the ominous axe-like flake above the chimney. Pro: to 3 inches. FA: Alan Vick and Steve Mackay, March 1972.
312. **Innominate II** 5.8 Follow the line of weakness up the slab right of *Little Murders*. Near the top are several flakes where pro can be placed for a lead. Numerous routes can be toproped on this slab (see topo).
313. **Descent Crack** 5.3 On the extreme right side of the slab is a low-angle flake/crack leading to a large tree about 40 feet up. This is used mainly as a descent route. FA: Unknown.

ROUTE NAME INDEX

SYMBOLS

The 5.7 Arete 73
10b or No 10b 144

A

Andy Dude 199
Angel's Fright 96
Angel's Wing 98
Angle Iron Traverse 105
Aqualung 173
Aqualung Direct 173
Archangel 142
Arcy Farcy 172
Arcy Farcy Direct Finish 172
Arcy Farcy Mantle 172
Arpa Carpa 134
Arpa Carpa Cliff 134
Arrowhead 163
Axe of God 191

B

B.C.'s Ouch Chimney 156
B.S. Arch 192
Baby Cobra 188
Baby Eagle Dihedral 199
Baby's Butt 128
Bacon Bits 172
Bam Bam 100
Barney 100
The Bastard 69
The Bat 83
Battle of the Bulge 150
Bedrock 101
Betty 100
Bibliography 109
Big Daddy 131
Big Momma 131
Birdman 43
Birdman Direct 43
Bitchin Lichen 43
Black Harlot's Layaway 124
Blade Runner 175
The Blank 92
Blanketty Blank 100
Blanketty Blank Direct Start 101
Blown Out 148
Bluebeard 171
Bocomaru 172
Bodacious 73
Bolts to Somewhere 142
The Bookend 113
Bookmark 115
Bookworm 113
Boomerang 142
Box of Rain 138
Break Out 206
The Breeze 190
Brilliant Disguise 140
BSSW Face 153
Buccaneer 171
Buffoonery 154
Bukatude 166
Bulge, Tahquitz 75
Bullocks 92
Bunny Slope 206
Burning Down the House 190
Buttress Chimney 168
The Buttress of Cracks 168
Bye Gully 179
Bye Gully Descent 179

C

Caliente 156
Captain Hook 171
Cat's Cave Inn 203

Cat's Meow 206
Cause for Alarm 85
Cerberus 142
Change in the Weather 183
Chatsworth Chimney 150
The Chauvinist 120
Cheap Day Return 190
Chin Strap Crack 85
Chingadera 124
Chisholm Trail 155
Chongo Arete 96
Chronic Dislocater 73
Clam Chowder 182
Climb with No Beginning 128
Clockwork Orange 156
Close Shave 198
Club Sandwich 172
Coffin Nail 106
Commencement 182
Compound Eyes 199
The Consolation 65
Constellation 65
Continuation 179
The Count 83
Coyote Girl 194
Crack of Noon 194
Crater Face 194
Crimes of Passion 103
Crimes of Passion Direct Start 103
Crucifiction 144
The Crucifix 83
Cutter 92

D

Daley's Direct 126
Dammit 138
Dave's Deviation 91
Dave's Deviation Direct Start 92
David 183
Decapitation 205
Deception Pillar 139, 140
Deck City Slab 138
Deep Vertical Smiles 168
Delila 185
Descent Crack, Suicide Rock 208
Devil's Delight 92
Diamond Lane 185
Dick Tracy 146
Dickhead 146
Diddly 128
The Dilemma 186
Dino 100
Dire Straits 182
Disco Jesus 144
Dog Bites Man 85
Dos Equis 105
Double Exposure 170
Double Exposure Direct Start 170
Down and Out 148
The Drain Pipe 158
Drowned Out 148
Duck Soup 182

E

Eagle Pinnacle 194
    Lower East Face 196
    North Side 199
    South Side 196
    Upper East Face 198
Eagles Nest 199
The Easement 176
East Buttress Gully 173
East Crack, The Far East 40
East Lark 50
The Edge, West Face 109
Edgehogs 58
El Camino Real 105
El Dorado 47
El Grandote 45
El Monte 47
El Whampo 45
Electric Razor 198
Endless Crack 153
The Error 55
The Escalator 185
Etude 203

Etude Direct Start 203
Euphoria 156
Eyes Wide Shut 179

F

The False Fitchen's Folly 128
The Far East 40
Farewell Horizontal 67
Faux Pas 126
Feeling Groovy 196
Fellatio 146
The Feminist 120
Field of Dreams 83
The Fiend 150
Finger Lickin' Good 198
Fingergrip 105
Fingertip Traverse 105
Fingertrip 103
First Pitch 166
Fitschen's Folly 128
Five Tree 146
Flake Out 202
Flakes of Rad 202
Flakes of Wrath 200
The Flakes, Upper Bulge 77
Flashback 115
Flatman Chimney 192
Flintstone Slab 98
Floating Log 136
Flower of High Rank 203
Flower of Low Rank 199
Flying Circus 117
Fools Rush 75
Forest Lawn 136
Fred 100
Free Lance 190
Freebase Variation 190
Freelove 96
Friction Route Descent 39
Friction Route, South Face, Tahquitz 128
Fright Night 98
Frightful Fright 98
Frightful Variation to the Trough 96
From Bad Traverse 87
Frustration 171
Funny Face 194

G

Gallwas Gallop 91
Garbage Gulch 155
Gates of Delirium 158
The Ghost 190
The Glossary 113
The Godzilla Face 186
Godzilla's Arete Variation 188
Godzilla's Descent 179
Godzilla's Return 188
Goliath 183
Goliath Direct Finish 183
Gone in 30 Seconds 200
Grace Slick 47
Graceland 190
Graham Crackers 205
Greasy Kid Stuff 205
The Great Pretender 140
Green Arch 117
Green Monster 182
The Green Rosetta 40
The Guillotine, Suicide Rock 205
The Gulp 65

H

Hades 142
Hair Face Variation 192
Hair Lip 192
Hair Pie 192
Ham Sandwich 172
The Hangover 106
Happy Hooker 80
Hard Lark 50
Harm's Way 206
The Heathen 120
The Hedge 113
Hedgehog 113
Heimlich Maneuver 73

Hell's Angel 142
Herkimer 192
The Hernia 171
Hernia Direct Finish 172
Hesitation 168
Hesitation Direct 168
Hey Dude 202
Hey Vic, Over Here 136
Hidden Crack 202
High Pressure Variation 173
Hillside Strangler 206
Hit It, Ethel 156
Hog Variation 60
Holiday 138
Hot Buttered Rump 192
Howard's Fifty-Footer 150
Hubris 52
Human Fright 98

I

The Illegitimate 69
The Incision 60
Initiation 196
The Innominate 124
Innominate II 208
Insomnia 170
Iron Cross 163
Iron Maiden 71
Ishi 158
It's a Bummer Please 75
It's a Mayracole 144
It's Showtime 192

J

The Jackal 190
The Jam Crack 91
Jammit 138
Javelin Variation 191
Jensen's Jaunt 106
Jigsaw 190
Jizz 199
Johnny Quest 200
Jonah 96

K

Kill Them All 154
Kiss of the Spider Woman 198
Kitty Litter 206
Knocking on Heaven's Door 144
Komodo Corner 188

L

Last Dance 148
Last Grapes 43
Last Judgment 106
Le Dent 136
Le Dent Pinnacle 136
Le Petite Gratton 136
Le Toit 77
Le Toit Direct 85
Le Toitlette 77
Left Ski Track 122
Left Wall, Open Book 109
Left X Crack 126
Lichen Lovers 198
Lik'en to Lichen 43
The Limp Dick 145
    North Side 146
    South Side 145
Limp Dick 145
Lip Up Fatty 52
Little Momma 131
Little Murders 208
Lizard's Leap 128
The Long Climb 67
Looking Backward 73
Low Pressure 173
Lower Bulge Buttress 85
Lower Royal's Arch 87
Lunch Rock 96
Lunch Rock Chimney Route 96
Lunch Rock Trail 37

M

Mad Dogs and Edgingmen 190
Magical Mystery Tour 58
Maiden Buttress 69
  Lower Maiden Buttress 71
  Right Side 73
Maiden Heaven 71
Maiden to Fool's Rush 71
Major 144
Man Bites Dog 85
The Man Who Fell to Earth 156
Mantle of No Return 178
Manwich 91
Mavericks 120
Mecca Godzilla 188
Mechanic's Route 115
Mercy of the Sisters 40
Mickey Mantle 150
Midnight Lumber Variation 185
Midnight Sun Variation 142
Mike and Larry's Excellent Adventure 154
Miller Time 154
Minor 145
Minuet 144
Miscalculation 144
Mr. Slate 98
Mogen David 185
Montezuma's Revenge 188
Moondance 163
Munge Dihedral 136
Mushy Peach 179
My Brothers 202
My Generation 166
My Obsession 153
My Obsession Boulder 152
My Pink Half of the Drainpipe 43
My Way 196

N

Narcolepsy 173
Nawab 173
New Generation 166
New Wave 117
Nirvana 166
Noondance 194
North Buttress, Taquitz 55
North Face, Suicide Rock 200
North Face Descent, Rebolting Face 183
North Face Descent, The Weeping Wall 179
North Face Trail 37
North Gully Descent 39
North Gully East 194
North Gully West, Eagle Pinnacle 199
Northeast Buttress, Suicide Rock 200
Northeast Buttress, Tahquitz 40
  Upper Northeast Buttress 43
Northeast Face East 47
Northeast Face West 47
Northeast Farce 45
Northeast Rib 43

O

Obscured by Clouds 205
Obscured by Time 205
The Offshoot 120
The Omen 198
On the Road 106
One Nut Willie 73
Open Book 109
  Left Wall 109
The Open Book 113
Orange Peel 128
Orange Roughy 145
Original Route, Northwest Recess 65
Original Route, Pas de Deux 126
Original Route, South Face Tahquitz 126
Ours 194
Over and Out 148
Overexposed 170

P

Paisano Chimney 156
Paisano Jam Crack 178

Paisano Overhang 176
Paisano Pinnacle 176
Palm Sunday 144
Pas de Deux 126
Pas de Deux Variation 126
Pass Time 171
The Passover 85
Pearly Gate 106
Pebbles 101
Peer Pressure 206
The Pharaoh 85
Philocetes Bow Variation 191
Picante 144
Pickpocket 186
Pieces of Eight 171
Pigs in Bondage 105
Pinhead 146
Pink Royd 150
Pink Royd Direct Finish 150
The Pirate 171
Piton Pooper 89
The Plague 173
Playing on the Freeway 185
Point Blank 103
Poker Face 92
Poppycock Arch 192
Powell Variation 120
Powell-Waugh Seam 153
The Price of Fear 77

Q

The Quarry 100
Question of Balance 189
Quiet Desperation 158

R

Race Bannon 200
Race with the Devil 166
The Rack 91
Raker's Escape 199
Rap Flake 186
Razor Burn 198
Razor Games 172
Razor's Edge 198
The Reach 124
Rebolting Development 185
Rebolting Face 183
Reckless Driving 185
Red Rain 163
Red Rock Route 131
Reunion 138
Revelation 182
Right Ski Track 122
Right X Crack 126
The Road to Nowhere 196
Rock Hudson 202
Rodan's Arete 188
Romeo Void 196
Root Canal 136
Royal's Arches 85
Running a Rig 140
Runout in Reverse 155

S

Sahara Terror 58
Sampson 183
The Scam 67
Scar Face 92
Scarface Slab 92
Schmooze 199
Science Friction 47
Season's End 186
Sensuous Corner 150
Serpentine 182
The Shadow 190
Shake Down 175
The Sham 65
Free variation 67
Shenanigans 154
Shit for Brains 103
Short Story 142
Show Stopper 194
Sideshow 192

Sideshow Slab 192
Sidewinder 163
Skigliak 179
The Slab, West Face Tahquitz 101
Slapstick 85
Sleepwalker 170
Sling Swing Traverse 120
Sloppy Seconds 198
Small Affair 196
Small Affair Direct 196
Smooth Sole Walls 146
  Left Side 148
  Right Side 150
Snakes on Everything 65
Someone You're Not 156
The Source 155
South Arete, Le Dent Pinnacle 136
South Face, Tahquitz Rock 122
  Left 117
  Right 126
South Pinnacle 196
The Souvenir 55
Spatula 173
Spatula Direct Start 173
Speaking in Tongues 168
Special K 69
Spiders from Mars 87
Spoodge 199
Spooky Spike 202
Spooky Spike Direct 202
Spring Cleaning 144
Stairway to Heaven 80
Standup Flake 85
Starburst Variation 156
Steal Your Face 138
The Step 77
The Step Away 178
Step Right Up 192
Steppin' Out 148
The Sting 67
Stinger 73
The Stretch 168
Subluminary Flight 198
Sugar Magnolia 138
Suicide Rock 132-208
  Arpa Carpa Cliff 134
  BSSW Face 153
  The Buttress of Cracks 168
    Right End 173
  Deception Pillar 139
  Eagle Pinnacle 194
    Lower East Face 196
    North Side 199
    South Side 196
    Upper East Face 198
  The Godzilla Face 186
  Le Dent Pinnacle 136
  The Limp Dick 145
    North Side 146
    South Side 145
  My Obsession Boulder 152
  North Face 200, 203
  Northeast Buttress 200
  Paisano Pinnalce 176
  Rebolting Face 183
  Sideshow Slab 192
  Smooth Sole Walls 146
    Left Side 148
    Right Side 150
  South Face 140
  South Pinnacle 196
  Sunkist Face 188
  The Sunshine Face 154
    Main Face 158
    Upper Left Side 154
  Tiny Pillars 194
  Upper East Buttress Ledge 172
  The Weeping Wall 179
  Winter Slab 132
Sundance 163
Sundance Arete 163
Sundike 163
Sunkist Face 188
The Sunshine Face 154
  Main Face 158
  Upper Left Side 154

Super Buzz 153
Super Pooper 77
Superfluous Bolt 205
Superfly 178
Surprise 182
Surprise Direct 182
The Swallow 60
Swashbuckler 171
Switchbacks 100
Switchbacks Direct Start 100
Sword of Damocles 171

T

Tabby Treat 206
Tahquitz Rock 37-131
  Bulge 75
  Descent Routes 39
  The Far East 40
  Flintstone Slab 98
  Lower Bulge Buttress 85
  Lunch Rock 96
  Maiden Buttress 69
  North Buttress 52
  North Face 45
  Northeast Buttress 40
    Upper Northeast Buttress 43
  Northwest Recess 55
  Open Book 109
    Left Wall 109
  Royal's Arches 85
  Scarface Slab 92
  South Face 109
    Left 117
    Right 126
  Tahquitz Summit Block 128
  The Y Crack Buttress 40
  West Face 87
    Center 96
    Left Side 89
    Right Side 101
  West Face Bulge 75
    Upper Bulge 77
  White Maiden's Apron 71
Tahquitz Summit Block 128
Tangled up in Blue 205
Tank Mechanic 52
Tar and Feathers 154
Ten Karat Gold 182
Ten Years After 103
Thin Man 206
Three-Hour Tour 58
Tiny Bubbles 194
Tiny Pillars 194
TM's Jewel 126
Toe Bias 50
Toe Tip 103
Too Biased 50
Torque Wrench 117
Toxic Waltz 152
Traitor Horn 106
The Trough 89
Tucker's Crack 186
Turbo Flange 109
Turn the Page 113
Twilight Delight 142

U

Ultimatum 150
The Unchaste 120
The Undertaker 175
The Uneventful 52
The Untickable 196
Upper Royal's 91
Upsidedown Cake 131
Urban Development 185

V

Valhalla 166
The Vampire 80
Vampire Direct Finish 83
Vampire Direct Start 83
Vicious Rumors 202
Voodoo Child 168

W

Walk the Plank 171
Warm Fuzzies 71
Warm Up 175
The Weeping Wall 179
West Face Bulge 75
    Upper Bulge 77
The West Face, Tahquitz Rock 87
    Center 96
    Left Side 89
    Right Side 101
West Lark 50
Wet Dreams 203
When You're Sap 172
White Line Fever 183
White Maiden's Apron 71
White Maiden's Walkaway 69
Whodunit 60
Wild Gazongas 134
Wild West 134
Wild Women 134
Wilma 101
Winter Flake 132
Winter Heat 132
Winter Slab 132
Winter Solstice 172
Wise Guys 178
Woodpecker Crack 154
Wong Climb 67

Y

The Y Crack 40
The Y Crack Buttress 40
Yaniro's Arch 156
Yellowjacket 67
Yours 203

Z

The Z Crack 69
Zeno's Paradox 71
Zig Zag 115
Ziggy Stardust 87
Zorro Zucchinis from Alpha Centuri Four 173
Zuma 73

RATED ROUTE INDEX

5.0

Northeast Rib 43

5.1

Minor 145
North Gully East 194
Tabby Treat 206

5.2

East Buttress Gully 173
Frightful Variation to the Trough 96
North Gully West, Eagle Pinnacle 199

5.3

Fingertip Traverse ★★ 105
Five Tree 146
Little Murders 208
Northeast Farce 45

5.4

The Trough ★★ 89
White Maiden's Walkaway ★★ 69

5.5

Bye Gully 179
East Lark 50
Maiden to Fool's Rush 71
The Uneventful 52
West Lark 50

5.6

Angel's Fright ★★ 96
Baby's Butt (R) 128
Break Out 206
Climb with No Beginning 128
Daley's Direct (R) 126
The Error 55
The Escalator 185
The False Fitchen's Folly 128
Fitschen's Folly 128
Fools Rush 75
From Bad Traverse 87
Garbage Gulch 155
Graham Crackers 205
Jensen's Jaunt ★ 106
Le Dent (R) 136
Left Ski Track ★★★ 122
Left Ski Track, Arete Variation 122
Left Ski Track, Slab Variation 122
Northeast Face East 47
Northeast Face West 47
Orange Peel 128
Spring Cleaning ★ 144

5.7

Angle Iron Traverse 105
Arcy Farcy Direct Finish 172
Chatsworth Chimney (R) 150
Continuation 179
David (R) ★ 183
El Whampo ★ 45
Eyes Wide Shut (R) ★ 179
Finger Lickin' Good 198
Fingertrip ★★★ 103
Flake Out 202
Goliath 183
Hard Lark ★ 50
Komodo Corner 188
Lunch Rock Chimney Route 96
Major 144
North Buttress, Taquitz 55

Red Rock Route ★ 131
Root Canal (R) ★ 136
Sahara Terror ★★ 58
Short Story 142

5.7+

Piton Pooper ★ 89

5.8

Axe of God 191
Buttress Chimney 168
Captain Hook ★ 171
Cat's Cave Inn 203
Cat's Meow 206
The Chauvinist ★★ 120
Coffin Nail ★ 106
Crack of Noon 194
Endless Crack 153
Fingergrip ★ 105
First Pitch 166
Goliath Direct Finish ★ 183
The Guillotine (R) ★★ 205
The Hernia ★ 171
Hidden Crack 202
Innominate II 208
The Jam Crack ★ 91
Le Toit Direct 85
Left Ski Track, Direct Finish 122
Lip Up Fatty 52
The Long Climb ★★ 67
Mechanic's Route (R) ★★★ 115
Mercy of the Sisters 40
Mickey Mantle (R) ★★★ 150
Mogen David (R) ★ 185
Nawab 173
Paisano Chimney 156
Philocetes Bow Variation 191
Pickpocket 186
The Plague 173
Poker Face 92
Rap Flake 186
Right X Crack (A2+) 126
Shake Down 175
The Shadow (R) ★ 190
Shenanigans 154
The Slab, West Face 101
Small Affair Direct (R) ★ 196
The Step Away (R) 178
Surprise (R) ★★ 182
Switchbacks Direct Start 100
Switchbacks (R) ★ 100
TM's Jewel (A3) 126
Traitor Horn ★★ 106
Upper Royal's Arch ★ 91
Wong Climb 67
Yours 203

5.8+

Hair Face Variation 192

5.9

Aqualung ★ 173
B.C.'s Ouch Chimney 156
B.S. Arch 192
Baby Eagle Dihedral (A3) 199
Bam Bam 100
Birdman Direct 43
Boomerang 142
Clam Chowder (R) ★★ 182
Close Shave (R) 198
Commencement (R) ★ 182
The Consolation ★ 65
Dave's Deviation (R) ★★ 91
Deception Pillar ★ 140
Delila 185
Eagles Nest 199
El Grandote ★ 45
Etude Direct Start 203
Euphoria (A1) ★ 156
Feeling Groovy 196

The Fiend (R) ★★ 150
Flatman Chimney 192
Flower of High Rank ★★★ 203
The Gulp 65
The Illegitimate ★ 69
The Innominate ★ 124
It's a Bummer Please 75
It's Showtime (TR) 192
Jammit ★ 138
Kitty Litter 206
Last Grapes ★ 43
Left Ski Track, Face Variation 122
Left X Crack (A4) 126
Lizard's Leap 128
Mantle of No Return (R) 178
Narcolepsy 173
The Offshoot ★ 120
The Open Book ★★★ 113
Over and Out (R) ★★ 148
Pass Time 171
Pearly Gate 106
Powell Variation ★★ 120
Razor's Edge (R) 198
Right Ski Track ★★ 122
Sampson (R) 183
Sensuous Corner ★ 150
Serpentine ★★★ 182
Sideshow (R) 192
Sling Swing Traverse ★ 120
Spooky Spike ★ 202
Spooky Spike Direct (R) ★ 202
Standup Flake ★ 85
Starburst Variation (R) 156
Surprise Direct ★★ 182
Sword of Damocles 171
The Stretch ★ 168
Thin Man (R) 206
Toe Bias (R) 50
Toe Tip 103
Too Biased 50
Twilight Delight 142
Warm Up 175
Whodunit ★★★ 60
Winter Heat 132

5.9+

Betty ★ 100
Gallwas Gallop ★ 91

5.10

Happy Hooker (A4-) ★★ 80

5.10A

Arpa Carpa (R) ★ 134
The Blank ★★ 92
The Breeze 190
Bullocks 192
Dammit 138
Diddly ★ 128
Dire Straits (R/X) ★ 182
Drowned Out (R) ★★ 148
East Crack, The Far East ★ 40
El Camino Real ★★ 105
El Dorado (R) ★ 47
Frustration ★ 171
Funny Face 194
Gone in 30 Seconds 200
Greasy Kid Stuff (R) 205
Green Monster 182
Hair Lip ★★ 192
Hair Pie 192
Hernia Direct Finish 172
Hesitation ★★ 168
Hey Vic, Over Here 136
Holiday ★ 138
Hot Buttered Rump 192
Human Fright ★★ 98
Jigsaw ★ 190
Last Dance (R) ★ 148
Lichen Lovers 198
Limp Dick ★ 145

Looking Backward 73
Mad Dogs and Edgingmen 190
Munge Dihedral ★★ 136
Noondance ★ 194
Obscured by Time 205
Paisano Jam Crack ★ 178
Peer Pressure ★ 206
Pigs in Bondage 105
The Rack 91
Revelation ★★ 182
Science Friction 47
Show Stopper (R) ★ 194
Skigliak 179
Small Affair (R) 196
Snakes on Everything ★ 65
Spatula (R) ★ 173
The Step ★★ 77
Step Right Up 192
Sundike ★★★ 163
Super Pooper ★★★ 77
Superfluous Bolt ★ 205
The Swallow 60
Ten Karat Gold (R) ★★★ 182
White Line Fever ★★ 183

5.10A/B

Original Route, South Face Tahquitz 126
Pas de Deux, Original Route 126

5.10B

The 5.7 Arete (R) ★ 73
10b or No 10b ★ 144
The Bastard 69
Bibliography (R) ★ 109
Big Momma ★ 131
Change in the Weather 183
Devil's Delight (R) ★ 92
Double Exposure (A1) ★★ 170
El Monte ★★ 47
Farewell Horizontal ★★ 67
Flower of Low Rank 199
Godzilla's Arete Variation (R) ★ 188
Grace Slick ★★ 47
Ham Sandwich 172
Harm's Way (R) 206
Hog variation 60
Jizz ★ 199
Johnny Quest ★★ 200
Lik'en to Lichen 43
Miller Time 154
Montezuma's Revenge (R) ★★ 188
My Pink Half of the Drainpipe ★ 43
Orange Roughy 145
Ours (R) ★ 194
The Road to Nowhere 196
Romeo Void (TR) 196
Shit for Brains 103
The Source (R) 155
Sundance ★★★ 163
Ten Years After ★ 103
Turn the Page ★ 113
Ultimatum (R) ★★ 150
Upsidedown Cake 131
The Y Crack ★ 40
Zig Zag ★ 115
Zorro Zucchinis from
Alpha Centuri Four (R) 173

5.10B/C

Bookmark 115
Kill Them All 154
The Jackal (R) ★ 190
Pas de Deux ★★ 126
Warm Fuzzies ★ 71

5.10C

Andy Dude 199
Big Daddy ★ 131
Bitchin Lichen 43
Blanketty Blank ★★ 100
Bluebeard 171
Buccaneer 171

Buffoonery 154
Chin Strap Crack 85
Dave's Deviation Direct Start ★★ 92
Deep Vertical Smiles (R) 168
Dick Tracy ★ 146
Dino 100
Dog Bites Man 85
Down and Out ★★ 148
Duck Soup (R) ★★ 182
Faux Pas ★ 126
Fellatio 146
Flakes of Wrath (R) ★★ 200
Free Lance (R) ★ 190
Herkimer (R) 192
Hillside Strangler ★ 206
Hubris ★ 52
Jonah ★★ 96
Low Pressure ★ 173
Maiden Heaven ★ 71
Man Bites Dog (R) ★ 85
Mike and Larry's Excellent Adventure 154
Minuet 144
Miscalculation ★★ 144
Mushy Peach 179
On the Road ★ 106
Overexposed (R) 170
Pink Royd Direct Finish (TR) 150
The Price of Fear ★★ 77
Question of Balance (R) 189
Sleepwalker (TR) 170
Spiders from Mars 87
Subluminary Flight 198
Tank Mechanic 52
Tucker's Crack 186
Vampire Direct Finish (R) 83
Wild Gazongas (R) ★ 134
The Z Crack 69
Ziggy Stardust 87

5.10C/D

Bodacious 73

5.10D

Angel's Wing 98
Blanketty Blank Direct Start 101
Blown Out ★ 148
Box of Rain (TR) 138
Clockwork Orange ★ 156
Club Sandwich (R) 172
Coyote Girl 194
Crimes of Passion Direct Start ★★ 103
Deck City Slab 138
Edgehogs ★★ 58
Flakes of Rad (R) 202
Flashback ★ 115
Godzilla's Return (R) ★★★ 188
The Hedge ★ 113
Heimlich Maneuver 73
Hesitation Direct ★★ 168
Howard's Fifty-Footer (R) ★ 150
Javelin Variation 191
Lower Royal's Arch 87
Mr. Slate (R) ★★ 98
Obscured by Clouds (R) ★★ 205
Original Route, Northwest Recess (A2, R) 65
The Passover 85
Pieces of Eight (R) ★ 171
Pink Royd (R) ★★ 150
Poppycock Arch (TR) 192
The Quarry ★★ 100
The Sham, Original Route (A2, R) 65
The Souvenir ★★ 55
Special K (R) ★★ 69
Spoodge ★ 199
Steppin' Out ★★ 148
Swashbuckler 171
Tangled up in Blue (R) ★ 205
Three-Hour Tour ★ 58
Torque Wrench ★ 117
Ultimatum (R) ★★ 150
Vampire Direct Start 83
Zeno's Paradox ★ 71

5.10D/11A
Arcy Farcy ★ 172

5.11
Bolts to Somewhere (A1) 142
Chongo Arete (TR) 96
Compound Eyes 199
Freebase Variation (TR) 190
Spatula Direct Start (R) 173

5.11A
Barney (TR) 100
Battle of the Bulge (R) ★★ 150
Bedrock ★★★ 101
The Bookend ★★ 113
Brilliant Disguise ★★ 140
Cerberus (R/X) ★★ 142
Chingadera ★★ 124
Decapitation (TR) ★ 205
Dos Equis 105
The Edge (R) ★★★ 109
Electric Razor ★ 198
Etude ★★★ 203
The Feminist (TR) ★★ 120
Fred ★★★ 100
Hubris ★ 52
Iron Cross ★★★ 163
Kiss of the Spider Woman ★ 198
The Man Who Fell to Earth ★★★ 156
Manwich ★ 91
Mecca Godzilla (A1) ★★ 188
My Generation (TR) ★ 166
Nirvana ★★★ 166
Race Bannon (TR) ★ 200
Raker's Escape 199
Razor Burn, Eagle Pinnacle (TR) 198
Reunion ★ 138
Rodan's Arete 188
Sloppy Seconds 198
South Face, Tahquitz Rock (R) ★ 122
Super Buzz (R) 153
Urban Development (R) ★ 185
The Unchaste ★★ 120
Valhalla ★★★ 166
The Vampire ★★★ 80
Wet Dreams ★ 203
Yellowjacket (TR) 67

5.11B
Arrowhead 163
Chronic Dislocater 73
Runout in Reverse 155
Baby Cobra ★ 188
The Bat (R) ★★ 83
Birdman ★ 43
Bunny Slope 206
Cause for Alarm ★ 85
Cheap Day Return (R) 190
Crimes of Passion ★ 103
The Crucifix ★★★ 83
Dickhead (R/X) 146
Disco Jesus ★★★ 144
The Drain Pipe ★★ 158
The Easement ★ 176
Field of Dreams ★★★ 83
Freelove 96
The Glossary ★ 113
The Heathen ★★★ 120
High Pressure Variation (R) 173
Last Judgment (R) 106
Midnight Lumber Variation (R/X) 185
Palm Sunday ★ 144
Rebolting Development (R) ★★★ 185
Red Rain ★★ 163
Voodoo Child (R) ★★ 168
When You're Sap 172
Winter Flake (R) 132

5.11B/C
Bacon Bits (R) ★ 172
Chisholm Trail ★★ 155
Cutter ★ 92

Green Arch ★★★ 117
Insomnia ★★★ 170
The Sting ★ 67

5.11C

Aqualung Direct (R) 173
Crater Face (TR) 194
The Dilemma 186
Diamond Lane ★ 185
The Flakes ★★★ 77
Floating Log ★ 136
Gates of Delirium ★ 158
Graceland (R) ★ 190
The Green Rosetta ★ 40
Hedgehog ★ 113
The Incision ★ 60
Initiation ★ 196
Le Petite Gratton (R) ★ 136
Le Toitlette ★ 77
Little Momma 131
Magical Mystery Tour (R) ★★ 58
Moondance ★★★ 163
My Way 196
New Generation ★★★ 166
The Omen (R) 198
Pebbles ★★ 101
The Quarry ★★ 100
Running a Rig (TR) 140
Season's End ★★ 186
Tiny Bubbles 194
Toxic Waltz 152
Turbo Flange (R) ★★★ 109
Vicious Rumors ★ 202
Wild Women ★★ 134
Wilma (R) ★ 101
Winter Solstice ★ 172

5.11C/D

The Sham, Free variation (R) ★ 67

5.11D

Archangel ★★ 142
Black Harlot's Layaway ★ 124
Bocomaru ★ 172
Bukatude 166
The Count (A1) ★★ 83
Crucifiction ★★ 144
Flying Circus (A4, R) ★★ 117
Frightful Fright (R) 98
Iron Maiden ★ 71
It's a Mayracole ★★ 144
Knocking on Heaven's Door ★ 144
Mavericks (TR) ★ 120
My Brothers (TR) 202
One Nut Willie ★ 73
Powell-Waugh Seam (TR) 153
Quiet Desperation ★★ 158
Race with the Devil (R) ★★ 166
The Reach ★ 124
The Scam (TR) ★ 67
Scar Face ★★ 92
South Arete, Le Dent Pinnacle ★★ 136
Speaking in Tongues (TR) ★ 168
Steppin' Out ★★ 148
Stinger ★ 73
Sugar Magnolia ★ 138
Tar and Feathers ★ 154

5.11D/12A

Playing on the Freeway ★★ 185
Sidewinder 163

5.12A

Arcy Farcy Mantle (R) 172
Blade Runner ★ 175
Double Exposure Direct Start (R) 170
Fright Night ★★ 98
Hell's Angel (R) ★★ 142
Hey Dude ★ 202
Le Toit (R) ★★★ 77
Midnight Sun Variation ★★ 142

My Obsession ★ 153
New Wave (R/X) ★ 117
Poker Face ★ 92
The Untickable ★★ 196
Walk the Plank ★ 171
Wild West (TR) ★ 134
Zuma ★ 73

5.12A/B

Constellation ★★ 65
Pinhead ★★ 146
Reckless Driving ★★ 185
Stairway to Heaven ★★★ 80
Yaniro's Arch (TR) 156

5.12B

Burning Down the House (R) ★★ 190
The Ghost (TR) 190
The Great Pretender ★★ 140
Hit It, Ethel (R) ★ 156
The Pharaoh ★ 85
Picante ★ 144
Point Blank ★ 103
Slapstick ★★ 85
Steal Your Face (TR) 138
Sundance Arete (R) 163
Wise Guys ★★ 178

5.12B/C

Schmooze ★ 199

5.12C

Bookworm ★★ 113
Caliente ★★★ 156
The Hangover 106
Paisano Overhang ★★ 176
Rock Hudson ★ 202

5.12C/D

The Pirate ★★★ 171

5.12D

Ishi (R) ★★★ 158

5.13A

Hades ★★★ 142
Someone You're Not ★★★ 156

ACCESS: It's every climber's concern

The Access Fund, a national, non-profit climbers organization, works to keep climbing areas open and to conserve the climbing environment. Need help with closures? land acquisition? legal or land management issues? funding for trails and other projects? starting a local climbers' group? CALL US!

Climbers can help preserve access by being committed to leaving the environment in its natural state.

• **ASPIRE TO CLIMB WITHOUT LEAVINGA TRACE** especially in environmentally sensitive areas like caves. Chalk can be a significant impact – don't use it around historic rock art. Pick up litter, and leave trees and plants intact.

• **DISPOSE OFHUMAN WASTE PROPERLY** Use toilets whenever possible. If toilets are not available, dig a "cat hole" at least six inches deep and 200 feet from any water, trails, campsites, or the base of climbs. *Always pack out toilet paper.* On big wall routes, use a "poop tube."

• **USE EXISTING TRAILS** Cutting switchbacks causes erosion. When walking off-trail, tread lightly, especially in the desert on cryptogamic soils. "Rim ecologies" (the clifftop) are often highly sensitive to disturbance.

• **BE DISCRETE WITH FIXED ANCHORS** *Bolts are controversial and are not a convenience* – don't place 'em unless they are *really* necessary. Camouflage all anchors. Remove unsightly slings from rappel stations.

• **RESPECTTHE RULES** and speak up when other climbers don't. Expect restrictions in designated wilderness areas, rock art sites, caves, and to protect wildlife, especially nesting birds of prey. *Power drills are illegal in wilderness and all national parks.*

• **PARK AND CAMPIN DESIGNATED AREAS** Some climbing areas require a permit for overnight camping.

• **MAINTAIN A LOW PROFILE** Leave the boom box and day-glo clothing at home.

• **RESPECT PRIVATE PROPERTY** Be courteous to land owners. Don't climb where you're not wanted.

• **JOIN THE ACCESS FUND** To become a member, make a tax-deductible donation of $25.

The Access Fund

Preserving America's Diverse Climbing Resources

PO Box 17010